MIGRAINE

Pain of the Body, Cry of the Spirit

*A Personal Guide to Healing and Preventing
Migraine Headaches*

Marian Frances Ordway

BookLocker.com, Inc.
2009

DISCLAIMER

This book details the author's personal experiences with and opinions about migraine headaches. The author is not a healthcare provider.

The author and publisher are providing this book and its contents on an "as is" basis and make no representations or warranties of any kind with respect to this book or its contents. The author and publisher disclaim all such representations and warranties, including for example warranties of merchantability and healthcare for a particular purpose. In addition, the author and publisher do not represent or warrant that the information accessible via this book is accurate, complete or current.

The statements made about products and services have not been evaluated by the U.S. Food and Drug Administration. They are not intended to diagnose, treat, cure, or prevent any condition or disease. Please consult with your own physician or healthcare specialist regarding the suggestions and recommendations made in this book.

Except as specifically stated in this book, neither the author or publisher, nor any authors, contributors, or other representatives will be liable for damages arising out of or in connection with the use of this book. This is a comprehensive limitation of liability that applies to all damages of any kind, including (without limitation) compensatory; direct, indirect or consequential damages; loss of data, income or profit; loss of or damage to property and claims of third parties.

This book is not intended as a replacement for medical therapy. The author assumes that persons with migraine have sought and continue to seek competent treatment from trained professionals in the health, counseling, and medical professions. Migraine is a neurovascular headache disorder that can signal severe, life-altering, and even life-threatening conditions, including stroke, brain tumor, and other illnesses. The author urges all persons who are suffering persistent headache or cycles of headaches to seek appropriate professional help.

You understand that this book is not intended as a substitute for consultation with a licensed healthcare practitioner, such as your physician. Before you begin any healthcare program, or change your lifestyle in any way, you will consult your physician or other licensed healthcare practitioner to ensure that you are in good health and that the examples contained in this book will not harm you.

This book provides content related to topics physical and/or mental health issues. As such, use of this book implies your acceptance of this disclaimer.

When you have a disease, do not try to cure.
Find your center, and you will be healed.

- Chinese proverb

DEDICATION

In Memoriam

To my teacher, the Reverend Linda Barnett

A Hasid asked his Rebbe:

"How can I best serve God?"

The Rebbe replied:

"One can best serve God with whatever

one is doing at the moment."

ACKNOWLEDGMENTS

My deep and sincere thanks to each and every person who gave of their time, energy and love when I needed to step back, away from the world, and penetrate the nature of my pain. A special thanks to the Lindas and Marks of the world, who are not rich and famous, nor are they ostentatious or boastful, but who offer to share their extraordinary healing gifts with those who are suffering. They walk lightly on this earth, and I have learned many important lessons from them.

Editing credit goes to Hella Rose Bloom, and cover art credit to Heidi Derstler, with many thanks.

CONTENTS

THE TOOLBOX

A Complete List of Healing Aids, Exercises, and Techniques for Migraineurs

PART I
Start a BEING Journal
A Beginning Exercise in Uncovering Essence:
      Examine the Garments, Lay Aside the Garments

Chapter 1
Record Your Migraine Treatments
Record Your Migraine Headache Healings

Chapter 2
Describe Your Migraines

Chapter 3
Remembering Wellness and Illness

Chapter 4
Energy Awareness Exercise
Color Energy Exercise

PART II
Mind Your Body: Drop Your Brains into Your Heart
      (A yoga practice to pull mind and body together)

Chapter 5
Morning Thoughts Exercise

Chapter 6
Test Your Fear Level: A Self-Survey

From the Author

A Word about the Word "God"

The trouble with the word "God" is that each and every reader comes to this book viewing the world through a personal veil of experience, environment and cultural associations. To one person "God" is the embodiment of patriarchal domination through the repressive doctrines of church; to another person God is unpredictable—loving one moment, and punishing the next. To me, God is an all-loving, all-forgiving force that cannot adequately be described in human words.

Throughout this book, I have needed to refer to the all-loving energy that drives the universe; the one unifying power and life-force; that which represents pure, divine goodness. "God" was one word I found myself using in this sense, along with the Creator, the One Power, the Almighty Spirit, and Father-Mother God.

Please, if the word "God" doesn't suit your needs, substitute whatever word does work in its place: You may be more comfortable referring to Great White Spirit (Native American), or One Love, One Truth, Divine Cosmos, or Buddha Consciousness. Rather than foisting any one preference upon readers, I chose to use the God reference because it is fairly common and because it carries power.

There are lots of authors of self-help and personal discovery books who prefer not to even deal with the "G" word—trying instead to strike a posture that allies with all-loving energy while avoiding references to words that carry too much cultural baggage—not all of it liberating in nature. I understand the need to get away from old, restrictive concepts, and deliberated long and hard about the wording of this book, particularly when it came to the Meditations section. Eventually, I decided it was good to use the word God, and that my internal understanding of what God is (was-is-will be) justified its usage.

In any language, my personal conviction remains the same: Divinity resides within.

It is up to each of us to remember that and consciously choose to ally with this wonderful, empowering energy so that we may feel, finally, all of God's attendant mysteries and everyday miracles— including that which we call "health." *–MFO*

Introduction

Considering Purpose

Each of us came to this earth for a purpose. We may sometimes, in moments of despair, deny that purpose exists, but deep in our hearts the word *purpose* resounds.

It is my conviction that uncovering that purpose, flowing with that purpose, and acting in accord with that purpose, will bring untold joy and health to each being on this planet.

You are the only one who can make the choice to discover why it is you are here. You are the only one who can ask yourself sincerely, "Who am I?" "What is my substance?" "What am I learning?" "What am I here to do within this lifetime?"

If you are a migraine sufferer, perhaps you have already quit asking "What is my purpose?" In your pain, feeling betrayed by this whole business called living, you have come to ask instead, "Did I come here to suffer? If so, I'm not so sure I want to stick around. It hurts too much."

Well, perhaps in some strange way you have come here to suffer. But is it divine will that you continue to suffer? Suffer and then die and be done with it all? The answer to that is No. Unequivocally, definitely, absolutely: No.

If you have chosen to read this book, and if this book speaks to you, there is every likelihood you have decided that you are tired of suffering. You are tired of drugs. You are tired of making excuses based on your disease. You are tired of not living a fulfilling, healthy life. Possibly you are just plain tired altogether.

If that is so, be grateful. If you have decided to look deeply at migraine and what migraine means to you, then you are a brave person. You are accepting a personal mission to take command of your own health. You have recognized that migraine belongs to you, not to your doctors or your mother or your minister. Migraine is totally personal. And because it is personal, it calls for a highly personal approach toward healing.

1

For me, the author, this is a personal book. I suffered from migraines for 20 years before I found the keys to long-term relief. I found my answers and attained healing in the face of incredible odds, and against all medical precedents. Since I am a woman whose mother also had severe migraines most of her life, I was told by doctors that I would probably be suffering from this disease until menopause, which translated into a total of 40 years of suffering.

...And even then there was no guarantee that the migraines would go away.

Somehow I could not face that possibility. I chose to reject that prognosis. I decided to not accept migraine as a permanent reality. Why? Because I was a parent; I needed to bring in steady income; and I desperately wanted to meet all of my commitments, professional and social. But being dragged down by onslaughts of headaches extracted a heavy toll on my mental and physical health. At times I felt I was not fit to be a wife or a mother or a writer or even a human being. On pain-free days I felt wonderful, though cautious; on migraine days I felt sub-human.

Only migraine sufferers know how a migraine feels. It's not just another headache. It's intense. It's frightening. It's debilitating. It makes you feel like you'd rather be dead. It can bring you to the point of total despair. The cycle of pills and pain can spiral you into depression. You who are very ill with migraine may feel that you are standing at the brink of a cliff, on the very edge of life itself. In many ways, you are doing just that.

In spite of all their good intentions, the healthy people around you cannot understand how these headaches (called "sick headaches," back in the day) can turn you into such a zombie. Hopefully, this book will be one that all persons—your friends, family members, and fellow workers—can learn from, regardless of their health status. But this book is written primarily for you, the sufferer.

I write this book out of love for all those who have migraine. It springs from a deep reverence for life, a reverence I had to locate within myself in order to begin the recovery process. I write this in accordance with my own purpose, as I have come to know it. I am eternally grateful for the guidance I receive when creating sentences, especially for being blessed with an inner, healing force that I refer to as, simply, the Bliss.

Your own personal bliss, or healing energy, is always within grasp. Yet healing comes not by force: it comes through only surrender. In that sense, the act of healing is a powerful paradox.

Just for a moment, to get the idea of what I mean by *surrender*, consider your life as a journey (a common enough image) in which you are driving a car. You drive this car down a road, a road you imagine to be your purpose, or your path. From time to time you take gigantic detours; and your car changes shape and color, from a red sportscar to a blue pickup truck, as in a dream. The car breaks down; it gets into minor accidents and major wrecks. You misplace your roadmaps, and panic, not knowing where you are or where you are going. People get in and out of the car, including children and seniors, whose lives you feel very responsible for; then, later, you feel like you are alone again.

All these things happen, but never for a moment do you take your hands off the steering wheel. You reason that, despite detours and hitchhikers and everything else, you are in the driver's seat because you are the one in control. It's all on *your* head. You take pride in that sense of control and power.

There's only one hitch—and you have a hard time explaining it to yourself, much less other people. It's such a long drive, you "know somehow" that you must be falling asleep at night to get your rest, in order to keep on going.

Yet you have no recollection of pulling over to a rest area or stopping at a motel.

The weirdest part is, when you are just in that space between Sleep and Awake, you sense that your hands are at your side, doing nothing whatsoever, and your head is thrown back on the headrest, as the eyes begin to open.

The car (representing your life) is still on the road (the road of your ultimate purpose, that is), and straight ahead is the most fantastic sunrise you have ever seen. It's wonderful to feel and see and drink in. There are shimmering pinks and streaks of deep purple and intense yellow rays of light that seem to warm your car, your whole body, everything. You could bask in the dawn forever, cruising easily down this magical road on this airy highway....

"Airy highway?" asks your Rational Mind, awakening fully from the sleeping body. "No such thing!" Mind, full of fear, calls to your hands, rousing them to active duty, "Quick! Take charge! Grab that wheel! No one's in control here and we're about to crash headlong into something really beautiful!"

BUT.

What if the mind is instead quieted at its most reactive moment just at that point—quieted by an inner voice from the heart, which tells it, firmly, "Mind, I insist that you take a break now. Go and sit in the back seat awhile."

This inner voice continues, speaking for the rest of the body, "Let me now surrender to this beauty here. Let me rest my hands for once, and keep very still. Let me give thanks that while I sleep, the hands of a powerful and good force not only keep me alive but guide me back to the road I am seeking in the first place. On top of that, this force, whatever it is, has shown me the most amazing sunrise, and I, for one, would like to travel straight into the center of that dawn and see what happens."

When this scenario occurs, the inner voice of the heart (by that I mean your highest spiritual self, the one aligned with all that is good and true and lasting and timeless) is asserting its place ahead of the self that is controlled by your rational mind, or your intellect. There is an acknowledgment, a clear realization that the intellect has not done all that well sitting in the driver's seat. There is the consideration, finally, that maybe all those detours and breakdowns along life's journey were part of an elaborate delusion or concoction of the mind, or the ego, or by an emotion such as fear.

This is surrender. And surrender is the only option left. When you try all the drugs, experiment with mechanical devices, cut out umpteen different food items from your diet, and still get clobbered by migraines, it is time to tell your mind, "Okay. You've done the best you can. Thank you for your good effort. Thank you for reading all those articles about headaches. Thank you for trying.

"Now go and sit in the back. Go rest. I'll call you when I need you. I am now going to listen to my heart for a while. I am going to try and hear what it has to say. If there is a cause for this pain, I want to know what it is. No more patch jobs for me. This is it. I'm going in."

Here's to the dawn, the journey, and the bliss up ahead.

PART ONE

ESSENCE VERSUS STRESS
Me, the Migraine, and That Person in the Mirror

"Esse" is the Latin word for "to be." Inside our hearts, the yearning to "just be" is irrefutable. It is so strong a drive, that anything interfering with it becomes our stress; in other words, a STRain on our ESSence. Over time, consistent strain on one's essence yields only one thing: physical pain.

Only migraine sufferers know what being in the middle of a migraine is all about. They find it impossible to explain to others, just as hurricane survivors are at a loss to talk about how a storm really felt: "It was like a freight train..." they start out. Then they shake their heads and stop. They start again, "You feel like everything you've ever been and everything you have will go at any moment, wiped out by the wind." Another shake of the head. "You had to be there," they end, lamely. Their silence speaks volumes.

In the past, as I struggled to get to the bathroom mid-migraine, propping myself against walls and groping along, eyes stabbed by the light in the hallway, the migraine was a giant set of pliers tightening fiercely around my head—gripping tighter, tighter, tighter... until WHAM! A brain-splitting blast that paralyzed, for agonizing seconds—an eternity—and then the pain lessened ever so slightly, just enough for me to make it all the way down the hall.

Many times too numerous to mention, there seemed to be three of me there in the bathroom. There was Me, there was the Migraine—an entity unto itself, and there was That Person in the Mirror. I would look at the person in the mirror—her face devoid of color, hair askew, dark half-moons under the eyes, and a prominent blood vessel visibly throbbing up and down on the temple—and I would whisper, "Who are you? Am I in there?"

Even after the migraine passed, I was haunted by those eyes— my own eyes. I wanted to find a way to reconnect the eyes to me, to self, and bounce the migraine out altogether. Unknowingly, I was onto something even then. Because ultimately, it was a personal search for essence—toward defining what be-ing was all about—that led me toward preventing and healing my own migraines. For the more I dug down to define what my be-ing was and what it was not, the closer I came toward feeling myself as one being whose soul, mind, personality and body worked together. Slowly, painstakingly, I began to see that when part of the whole combination that makes up a person is not in accord with essential self, other parts function at odds within the system.

In the beginning of my quest, I did not know what to do. It was just me, struggling to understand me. I began asking serious questions of myself. And I began to strip away the identities I had grown accustomed to. I had a hunch that if I could be reduced to a mirror image by pain, then there was something in that stripped-down version of me that could lead me somewhere. It did not matter where I was going: I just knew I had to go there. There seemed to be no other place to go.

After all, I told myself, it does not matter what you can do, or what your talents are, what your potential is, if you are constantly battered by pain. People subjected to sudden, debilitating pain cannot be counted on to perform. They cannot even count on themselves. They begin to ask: What part of me is real? Is there something about me that I can count on? Can I define myself in a new way, a truer way?

Being a writer helped. I imagined I was a novelist writing about myself. I watched myself go through the day. I noticed how many personalities there were. I was confused by the many things I was able to be: mother, wife, lover, daughter, businesswoman, author, cook, teacher of Japanese language, dancer, tennis player, swimmer, editor, communications and promotions consultant, thinker, achiever, loner, extrovert... The list went on and on.

From there I began to put all of those roles aside, one by one. In a way, the migraine experience helped me do that. Over and over again, I saw that migraines had consistently led me to a side of myself that I had been avoiding for years. Underneath every migraine was a frustration. I could not always put my finger on it, but I felt it and knew it with all my heart. One particularly severe migraine, which landed me in the hospital in 1986, had led me to put aside commercial writing. It told me it was time to clear the decks and allow another kind of writing—personal, creative writing—to claim my time and energy.

I guess that hospital experience was something like being in a bad car wreck. If you survive a wreck, you come out knowing that you do not have a lot of time in this world, and if you are not doing what you are "essentially supposed to be doing," then you are not ever going to be happy and whole. Worse yet, you will never achieve what you came here to do.

To be honest, I was not comfortable with the sacrifices that came along with discovering essence. I was unused to acting on intuition rather than established norms. It was a very frightening time, and I would make great progress only to slip and slide back again into what I thought was familiar territory.

In fact, though, I discovered that what formerly seemed familiar was not really very comforting or nurturing to me after all. What I had defined myself as for many years began to feel heavy. It was more of a burden than a pleasure. It was stressful.

The journey home to what is truly familiar, truly comfortable within oneself, is arduous. But it is immeasurably rewarding. When at last you physically experience a feeling of true familiarity within your self, you will experience essence, essential self, the pure self that is, as opposed to the self that is trying to be, or convincing itself that it is what it is not.

Beneath the crisis of migraine, then, is a crisis of essence: *How can I be, so that migraine will cease to be?* That is a question migraine sufferers ask themselves over and over again.

Stress Equals STRained ESSence

Migraine sufferers are usually counseled to reduce the stress in their lives, or to find ways to cope with it in a healthy fashion. But rarely do we operate with more than a superficial definition of what stress is. The common media definition, and certainly the mainstream medical definition of stress focuses on outward influences that have an impact on us: work, monetary troubles, relationships, traffic, and so forth.

However, would not all these outer stresses of the world be far more manageable if we, as individuals, first attended to the innermost needs of our soul? How can we possibly begin to cope with the stresses hurled our way, if our core is unsettled, or off kilter?

"Stress occurs from trying to be someone we are not." So writes Jacquelyn Small, a California therapist and author of the book *Transformers: The Therapists of the Future* (DeVorss & Co., Marina del Rey, CA, 1982). Furthermore, Small says, when we seek to discover the meaning of our experiences, we come to the reawakening, the transformation. And in changing our sick bodies to healthy bodies, nothing short of transformation will do. To find the answer, one must become less and less. The Old Self must die so that Essential Self can come into full view.

Fortunately for me, I did find essence. I found full-scale essence, and it is far less and far more than I could have imagined. Far less, because not even DNA counts in the final paring down; far more, because the "stuff" we are made of, once we tap into it, is virtually unlimited in its power, breadth, and depth.

First Step: Start a BEING Journal

However you find Essence is an individual matter. But just thinking about it will get you nowhere. As you begin exploring the nature of your self, your migraines, and your body (that person in the mirror), record the process. Purchase a good composition notebook to write in, and/or a sketchbook to draw in. Or you can use an audio or video tape in which to record your quest for bare essence. Do not label this journal with your name or your title or phone number, however. Instead, call it "BEING."

Unlike most migraine journals, the Being Journal (or tape) does not require you to note when you got a headache, and what foods you have eaten, or what drugs you took to quell the pain. You may choose to write as much or as little about the circumstances of your life as you wish. But in order to step away from pain, you must allow yourself to walk more deeply into your core.

Guided journal writing is one good way to open up. When you follow a specific format, with the ultimate goal of hitting an important target, you empower yourself with a real prescription for action. Since you desire to make a change from being ill to being well, you must first act to shake up the energy that has become so desperately "stuck."

If you suffer migraines, especially recurring ones, it should not be hard to visualize yourself as being literally in gridlock. (Gridlock is that traffic phenomenon which happens when cars are totally unable to move forward or backward in an intersection.) What you must ask is: "How did this gridlock happen?" Or, "How have I come to be controlled by pain? Can I blame it on my heredity? Is it in any way possible that this gridlock is of my own making? And if so, how can I extricate me—my good self—from this mess?"

Surely many individual components, like so many cars, all ended up converging on the same street corner to cause this situation in your life. And in order to get out, a traffic cop has to show up and call forth the cars, one by one. That is what journaling is for—it's a self-help cop.

The following guided journal exercise, "Examine the Garments"—which may entail weeks or months of ongoing writing and drawing—focuses on uncovering essence. Why do it? The reason is simple:

YOU are not your migraine.

Unwittingly, and quite in spite of your best intentions, you may have grown accustomed to defining yourself in relation to migraine. Along with doing what you do and being who you are, you think of yourself as a person who suffers greatly from debilitating headaches. That's the cross you've come to bear. And the chance of migraine raining on all your parades severely compromises your personhood, and of enjoying life in a simple fashion.

11

In fact, chances are good that you have forgotten much of what you actually are. Prepare to ask yourself, then, for the deepest answers to the famous question: "Who am I?" At first it may feel like there is too much material. But remember, inherent in the question is a denial—a letting go of old notions of self.

Underneath it all, you can be sure there is a beautiful, pain-free soul, longing to be.

A Beginning Exercise in Uncovering Essence:
Examine the Garments, Lay Aside the Garments

Set aside some time for yourself, when you know no one will disturb you. Then, use this exercise to begin the process of becoming more fully you. If you like, you can read this exercise aloud into a tape recorder, then lie down or sit quietly and play it back to yourself. Or you can simply read one paragraph at a time, then close your eyes and experience the images that come to mind. Keep your BEING journal handy for writing or drawing. You can go back to this again and again in the weeks and months to come.

The Garments Exercise

In order to strip away layers to discover the essential truth about your self, first picture yourself wearing a coat. It is a very big, warm coat. Under that coat see that there are many, many garments. Other coats, jackets, sweaters, etc.

In fact, there are too many garments. You realize you feel weighed down by all these garments. It is time to take them off, and see what lies underneath. It is time to get lighter and lighter.

Do not undress too quickly, however. Spend as much time as you need to with each garment. Using your imagination, describe, draw, or simply list an item of clothing that represents what you do for a living.

Next, imagine a garment that represents each of your jobs, skills, hobbies and interests. Record what enters your mind. Take as much time as you need—whether it is hours, days, weeks, or months.

In each "garment," envision the people and situations and the course that your life has taken—going as far back into your past as you can. Write down the names of the people associated with these garments, and reflect briefly on the moods that they evoke in you.

Look at each of your roles as an item of clothing. Recall the many responsibilities in each role. Draw or write about the various roles you play: parent, worker, child, volunteer, and so on.

Each time you are ready to move from one garment to another, visualize yourself gently removing it and then lay it aside carefully. Feel your heart release it lovingly. Say to yourself, "This garment has served its purpose."

When at last you feel you have finished removing garments, tell yourself aloud and/or write down: "These have served me well. I am releasing them into the loving arms of the universe. Whatever it is that I am, is now being revealed to me, more and more each day."

Chapter 1
The Cloud That Lifts

I was with my family on a social visit. I think we had been invited for dinner. The migraine that had been hanging around most of the day now was moving rapidly into high gear. I knew I had to get home soon, first to get to my bottle of Fiorinol (a painkiller), and then to prepare the children for bed, and get myself into bed for what promised to be another bout of 48-hour agony. This was no small headache. It was what I termed "full-blown."

I knew from experience what lay ahead. In the days, months, years preceding this, the kind of pain I was feeling typically lasted two days on one side of the head. Then there would be a day of clearance in between, followed by a migraine attack on the other side of the head. A Double Whammy.

I worried about the amount of painkilling pills I had left. *Would I have to call my doctor for a refill of the Fiorinol prescription? Would I even be able to make that call?*

I had one pill in my pocket, but I wanted to save it, to take it in conjunction with another Fiorinol for best effect. Everyone was having such a good time, but I had no choice. I announced to my husband and children, and our hosts, that we had to go, that I was getting one of my headaches, and I had to get back to my own house.

One of our hosts, whom I shall call Martin, took a long, compassionate look at me. I just shook my head. "I'm sorry," I said. "I know it's early yet."

"Listen," said Martin, "I don't know if this will help, but I think I can try to do something about that pain. I have a way of helping people with their pain sometimes. Sort of a massage. It's not something I tell many people about, and I can't guarantee anything, but if you'd like to give it a try..."

His wife nodded. "He's pretty special," she said. "Martin has this gift. Like he says, it's not something he talks about or wants blabbed to the neighbors, or even to people in his family."

I assured them both that I would keep it to myself.

She encouraged me, "Go ahead, I'll keep an eye on the kids." Everybody but Martin and I left the room.

"OK, what do I do?" I asked Martin. I was desperate. I was also skeptical. *But*, I reasoned, *maybe I should just get this massage, relax a little, and then get home to my drugs.*

Martin told me to stay still on the sofa where I had been sitting. He stood directly behind me and told me to close my eyes and just breathe in and out. He put one hand on my head, near where the pain was centered. He placed his other hand loosely at the back of my neck. Unlike other people who had worked on my neck and head to try to relieve my pain, Martin did not probe pressure points or massage my skin. He said quietly, "Keep relaxing, keep breathing. This will take about five minutes or so."

Nothing much happened. Everyone went on their business around us in the other rooms of the house. All I felt from Martin was a very slight shaking in the hand that was centered on the nape of my neck. Although wide awake, I felt more and more relaxed, and my mind began to wander off.

After a few minutes the strange massage was over. Martin went off somewhere, perhaps to the kitchen. I opened my eyes, felt my head still throbbing. Pain briefly pierced me in the eye.

It was a nice try, I said to myself. *But now it's time you got yourself home to your pills. Something you know will at least dull the pain and put you to sleep.* I gathered my things to leave, signaling to my family that it was time to go.

"Did it help?" asked the hostess.

"Yes," I lied. "The pain seems to have gone down a bit." I didn't want to be impolite. I even managed a half-smile. In truth, though, I couldn't wait to get into the car, to get home. I felt sorry for myself. And I was deeply disappointed. One more therapy that didn't work. This pain was bigger than everybody and everything.

Martin and his family kissed us all goodbye. I thanked Martin. He sort of shrugged it off, saying, "I hope you're feeling better." He was sort of a shy person. Doesn't like too much attention focused on him. Never did.

Silently we drove home. It was a short ride—15 minutes at most. I must have fallen asleep in that short time. I remember waking up back at the house and saying, "You know what? I think I'm feeling a little better."

I felt like lying down on the sofa. Before doing so, however, I opened the high kitchen cabinet where I kept my Fiorinol handy, and looked hard at the prescription bottle. *Should I take two pills anyway?*

I closed the cabinet, deciding against the drug. I headed for the couch. I was beginning to feel better and better. *What was going on?* I asked myself.

Physically, it felt as though a cloud was lifting off my head and gradually moving off and away, like a giant storm system carried out to sea by the wind.

This healing I was experiencing was unlike anything that had ever happened to me. *If there is a miracle*, I told myself, *I want to know it completely. If I get through this without drugs, I will know this miracle is true and fantastic.*

I fell asleep. My dreams were pleasant, not frenetic as migraine dreams sometimes are. Two hours later I woke up, aware that I felt no pain whatsoever. I felt tired but refreshed. The first thing I did was cry, I was so happy.

I went through a thousand emotions and as many scenarios of doubt. *If I move, maybe it will come back.* It didn't. *If I dare to believe this migraine is gone, maybe I will get another one next on the other side of my head.* But that did not happen.

When I checked my face in the mirror, I saw nothing but serenity. A beautiful sense of relief washed over me.

I called Martin right away, overcome with emotion, and gratitude. I told him that the pain was completely gone. He told me he was glad, and that I could call him if it ever got that bad again.

"You don't know what this means to me," I said. I felt sort of dependent on him, guessing that I might have to call him again in the future. But underneath everything, I knew that a connection had been made on my behalf. If a five-minute laying on of hands could cure the worst, most dangerous pain I knew, then there was a way through pain. A non-medical way through. Something that I knew very little about. But something that I could testify to, with complete faith and conviction.

I knew that energy—perhaps electrical energy—was involved. Beyond that I knew nothing. Martin himself would not discuss the subject. He made it clear that it was a private matter. And I respected his wishes. I did not probe. After all, he was a quiet family man, a working man, a former helicopter pilot who flew rescue missions over VietNam.

Above all, he was a man of infinite compassion. He gave me the initial inspiration to learn more about the energy of migraines, and helped me find the courage to learn to heal myself.

I called on his help in only two subsequent circumstances (once at 11:30 P.M.). In truth, I wanted to call on him many more times than that, but I was afraid he would think I was intruding on his private life. I continued to suffer from frequent migraines, always drugging myself to get through them. In these two particular instances, though, I called Martin as my last resort. On these occasions, even heavy medication had made no dent in my pain, and I was severely nauseous. I was very, very sick. I was prepared to check into the hospital if his efforts failed.

In retrospect, I have considered that perhaps I needed to go through these crisis experiences, to prove to myself once and for all that a simple laying on of hands, done by the "right" person, was enough to lift the worst type of pain. As before, the treatments worked. Shortly thereafter, putting aside my last shred of skepticism, I turned in earnest to discover what this phenomenon was all about.

I began my journey of self-healing. Incredibly, once I decided to learn about the energy that lifts off pain, I immediately began to meet people that could help me on each step of the journey. Books that guided me along were simply handed to me. If I envision my journey as something painted on a game board—like Candyland or Monopoly—the first square to land on would definitely be labeled Blind Faith. Blind faith in a light touch/massage method that completely baffled and amazed me.

What Martin does cannot be packaged. It is difficult enough simply finding the English words to express what he does. However, I have discovered that the essence of what he does, as it relates to healing energy, is present within every human being. Furthermore, this ability can be explored and developed on one's own using a variety of tools and techniques. The process is fascinating, challenging, and, in my opinion, lifesaving.

With sincere and devoted commitment, theoretically, anyone can claim access to his or her physician within. The following chapters describe critical aspects of the process involved with becoming an agent of your own healing.

Two Exercises for the Record

#1. Record Your Migraine Treatments

In your BEING Journal, set aside some pages where you can record all the types of treatments you have undergone and sought for your migraines. It's important to be able to refer to what you tried in the past, and over how many years. Leave lots of blank space, since it's unlikely you'll recall all the treatments (drugs, hot and cold showers, acupuncture, sumatriptan injections, homeopathic remedies, etc.) all at one sitting. Jot the treatments down as you remember them so that you can build as accurate a medical history as possible. Also, record (if you can remember) when migraines have bothered you the most in the past, starting from when they first began.

#2. Record Your Migraine Headache Healings

In your BEING journal, set aside a separate section of blank pages where you can record any memorable healing experiences which resulted in your migraine being completely healed more quickly or more completely than usual. Start out by discussing how long it typically takes for a migraine to heal using no painkiller, using painkilling medicine or even a combination of medicines (list approximate dosages), using a prescription migraine drug (spray, injection, pill), and so on. Continue on by noting any other types of healing experiences—describing what happened, how much time was involved, and your feelings about the event.

Chapter 2
Mystical Migraine

Migraine can be such a terrible phenomenon, with its pain and unpredictability, that some migraine sufferers—even though they genuinely want to know more about migraines—will find it hard to get past the front cover of this book. The slightest reminder of migraine makes them feel sick. To them, migraine is a *terror*-ble thing. Deep fright kicks in when migraine strikes. Intense fear is at hand.

One way to begin conquering a fearful thing is to examine it closely, and deal with it directly. For example, if you have a fear of dogs, perhaps from a childhood encounter with just one vicious dog, it is possible to get a handle on that fear by raising a puppy to adulthood. Your dog becomes familiar. Its mystery is gone. The master is now you, not the beast that inspired fear.

Likewise, terror-ble headaches demand to be taken apart and looked at very closely. Instead of running away from the phenomenon, each of us must boldly explore what migraine really is, for each individual sufferer, and try to identify its various properties and even its possible merits. We must finally consider that migraine is more than a hateful experience. This is not to say that we must embrace migraine but rather that we must put it under our personal microscopes and view it as best we can.

Moreover, since only migraine sufferers really know what's going on when an attack hits, they should be the ones telling everybody else what migraine is or is not—remembering, of course, that each person feels it differently.

The word migraine comes from the Latin words *hemi*, meaning "half" or "one side" (as in *hemisphere*, one half of the globe), and <u>*crania*</u> meaning "head." In migraine, half of the head is affected, and pain is distinctly located on either one side or the other. The ailment is described from ancient times, so we know it is not a modern phenomenon.

In medical terms, migraine is a physiological reaction that causes blood vessels to swell, putting painful pressure on tissues around the brain and on head and neck muscles. It is sometimes preceded by distortions in vision and speech, which is referred to as an 'aura.'

Since migraine involves the blood vessels, it is classified as a vascular disease. When the migraine begins, typically there is first a sudden constriction, or narrowing, of the blood vessels in the head and neck. This brief phase is followed by a sharp swing in the opposite direction as the blood vessels then dilate, or open out widely, touching sensitive nerve endings and inflicting intense pain.

The constriction phase is when some migraine sufferers experience an aura. Depending on the individual, you might see blinking or flashing lights, jagged lines, and other visual disturbances, or have some temporary blinding. You might also experience some numbing of the face, mouth or hands, and find yourself unable to express yourself clearly in speech. An aura may occur before a migraine, but not necessarily each time one is experienced. When an aura occurs without the painful headache, it's called a migraine equivalent.

Other symptoms of migraine, which can be as difficult to handle as the pain itself, include nausea, vomiting, general malaise (feeling poorly), and confusion. In many cases the sufferer finds herself/himself unable to bear ordinary light and sound. Sunshine and office lights are painfully bright, to the point where an ordinary washtowel covering the eyes can be inadequate: any light at all sears into the eyes, furthering pain. Sometimes only a black cloth draped over the eyes will help eliminate eye discomfort. Sounds are horribly amplified so that a whisper across the room is clearly heard and is received by the ear as if it were spoken aloud.

Further symptoms: For years I also experienced clogged sinuses while in migraine mode, and had frequent urination. During the aura phase, I found myself unable to concentrate and I was unusually clumsy. Since those conditions can exist without signaling the onslaught of a migraine, I frequently had to rely on other indicators to be sure I should treat myself with a migraine-prevention drug. For there are certain medications—the ones containing ergotamine, such as Cafergot, Bellergal, etc.—which can head off a migraine attack if taken in the aura phase just before the headache pain hits. In my experience, there were only about 20 minutes' worth of warning time.

I discovered that one sure migraine indicator was a certain crackly feeling at the back of my neck. Also, clumsiness resulting in pain served to clue me in. I have been known to walk into closed doors, not connecting mentally that the door was not open, or walls and doorjambs while aiming to get from one area of the house to another; then several minutes later, I found myself with migraine pain. Over time, I began to take my medicine faithfully whenever such blatant lapses of kinesthetic sense—my awareness of my body's position in space—occurred.

Migraines are dangerous. Not only can they link up with depression and other serious psychological states, but medical documentation shows that people who get migraines run a higher than normal risk of suffering from stroke. (And a smoking habit really ups the ante.) Medical professionals are very concerned about that fact. Gynecologists, for example, are reluctant to prescribe birth control pills for patients who suffer from migraine. According to Dr. Judith Reichman, whose article (September, 2005) on migraines and birth control pills can be found online, women who get auras preceding migraine may be more susceptible to stroke if they go on the Pill. (Refer to http://www.msnbc.msn.com/id/9493518.) She writes, "If you have a migraine with aura, don't use birth control pills before consulting a headache specialist. And under no circumstances should you take birth control pills if you smoke and have migraines of either type"; those types are no-aura migraine and aura-related migraine. (More information on auras follows.)

Prudent doctors conduct thorough examinations and tests with their migraine patients, including tests that would reveal an underlying cause based on head injuries, diseases, brain tumors, aneurysms, or what have you. I know migraine sufferers who have been through every battery of test there is: EEG, EKG, CAT scans, and so forth. And for good reason. A severe headache, or frequently recurring headaches, can signal a dire emergency or even impending death.

But the majority of migraine sufferers are eventually not ruled to be in a crisis situation. They are given medication to control their symptoms, and go back to their doctors for periodic checkups.

If the headaches keep coming back, after all serious disease states have been ruled out, doctors usually counsel their patients to reduce stress. They continue to prescribe a variety of different drugs and medical therapies in an effort to alleviate their patients' suffering. The treatments meet with varying degrees of success, depending on the individual patient. To treat migraine that strikes during menstruation, for example, some doctors have tried prescribing calcium channel blockers (drugs used to control high blood pressure) and beta blockers, blood pressure medications that women take for a certain number of days prior to their period. Doctors also prescribe a nasal spray medication that is designed to reach the pain faster. They may prescribe three medications for chronic migraineurs: a preventive pill for the aura phase, a painkiller for those headaches that charge on past the aura and become full-fledged monsters, and a suppository to control nausea from the painkillers or the migraine itself. In recent years, medicines have been developed to specifically target menstruation-related migraines.

There are no statistics regarding the cure rate from migraines. What we do know is the suffering rate: Some 24 to 26 million Americans keep on getting migraines. The world rates may approach 200+ million. We also know that more women than men suffer from migraine, experiencing three times as many migraines as men. The medical literature reports that boys in puberty may get migraines for a few years, then never (or rarely) experience them again. Many, many women report that the headaches often precede or accompany menstruation. Sometimes the incidents disappear or happen less frequently after menopause. Children can get them. And migraines seem to run in the family, indicating a genetic predisposition.

People with migraine have highly individual histories related to the disease. I believe it is important to value everyone's individual experiences, and not to discount them in any way. In the past, doctors were openly skeptical about the aura phase, describing visual disturbances that their patients had as "illusions" or "hallucinations." There was much veiled doubt on the part of physicians as to the realness of the migraineur's expressed experience.

In recent decades, however, there have been great advances in the study of headaches, including migraines. Doctors know, finally, that their patients aren't "seeing things" but are actually experiencing sensory disturbances relating to physiological changes (involving chemicals, blood pressure, and so forth) in the body's internal system.

Nonetheless, the migraine experience is still mysterious, and little understood. It is at once fascinating and it is frightening because it still falls outside the realm of the tangible or measurable.

There is no question in my mind that migraine experiences can involve strange lights and sounds and wooziness and weird dreams and all sorts of interesting phenomena. My mother used to report seeing lights go popping on and off: "It's like when you take a flash picture in an old Kodak camera," she said. Symptoms like these were traditionally downplayed by the medical establishment.

To my way of thinking, if you report that you see blinking lights, then it is true that you see blinking lights. You do not "sort of" see them, you actually do see and experience them with the visual capability at a given time.

Likewise, if you see something out of the ordinary, such as all kinds of colors flashing in front of you on the road as you are driving, then you are not seeing an illusion, but you are actually experiencing colors flashing. Your experience is real to you, no matter how it is perceived by doctors or friends or others. In other words: *It is time to accept your migraine experience exactly as you know it to be.*

Above all, migraine is characterized by heightened sensitivity. What does that mean for a migraineur? Face it: you are a sensitive person. Accept this truth about yourself once and for all. Respect it. Absorb it. Give it thoughtful attention.

Next, allow yourself to take this sensitivity aspect a step further. You don't have to look far to see that there is an enormous realm of mystical events connected with migraine, and, interestingly, these events often take place right in the middle of the worst pain.

Migraineurs have extraordinary tales to tell, if prompted to do so, for the world of migraine is made up of far more than its tortuous image suggests. Migraineurs have been known to see and experience all of the following: vivid visions and amazing dreams; brilliant ideas; business and political schemes both fantastical and practical; the answers to problems long-unsolved; flights into the past and future; and the beginnings, middles and ends of intensely creative works of art such as paintings, films, poems, dances and even art forms not yet revealed on this planet.

Some migraine people utilize their visions consciously. They say afterwards, "Gee, I have this great plan I'm going to work on." Others are completely frustrated by not being able to remember all the complex detailing that seemed so easy while they were in the throes of the migraine. Still others dismiss all that as machinations of the mind, and tell their spouses or friends, "I had some crazy thoughts while I was sick. But don't worry, I'm okay now." They rarely convey such information to their doctors, fearing, perhaps, that it does not hold any worth, and that it is not believable.

Think for a minute, though, about the case of one famous migraineur: Lewis Carroll. Had Carroll not "believed" what he saw in his many migraine-related visions, *Alice in Wonderland* might never have been written. Consider, too, that what can seem very wacky in the bright daylight of the rational, physical world—by wacky I mean the idea of a full-sized girl following a talking rabbit down the world's deepest rabbit hole—can, over time, come to be accepted as a masterpiece. It can be a Disney movie, an epic fantasy, and the subject of political and philosophical debate.

I do not mean to imply, and never let it be said, that migraine is to be glorified. Nothing so painful, so damaging, can be good for you. But perhaps it is time to acknowledge that there is some good that has come from migraine energy. Perhaps we can even celebrate this phenomenon in a healthy fashion. At the very least we can work toward understanding and appreciating its mystical side, since that is very real and it does not go away.

Migraineurs can begin to feel better about themselves. For a long time we have been keeping our visions and insights to ourselves because they are so incredible to others, so unbelievable. They defy explanation. But that does not make them invalid. Migraine experiences are not less real than any other experiences. They just are.

I think it is very important to talk about migraine thinking, or what kinds of thought processes occur during migraine, as well as migraine monsters, too, including the ideas and visions and dreamlike states that can be very disturbing. You can actually feel like you are losing your mind in the throes of migraine. I have memories of my brain racing a million miles a minute for hours on end. I used to tell my family, "It feels like my brain is on overdrive."

Not surprisingly, one of the treatments some specialists use today with migraine patients is art therapy. The migraine sufferers paint to express how they feel about their migraines, or they paint how the migraine would look if it were an abstract piece of art, and so on. Of course, the art program is much more complex than that, and there are many levels, including working toward feelings of rage, expressing fears, and, in the act, giving credence to the migraine experience. All of this important psychotherapy has come at a late date, but at last it has finally arrived.

I am not sure what art therapy will mean in terms of curing and preventing migraine. But it has very promising implications for doctors and other medical professionals who, at present, exhibit very little direct knowledge of what migraine feels like and how very complex it is.

Think how much fuller our comprehension of migraine would be if we lived in a country where migraine patients were counseled by their doctors to recount the images they see! Suppose people could capture the words that tumbled through their mind during migraine, writing them exactly as they came into the head, freeform, without judgment? Or what if paints and paper were always within easy reach of the sickbed? What powerful energy would be unleashed.

Migraine is still considered a medical mystery. The physical aspects of the disease are fairly well researched and well documented, but we still do not know what is going on. That is how I came to study the unseen. This book is about the unseen aspects of migraine, where uncovering the cause and discovering the healing are flip sides of the same coin.

Describe Your Migraines

Take time to describe and record the experience of migraine—beyond just the pain details. If you are comfortable writing about this, add these descriptions to your Being Journal or in a document on the computer. If talking is an easier form of expression for you, share your migraine experiences in depth, possibly to a close friend or relative or a support group.

If you choose to speak instead of write, consider recording your conversation. Many times, migraine experiences are much like dream experiences. They don't make much sense, and they are hard to describe because they fall outside the realm of what feels like normal perception of the world around us. Nonetheless, it is valuable to see more clearly those aspects of migraine that bring us into mystical aspects of ourselves.

Chapter 3
Dis-Ease

"Migraine is a disease." When a doctor first told me this, I was in the hospital. It was the winter of 1986. In all the years I had been treated for migraine, I had never heard a doctor describe my condition as a disease. It felt strange to think of myself as a person with a disease. It was not like measles or chicken pox, which go away quickly. The seriousness of the situation was hammered home by this word: *Disease*.

I thought about how this word affected me. First of all, I realized that it legitimated my suffering. I was not having headaches because I "wanted attention," or because I "had stress." I had a disease.

Also, migraine seemed more formidable than before. A headache, I reasoned, is something you should be able to figure out. But a disease.... That was positively medical territory. I felt more and more disabled just thinking about the word.

Accepting that I had a disease had a profound effect on me in another way: I was scared. I thought about why I was in a hospital, vomiting from the Demerol, hooked up to an IV pole, with medicine pumped in to drug me out, combined with another medicine to keep down the nausea.

After I got out, for the next two weeks I had two constant reminders of the event. The top sides of both my right and left hands were completely bruised black and blue, and so was the skin extending from my wrists all the way up my forearms. That's because the nurses who were in charge of sticking the IV needle in had tried repeatedly to find a decent blood vessel in my hands, but failed entirely. Frustrated, they ended up going into the crook of my arm.

In those two weeks I made a major decision. I would cut out stress in any way I could. I picked on the most stressful "thing" I could pinpoint leading up to the hospitalization. It was a book project. I had been on deadline writing a book for a publisher, and when I finished the manuscript, the migraine struck full force. (Many other

28

migraineurs confirm that migraines hit them after the stress is over.) I was feeling the stress of meeting that deadline, and I was very unhappy with the conditions of the book contract, plus I had had to schedule my work around two preschool-age children. It was all too much for one person to handle, I decided. I was not Superwoman after all. So I announced to myself and anyone who would listen that I would no longer accept commercial assignments. Despite financial difficulties, I would keep on being a conscientious mother and I was going to start writing things that I wanted to write. Creative work only. "When I have time," that is. No more assignments from publishers. No more superhuman deadlines.

This was a major decision for me. I got out an old manuscript, a novel I had begun in 1979. I dusted it off, read it over, and knew that I was on the right track.

Yes, I had a disease, I admitted. And somehow commercial work was making it worse. For whatever reasons, I told myself, I cannot cope with doing that sort of thing. Not now. In effect, I gave myself permission to take a break, to think about writing, to get back to doing something that felt good.

Right around that time, out of the blue, my mother sent me a small blue examination notebook that had my name on the cover. (My father and mother, both college teachers, used to have unused or half-used exam booklets around for me and my siblings to draw in.) This particular booklet contained an entire collection of short stories written in a childish, scrawling cursive hand. I was surprised by the date on the cover: it told me that I had been creating stories since I was five years old.

I wrote that when I was five, I said to myself, *and now I'm going back to being five. To doing what I like to do.* Forget all the hoopla in between then and now, working as a translator or a dance teacher or editing university catalogs, etc. That winter signaled the beginning of my search for essence. But it was to be more than two years before I ran into the person who helped me pull myself all the way out, a spiritual teacher and counselor named Linda Barnett.

Linda's work as a healer and teacher spanned 40 years. She passed away in 1997. Already in her 70s when I met her, Linda lived in the Southeast U.S., conducting her life quietly (her main companion was Kodata, a Chihuahua); modestly (she was a minister who disliked being called Reverend); and, above all, busily. It was not unusual for her to drive on Sundays to Fayetteville, North Carolina, where she occasionally conducted morning services at a church, following up with one-on-one spiritual counseling with folks there, and then head three hours back to Charlotte, where more people in various stages of crisis awaited her loving teachings.

I remember clearly what Linda said about this word "disease." A gifted psychic, she asked me right away about migraines when I met her—even before I had had a chance to discuss my physical problems with her. She referred to them as my "headaches," and I quickly corrected her (I had gotten into the habit of correcting people), saying, "You mean migraine? It's a disease."

"Honey," she laughed, "Of course it's a disease. And have you thought about where they get the word disease? Dis. Ease. Something is not calm with itself. That's why it's called dis-ease."

The year was 1989. By that point I had gotten so comfortable with knowing I had a disease, that I was not at all happy with this new twist on my word. But from that moment on, she referred to my dis-ease, speaking the two syllables so distinctly from each other, that over the weeks to come I became familiar with the idea. And I began to consider what dis-ease meant. How big, how deep was my dis-ease?

"I know this is going to sound simple, dear," she said gently, "but dis-ease is a manifestation of the body not being in touch with Spirit. And the mind, well, it's doing its best but it thinks it has a lot of power when it really is just a tool. It, too, needs to get in line with Spirit, so that body, mind, and spirit can act together, the way they're supposed to."

She said that all disease is an illusion. At first it was impossible for me to believe that. After all, I was in very real, excruciating pain. Nonetheless, I found myself unable to forget what she said, because she treated me mercifully, with tremendous compassion for the pain I was suffering. In addition, she commenced healing my sore head using the same type of energy work that Martin had exhibited when he set about dislodging my headache. Every time I left Linda's house, or was in her company, I left feeling immensely better than when I walked in. It was a powerful testament to her being.

The philosophical position of this master healer and teacher— that disease is an illusion which we do not have to accept—gradually became clearer over the many months I spent learning from her. She explained, "All disease, pain and suffering is a result of our not remembering our oneness with the Creator."

Though I had a hard time swallowing what she said, in light of my own pain, something about that last statement resonated within my heart. I instinctively knew its truth. Furthermore, I eventually came to think that before I could completely remember my oneness with a Creator-force, I had to consider that I had been actively denying myself divinity.

In American society, especially in the North where I grew up, one may not confront questions about God on a daily or even a yearly basis. But at some point, someone will ask, "What do you think? What's your take on God?" I used to tell people that "God lives inside," but I did not really feel that way. I did not feel it in my body, which is where it counts if you are a human being. It was all an intellectualization. If I had explored my own statement more honestly, I'd have had to admit that somewhere deep in my body I harbored resentment. If God is inside, why is He punishing me? The child-self in me reasoned, God must be like an angry parent. Here I am, trying to be so good, and all I get are a few crumbs of good, painfree moments in between all the torture.

My experience was characteristic, I guess, of a person in a society caught in a trap of religious dogma, a trap of its own making, in which God is Other. A system in which God punishes, and God is mighty, and (in some traditions) God would never forgive you if you got divorced, and so on. This God is the one I learned about, but fortunately, thanks to no sustained, early indoctrination during childhood, I was never too comfortable with this outside God. This God of the society in which I lived was like a "good parent, bad

31

parent" God. And it was male. I felt very removed indeed from that God.

I was not sure what all Linda was talking about when she told me about dis-ease. I did acknowledge that there were energy forces at work in my life—energy forces that I did not understand, nor could I see. I could feel their physical effects, however. There was a miraculous, unseen *alignment*—that's the best word I could come up with—though, happening to me when people like Martin or Linda performed their "laying on of hands" (for lack of better description). And these modest, healing folks who worked on me always told me the same thing when I thanked them for healing my headaches. They said, "It was you who healed yourself. I am just a channel for your own healing to become activated."

Deep down, I did not believe them. *They were born with healing gifts, not I*, is what I told myself. And it was only because I feared migraine so greatly that I first asked Linda to teach me the ways of healing myself. After all, I thought, these nice people might not always be around for me! I feared growing dependent on them. I began to consider, finally, that if they refused to take the credit for healing me, claiming they are mere vessels for healing, maybe I really could learn how to become my own vessel for healing. That way, I reasoned, even if I had headaches till the end of my life, I could access this physician within.

And so it was that I turned from being helped by others to helping myself. In the process of learning how to go within the self, which is essential to accessing the physician within, I discovered the causes of my dis-ease, and began working my way toward balance. Today, people call on me for healing, and I pass along the lessons and teachings that Linda willingly gave to me.

Some of the people who call themselves healers are very misguided folks who would just as soon have you keep on coming back for more and more so-called cures. I was always conscious of the fact that I was very lucky—destined, I guess—to meet up with teachers who saw their purpose as twofold: to facilitate healing for others by lending their personal help, and to encourage people like me to move from the role of being a patient (one who is being helped) to being self-empowered (one who actively employs his/her innate healing gifts).

The connection between spirit and health kept right on opening up to me. Wellness and illness were not strictly clinical matters. Pain, I felt, was a signal—a cry of the spirit, aching to be heard. It was high time for me to investigate this invisible realm where healing occurred.

Confirmations for what I was doing came from the oddest places, including mainstream publications. Among them was an article in *Newsweek* (Sept. 24, 1990, pp. 39-40) called "The Power to Heal." It was the cover story. Inside were the following words by Wade Davis, Ph.D., who has studied the cultures of Haiti and the Amazon River region and is a Harvard-trained ethnobotanist: "For most societies around the world today, priest and physician are still one. The state of the body is inseparable from the condition of the spirit. Sickness is disruption, imbalance, the manifestation of malevolent forces in the flesh. Health is a state of balance, of harmony, and in most cultures it is something holy."

I also came across a book by Andrew Weil, M.D., entitled *Health and Healing* (Houghton Mifflin, 1988), a whole treatise of what health and disease are, and how health and healing are viewed by various cultures, our own included. Dr. Weil's summary of the Chinese acupuncturist's basic view of health relates closely to principles of health and disease explored in this book about migraines. He has written:

> A Chinese acupuncturist would say something of this sort [when defining the theory of health]: health of the body is the microcosmic reflection of the harmony of heaven, representing a state of balance in the complementary and opposing forces of the universe. Disease begins as an imbalance in those forces, producing either excesses or deficiencies of basic life energy in particular organs. If not corrected, these imbalances eventually produce physical changes in the material body. Treatment consists of manipulating energy flow around the body in order to draw excess

energy away from organs with too much and redirect it to organs with too little. (113)

The Chinese are not the only ones to point to energy flow as it pertains to health and healing. In fact, most cultures operate knowing about subtleties of the unseen, taking for granted that energy does not have to be seen to be believed. It is this relatively young Western culture here in the USA that has systematically undermined and denied outright any approaches to health and illness other than what can be strictly measured using scientific instruments.

For cases of advanced illnesses and other medical crises such as burns and broken limbs, American allopathic medicine (mainstream medicine) is very, very useful. But it can do little to rectify chronic pain such as migraine, precisely because it has no way of measuring what is going on. Moreover, we Americans have grown accustomed to treating symptoms even as we say we are curing the problem. Doing this is sort of like throwing on a blanket when it gets cold, only to find ourselves cold and shivering when the blanket gets kicked off in the middle of the night. We use surface solutions to provide temporary relief, but the original problem still exists because the cause was never addressed.

There can be no deep understanding of migraine on the part of the majority of American physicians because they do not even wish to consider that the body's energy system might be awry. Most doctors will look at heredity, brain chemistry, and vascular dilation (the expanding of blood vessels) every which way they can, but they have, for the most part, little or no experience with what doctors from other cultures refer to as invisible illness. Were they educated to see the invisible illness that precedes visible illness, and trained to "read" or sense the essential energy patterns of individuals, they would be very different healers, indeed. But as of this writing, most American doctors are still very convinced of the notion that outside agents cause disease and, therefore, people get sick.

People with chronic pain—especially chronic migraine sufferers—have little choice but to explore their personal architecture of energy as it exists within their minds and bodies, if they ever want to get off drugs and live a full life. Then, and only then, will individuals be free to detect invisible stages of energy imbalance—the early dis-ease—before that imbalance becomes manifested as disease.

Remembering Wellness and Illness: An Exercise

Explore the notions of disease and wellness for yourself, in your journal, or through talking with a counselor or close friend, or using any mode of expression that feels right.

To recall times of wellness, feel free to jog your memory by reading over old diaries or poetry you've written, or to talk with family members who have known you for a long time. You may even wish to look through old photographs of yourself to see if you can identify any that showed you at a time when you felt and looked healthy and well.

Think back to those times in your life when you did not feel at the mercy of an oncoming headache. List the people and the circumstances, the scenery, and any feelings you have relating to what wellness means to you.

Next, balance this "wellness autobiography" with your thoughts, memories, artwork, conversation, and other expressions about being unwell, and feeling out of control due to migraines. This will be your "dis-ease autobiography," so to speak, and—just as you described circumstances surrounding your wellness—your aim is to record your impressions about being a migraine sufferer. The information may surprise you—it may seem insignificant, or it may be revelatory. For example, you may recall, "I remember that I was wearing a red shirt when I had my worst migraine bout." Or, you may recall that you had no migraines at all while you were pregnant, but the minute you stopped nursing the baby, the illness started hitting you again. Pay special attention to circumstances in relation to illness—your home and work environments, feelings, events, and so forth. Do not judge what you record—just get it out. On paper is best, since you can review it later.

Since this wellness and illness information may come back to you in dribs and drabs, and at odd times of the day or night, give yourself permission to regard this exercise not as a homework assignment, but as a fluid dialogue that continues over time.

Chapter 4
Energy

Everything that we experience, and all that we are, carries energy. Migraine is no exception. Migraine's vibrations and lights and thoughts all whirling inside the head are energy occurrences. These are very high in frequency, swooping in so hard and fast you may not be able to catch hold of them.

Martin was able to describe one thing about his healing gift, which he shared with me. He said, "I just push the pain away. It's something to do with energy."

The incredible thing to me is that this speedy, total-relief healing comes from seeing/sensing pain as a cloud that can be dislodged and gently lifted, or pushed up and away. I did notice that Martin took a long walk after treating me at one of my worst crisis times. He said something about needing to take a walk. My guess is that he shakes off any negative energy that might have been transferred, to protect himself from any bad effects. His fingers kind of shake and tremble where the energy transfer is happening. Quite definitely he is not massaging at all, in the flesh-kneading fashion (such as Swedish massage) that is our common image of massage therapy, but opening himself to a rare healing gift.

The gift is rare. Yet I have come to believe that all people possess the potential for developing their own unique healing gift. The ability to heal is rare because only a few of us discover it, accept it, realize we can help ourselves and other people, and foster it. Once we have accepted the healing gift that is innately ours, we find teachers all around us who can help us learn to nurture and direct the healing current.

Linda was able to tell me much more about these healing energies I had encountered. I had described to her what Martin had accomplished. How I was amazed. And how I was amazed at the similar way in which she treated my migraines, with total relief, within a short span of time, and with no drugs in sight. Linda became the primary person to lovingly, persistently, work with me over two and a half years, using her healing energies to work miracles on my aching head and teaching me the way to access my own healing powers.

"Migraine," Linda insisted, "is spiritual energy misdirected."

Migraine is *spiritual energy misdirected.*

When I first heard this phrase, I resisted the idea vigorously. I argued about this with Linda, and I argued inside my head about it for over a year. I had been a health writer for many years, and had read everything there was to read about migraine in the medical literature. This new approach—one based on looking at migraine as a spiritual crisis, essentially—seemed too far out in left field. The difference was, medical approaches had not worked for me: they only masked the symptoms. The headaches always came back. Here was a chance to get at inner cause, and open up to something deep within the self.

"Migraine is spiritual energy that is horribly, destructively manifested," asserted Linda. Gradually, over time, I came to know that she spoke the truth.

This is basically what happens. (Chances are this material will not be immediately clear, which is why later chapters describe various aspects of this energy event, and why we must, as migraineurs, concern ourselves with energy consciousness.) Our long bodies function as a vessel—like a tube or a drinking straw—where energies constantly enter, flow and exit. In migraine, energy turns in on itself. As spiritual energy, or energy from the higher self, enters in its usual fashion through the crown (the highest spiritual center of the body), it encounters blockages, and redirects upward, circling and circling back on itself in a flawed attempt to flow freely through all of the body's energy centers.

Linda was one person who could physically see this energy. I recall her describing the energy of one migraine, which circled the migraine sufferer's head like a big figure eight. Breaking that flow involves centering and anchoring that person back into his/her highest spiritual centers: the crown, the forehead, and the heart.

When the energy paths are cleared by a healing practitioner, the physician within is able to take over and channel the entering energy harmoniously throughout the body, in through the head and out through the feet.

"Can an ordinary person learn to clear her own channels?" I asked Linda.

"Anyone can learn," Linda laughed. "But first you have to choose to learn." She told me that a person who has learned to open and keep clear all her or his energy centers and be receptive to this energy is capable of receiving and transmitting messages from the cosmos—tuning into a band on the radio is analogous—without feeling pain.

"People who get migraine tend to be highly spiritual people," Linda told me. "But they are blocking that spiritual side from coming through. It keeps on pushing, and when they're tired enough, just like you, they start to accept that maybe they can let go. They can let that energy in, and if they keep themselves clear, it can be a fantastic power instead of a fantastic pain. It all is a matter of energy."

Taking workshops that teach the ancient Indian chakra (pronounced "*shah* kra") system helped me understand more about energy and how energy operates in the body and outside one's self. The chakra system delineates the energy centers in the body, with particular focus on the seven main centers. In India and cultures outside the West, study of the chakras is not new. Healing practitioners in Eastern cultures seek to balance the seven major centers of energy through various techniques, including yoga, breathing exercises, meditation, and focusing on colors or sound tones. Today, there are people giving workshops on how to activate and balance the chakras in probably every major city in the United States.

The illustration at the end of this chapter shows the chakra system in detail. The word chakra is Sanskrit for wheel. Like a wheel, each chakra is a spinning vortex of energy.

What does chakra have to do with migraines and healing? Quite simply, when you begin to spend time on yourself, on your body, with conscious focus on the unseen, you begin the process of locating the keys to cracking your personal migraine code. Instead of spending your energy restricting your life more and more (cutting out foods, avoiding people who make you upset, staying out of the sun at high noon, or whatever), you walk into the heart of your own energies to bring the spiritual, the unseen, part of yourself to the fore. Meditating on the chakras has the direct effect of bringing the physical body in touch with the spiritual self. Eventually, with practice, you start restricting yourself less, and allow the self to unfold and breathe more fully and expand again.

Living with migraine is akin to living with a time bomb. Certain situations or events or foods may set off this bomb, we are told. For example: a stressful day plus a chocolate bar plus a strong perfume in the elevator equals migraine. Or, a hereditary tendency plus PMS (premenstrual syndrome) equals migraine. One migraine specialist has posited that the elements that precede an attack may be isolated, but when put together they can be devastating. He compared the headache event to striking a number of piano keys all at once to produce a certain chord. In other words, you might be able to eat chocolate bars for three days straight and feel fine, but if you get PMS on that third night, you might conceivably get a migraine—just when you assumed it was safe to eat chocolate again. Whether he was right or wrong, it is clear that migraine is an individual matter. The chord that sets you off may not set off another migraine sufferer.

Your doctor generally does not have the time or the training to help you pick apart that unique combination of "piano keys." Counseling and psychotherapy can help you make tremendous headway, so that you can recognize the role your emotions play. In the end, it ultimately is up to you to seek ways to integrate all the scattered parts of yourself so that you can feel a sense of wholeness.

Rather than worrying yourself sick over the elements that seem to produce this bad combination or chord that leads to misery, it is time to take another tack altogether. Focusing on what hurts you will not lead to healing. Focusing on what feels good to you, and sets you at ease, will lead to healing.

One thing you must do is begin to pay attention to your body's energy centers. The energy-center (chakra) meditation at the end of Chapter 16 in this book is not a one-time meditation that you try and see. If you have never before dealt with your body's unseen energy, you will benefit greatly from practicing this meditation daily for many days, weeks, and even months before turning to other meditations and energy-balancing techniques.

Fortunately, there are several good audio- and videotapes and DVDs on chakra balancing available these days. One of the first fine videotapes on chakra balancing was "Shirley MacLaine's Inner Workout," done in 1997. This production takes the viewer deep into meditation. MacLaine's excellent book *Going Within: A Guide for Inner Transformation* (1990) also contains a strong chapter called "Meditating on the Chakras."

The Legion of Light's *Chakra Awareness Guide* is a helpful chart available for purchase online and in health stores. It describes the chakra system as follows:

> Each chakra in the body is recognized as a focal point of life-force relating to physical, emotional, mental, and spiritual energies. The chakras are the network through which body, mind and spirit interact as one holistic system. The seven major chakras correspond to specific aspects of our consciousness and have their own individual characteristics and functions. Each has a corresponding relationship to one of the various glands of the body's endocrine system, as well as to one of the seven colors of the rainbow spectrum… The main purpose of working with and understanding the chakras is to create integration and wholeness within ourselves. In this way we bring the various aspects of our consciousness, from the physical to the spiritual, into a harmonious relationship. Ultimately, we begin to recognize that the different aspects of ourselves (physical, material, sexual, spiritual, etc.) all work together, and that each aspect is as much a part of the whole as the others. We must be able to acknowledge, accept and integrate all levels of our being.

(©1988 Legion of Light Products)

Energy in Action

If thinking about your world in terms of unseen energy is foreign to you, perhaps some concrete examples can pull you closer to accepting the concepts presented here.

Imagine you have a friend named Julia. Julia is angry with you. Not knowing she is angry, you go to her house to visit and you walk in with a big smile on your face, calling out, "Hi, Julia!"

Julia is in the kitchen with her back to you. She says, carefully, "Oh, hi." You start to cross from the living room into the kitchen but something stops you. Julia hasn't once looked up, and her back is stiff. Although she has not said one single word to indicate her mood or attitude, you already know something's wrong. You can feel it. You can sense her negative energy from across the room, yet you cannot touch it or prove it with any mechanical instrument.

There's an energy at work there. And it does not stay still. It passes from her to you. Why? Because you care about Julia. How she acts in relation to you affects you deeply. An anxious energy begins to consume you. Now there is different, uncomfortable energy going on: her anger, and your anxiety.

Julia's kids walk in from school. They are bouncing around, throwing off exuberant, after-school energy. Julia snaps at them when they throw their bookbags on the floor instead of hanging them neatly in the hallway. One child starts to grumble and the other whines, "Mommy, my stomach hurts!" Now the angry energy has affected four people.

Julia herself cannot stand to be angry with you for long. That's because she cares for you, and she knows she has to settle this problem. She looks you square in the eye... And now you identify a new energy in yourself, one that is an unsure combination of fear and hope. Fear that she will hurt you by saying something unkind or untrue or that she doesn't like you any more; and hope that you can work things out and everything will feel okay. Julia senses your fear/hope energy, mixes it with her angry/negative/hurt energy, and releases what made her so upset. She starts talking.

The air has been thick with all this emotional energy. It has even entered the bodies of all those in contact with it. There are knots in your stomach, Julia is all choked up in her throat region, and one child has an out-and-out bellyache.

Skipping ahead to the good part...

When you and Julia resolve your misunderstanding, you hug and reaffirm that you are close friends and would never knowingly do anything to hurt each other. The children, who rapidly sense the energy change in the house, are getting a snack for themselves and are beginning to regain their good humor. Love energy, which has replaced all the other energy, is infectious.

Love is located in the heart chakra (chest area). It is the kind of energy that serves to clear and balance all of the body's other chakras, in an absolutely boundless, beautifully healing fashion. The highest spiritual chakras—the crown of the head (spirituality), the forehead (representing third eye awareness and/or intuition), and the throat chakra (the site of personal power, where truth becomes expressed in the form of sounds and words)—meet up in the middle zone of the heart (seat of unconditional love) with the lower chakras—the solar plexus (representing feelings and emotional self), the sexual organs (site of reproduction, carnal self, and creative self), and the groin area (which is the body's center for elimination functions and for feeling grounded, active).

Results from love energy can be measured and counted, to some degree. Once you become intimately familiar with chakra meditation, which comes from regular meditation practice, you will be able to measure these results for yourself.

There is no substitute for energy work, for dealing with energy. There is energy in the emotions of other people who live with you. Energy exists in the chinaware that was once your grandmother's, or the piano played by your sister. There is an energy impact on your body as a result of the foods you habitually eat.

Somewhere in the future, when you feel uncomfortable or agitated, you will be able to dissect those energies dispassionately. Turning inward, to your highest self, you will recognize that agitated energies are not your true energies, but ones you picked up from reacting to the outside world. Since you are the one affected, it is your responsibility to practice ways of clearing unwanted energy from your body and allow positive, healing energy to take its place.

Energy Awareness Exercise

The following is an exercise in energy awareness. Sitting down in one room of your house, perhaps your bedroom, list 10 to 20 objects you see in your journal. Then, pick one or more items and describe the feeling that emanates from each object. Remember where you got it, who was associated with it, and whatever memories come to mind regarding the object. Then, list a few adjectives that best describe your feelings toward it. For example, a scarf that you received as a birthday gift from your children may feel "dear" to your heart. Or, if it has a paisley pattern that reminds you of your teenage days, you may have a "pleasantly amused" feeling as you recall a time when you wore it every day to school, as a symbol of your emerging self.

Now look at one object. Ask yourself, "How far can the energy in this object go?" If it is a knickknack that your sister gave you, imagine its unseen energy radiating out in waves as far as your sister. Imagine her buying it for you. If you know that your sister got it as a souvenir on her trip to Spain, let your mind fly across the ocean and land in Madrid. You can even imagine the shop, the shop owner, his family—even the factory and worker who created the object, and what materials they used.

What you're doing is exploring energy in relation to physical objects. You can feel for yourself how the object transcends its borders through the workings of your mind and heart.

To go a step further, list five people whom you know (you can even pick their names randomly from your personal address book). Think of the energy they exude, and write down several adjectives or other words beside their names. When you think of your brother Billy, for example, you might relate that he has a cheery exterior—he's always smiling—but underneath you have always felt an undercurrent of unrest or unhappiness in him. List what you feel. Explore what you've always felt lies beneath the surface of those closest to you.

Now, pick out an event that happened today. It doesn't need to be earth-shaking— just something that happened which stuck in your mind. Describe how the event affected your feelings, and colored your day in either a more positive or more negative light.

Color Energy Exercise

Over the next few weeks, take some time to assign colors to persons you know and experiences that were important in your life. It might help to buy a large box of new crayons and then open your journal to the pages where you did the above Energy Awareness Exercise. As you pore over the colors in the crayon box, pick out three or four colors that seem to "describe" persons and events for you, then narrow the choice down to the one color that seems to be truest. You can draw that color directly next to each particular section in your journal, or merely think about it.

Anther method is to lie down quietly at the end of the day, before you drift off to sleep, and mentally paint a color corresponding to particular individuals and experiences that affect you deeply. You can even think to yourself, "What color comes to mind when I consider that person's attitude?" or "What color would I paint this day?"

Note: The above exercises sometimes have the interesting metaphysical (beyond the physical) effect of drawing synchronistic events into your daily experiences. If someone you've been focusing on calls you up "out of the blue," chalk it up to the power of energy— and note the event in your journal.

The Chakra System

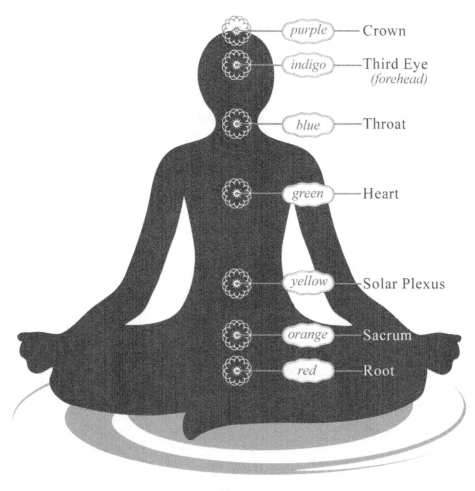

purple	Crown	
indigo	Third Eye *(forehead)*	
blue	Throat	
green	Heart	
yellow	Solar Plexus	
orange	Sacrum	
red	Root	

PART TWO

CAUSE AND EFFECT
Mind Is Body

All of our experiences become seeds for a memory garden, which is never just thought but involves a chemical process that is fascinating, intricate, and nearly impossible for humans to fully comprehend, affecting both mind and body.

In nature—outdoors in the realm of earth science—it's easy to see what happens when it rains: The skies start off being cloudy, soon small droplets of water descend, the people get out of the way, and the soil drinks up moisture, becoming muddied and dark. You might say to yourself the familiar, "Good, we needed a rain. Now my tomato garden has a chance this summer. Maybe I'll put up 80 quarts of sauce this year, instead of the usual 50."

You've got the above scenario all figured out. Sure, something bizarre could happen—the rain might not stop for two days, and the ensuing flooding could wash out all the seedlings you planted. Or it could rain once and not rain again for two months. Or it could keep up a nice pattern—sun, rain, sun, rain—until every last tomato plant gives its all and the yield is 100 quarts of sauce this year. All those possibilities exist.

So why is it that these laws of nature—cause and effect— apply 100% to earth sciences but apply only 50% (if that) when it comes to our personal conclusions about the events in our own lives, especially the events of our own making?

Example: Let's say you decide one day that you are sick and tired of being the only one to put up the tomatoes. You say to yourself, "No one helps me with them anyway, and no one will notice the difference if I buy canned sauce. It's probably cheaper anyway, considering how much time I spend slaving over a hot stove stirring down the sauce all night." You don't tell anyone about your decision, and no one asks about the garden. Usually that's the way it is anyway—people don't ask until after the garden is well under way, with the soil all tilled, the seedlings all dug in and lined up.

It feels like the tomato-canning deal is over and done. In your mind, you have already quit. You get involved in other things, other activities. But what you did not count on were the cause and the effect of your decision. To be inactive with regard to the tomato garden was not an inactive event at all. The energy of that event—that non-action—is active on many levels. When harvest time arrives, you find yourself staying up later than usual, and heading out to the kitchen in the middle of the night. (And chances are, you won't even be aware of why you are compelled this way.) When you go to make spaghetti, you can't just head to the pantry shelf to pull out a jar of sauce already made up. When you go to buy sauce at the store, something inside you recoils at the price tag. And none of the brands have quite the right combination of ingredients you're accustomed to.   "Never mind," you tell yourself. "It's better this way. Think of all the extra time I had to do other things this summer, without having to be chained to the weeding and harvesting chores."

Still, events related to your non-action are happening to you. Some of them are "feeling events" that sweep over your body. Anger is one of those feelings. "Why am I feeling angry about this?" you ask yourself. It's not a big feeling, but a vague, nagging one. "Am I angry at myself? Am I still angry at everybody for never volunteering to help out at harvest time? *Am I angry for never actually asking them to help?*" Bingo. Something rings true.

Another feeling you get has to do with family, childhood, and your mother, and your grandmother (and possibly your grandfather). Before you know it, a wave of memories is flooding your body system; if you had the ability to see into your bloodstream you could see the particle stream of chemicals coursing through you from head to toe. They are chemicals put out by the brain relating to love, familiarity, and sadness for things past, and body memories from the days of your girlhood when the women in the family stood in the kitchen chopping up tomatoes at summer's end, wearing aprons, with their hair tied back, sweat collecting in beads along the forehead and glistening off their arms.

48

"It's just a memory. Old, stale sentimentalism," you might say to yourself at first.

Then, halfway into the winter, when someone in the family starts complaining about storebought sauce, and calls you lazy and selfish because you decided against canning your own tomato sauce, well.... That's when the storm hits. There's no escaping this time. You counter with the same accusation—feeling bitter and self-righteous. "Who are the selfish and lazy ones around here? I'll tell you who..." And on it goes. Until all the fury and resentments and pent-up hurt gets spewed forth, looking (to the mind's eye) very much like the big, boiling red bubble of the tomato sauce after it's been on the stove in a slow-cook for several hours.

In a giving family, where love reigns over pride and self-righteous energy, the members would find a way to come together in the end with a new plan for support, sharing and new expressions of appreciation for the old traditions that bring so much pleasure to them all. The family members who choose to get involved in the planting next summer will begin planting their own memory garden—a memory garden that is never just thought but involves a chemical process that is fascinating and intricate and nearly impossible for humans to fully comprehend, affecting both mind and body. The senses are on full alert, storing all the associations of earth and sky, the rich reds and yellows of the tomato crop, the sound of bees humming, the back's aching from toil, the laughter and joking among familiar people, the pungent smell of tomato leaves and stems. Can we truly know how deeply these experiences sink into us? Is there, after all, a separation between body and mind?

It seems that no matter what, we are destined to feel the cycle of cause and effect. We can fool ourselves for only a short while, if we continue to insist that our thoughts do not carry much weight or our actions "do not matter." All of it matters, eventually.

In terms of health and wellness, scientists are only beginning to discover the mechanisms and interconnections between mind and body. They are beginning to see empirically—that is, in the laboratory—how mind and body are not only connected, but inextricably interconnected.

In other words, mind and body cannot be separated. It was only recently that scientists discovered that nerve cells exist in the workings of the immune system. "Can that mean," ask some doctors incredulously, "that the cells of the mind 'talk' to the cells of the immune system—telling it to react in certain ways?"

Why not?

Doctors are pursuing this research because of a phenomenon they cannot explain. It seems that the will to live, the will to survive, in critically ill patients is a major determinant of that patient's prognosis. That is, a patient who is determined to live has a far better chance of surviving a disorder or major surgery—or at least extending his/her timeline—than a patient with a similar condition but possessing a defeated, death-oriented mental state.

If the mind can think in symbols of living and surviving, and if those symbols activate a chemical response that is then sent to the immune system where nerve cells begin responding, and if this process continues on unabated, then the laws of cause and effect are not only in play, but are in command.

It is conceivable that we literally can talk our bodies into health—that we have the power to help self-correct certain physical disorders in this fashion. Why we do not give our bodies more credit is absolutely beyond me. One look at a cell under a microscope should be enough to convince anyone of the wonderful potential we possess as human beings. It is an awesome life force we possess, with powerful causes and powerful effects, that moves through us at all times. *If only we choose to become aware.* Then, and only then, will we internalize the concept that some of our top scientists are coming to realize—that mind and body are one. Mind is body, body is mind. What you think affects your body; how your body moves or does not move affects your mind.

But even that last statement feels a little separatist—as it assumes there is first one event, then the other. Perhaps a person who has released into a state of true mind-body-spirit awareness does not contemplate "first one thing, then the other." Instead there is be-ing. Only being. In that state, all is one. It is the ultimate wellness—to feel that oneness. There are ways to open into that type of wellness, but before we get to those techniques, it is important to examine the elements of cause and effect. That is what this section of the book is all about.

It is said that to conquer the enemy, you must first think like the enemy. Moreover, if it turns out that the enemy resides within, you must learn to recognize its disguises, so as to be able to cast out the old, destructive, enemy ways. These are ways of behaving and thinking that have become habitual but are not essentially you.

With their purging comes the sweet release from pain's prison.

Mind Your Body Exercise:
A 5-Minute Technique to Collect Yourself Anywhere, Anytime

Find a quiet spot where you can sit very still for 5 minutes. Imagine that you are dropping your brains into your heart. Mentally announce to yourself: "I am dropping my brains into my heart." As you close your eyes, sink more deeply into this image—allowing each thought, each idea, each sound, mental image, worry, feeling, and care to become redirected from your head to your chest area. Imagine the heart as a deep, loving receptacle that holds and softens all the thoughts that your head can drop into it. Feel the heart envelope your concerns. Know that the love that drives your heart also serves to drive your body. Allow the natural quiet of your loving heart to calm your mind, and feel that quiet love-force permeate every cell in your body from head to toe.

As you emerge from this powerful mini-meditation, tell yourself: "I will walk with my heart first today." In doing this, your mind and body can more easily feel the deep interconnection that always exists between them. Whenever your mind starts working overtime and you feel distraught and too full in your head zone, tell yourself once more: "I am dropping my brains into my heart." After a while, a simple reminder is all you'll need to walk through the day heart-first.

(Don't worry—the head will follow.)

Chapter 5
Thoughts

Thoughts are things.

If you hold tightly onto what you think as real and true, simply because it comes into your head, then you are doing what I call bronzing your thoughts. You think, therefore your thoughts have merit. You hold tightly to what you think, what you have reasoned out to be correct. Each thought becomes a bronze statue of your own truth. And when others challenge your statues with their own statues, you attempt to keep your collection intact. You fight the others, using intellectual weaponry. Or you ignore them, with righteous rectitude. You dismiss others, or avoid others who might not appreciate your bronze statues, your valued artwork.

In the end, if you are lonely, and feel friendless, it is no wonder. The bronzing of your thoughts has coated you in a suit of armor that none can break. All because of this habit of placing thoughts on a pedestal.

Of course, there is a wondrous quality to thinking and thoughts and ideas. Thoughts are necessary for living. They're necessary for making changes. But thoughts are, nonetheless, just things. When a destructive or negative thought becomes internalized, deep trouble results. It may be an inner trouble at first, but if it crosses into the physical realm, and you act upon it, there will always be hell to pay. "What goes around, comes around" is an old saying. It means that whatever energy you put out into the world, like energy will come back to you, in circular fashion. No action is without consequence, seen or unseen. That is one reason to look carefully at thoughts and their role in life.

There is a way to deconstruct the attachment we feel to thoughts. I use the following exercise to see thoughts for what they are. It involves some creative visualization, as if you are in a play.

Let's say you have the option of going out to eat with a friend, or staying home to eat with the same friend. You have two thoughts: "I will go out" and "I won't go out." Mentally hold those two thoughts in either hand, with the "I will go out" thought in your right hand, and the "I won't go out" thought in your left hand. Hold them out at arm's length and look at them, distancing them from your body.

The two thoughts have totally equal weight. At last you decide "I will go out." Now, feel the two thoughts. Suddenly the other, "I won't go out," has little or no weight. No value. Why? That is because when you accepted "I will go out," you took it into your heart. You took it away from the space outside your body and pulled it toward you. Visualize how you pulled that thought, represented by your right hand, in toward your heart.

We sometimes think we corral thoughts in the head area. This is not entirely true. We pull them in to the heart or chest area, too, and hold them in that energy center, which serves as our body's true biocomputer.

Now you are involved. You begin to plan where you might go. You imagine the food, your friend, the outfit you are going to wear, and so on. You talk it over with your friend, and the two of you make a plan to meet at a certain restaurant. Then, an hour before you are to leave your house, the friend calls up to cancel. Her babysitter couldn't come.

At this moment you feel something tug at you. You are hurt, or sorry, or disappointed, or even angry. But that is only because you took a thought and directed its energy into your heart. That thought led to other thoughts which you embraced, thoughts that became expectations. Suddenly you are stuck.

This is why seeing thoughts as things is very useful. If you view thoughts this way, instead of focusing on how disappointed you feel, you can now take yourself back to the point where you had two thoughts in your hands, two thoughts of equal weight. You made a decision then, took it into your body's energy, and made more energy around it (the expectations). In order to release all that from your heart, send it back out with love, the same way it came in. See the thought as a thing, and send it back out into that space in front of you, that place where the whole thing began: "I will go." "I won't go."

See the two thoughts in front of you, and reel in the "I won't go." You take it into your heart with love, knowing that your choice was influenced by the Providence of all things. Providence bid you not to go, even though you thought you could, so now you are regaining your center, your balance, by accepting that you cannot always know what lies ahead. The result is you will be free of the web of expectations that caused you to be sad. You will harbor no regrets, but peacefully continue on with your evening, open to the joy of living in the moment.

When you create an open pathway for grace to walk into your life—unobstructed by mind-chatter—grace will do exactly that. For you can never be at peace by resisting what is beyond your control; rather, by embracing a sense of divine providence you will remain open to the beauty of all that lies ahead.

See your mind's expectations for what they are: mere constructs of the mind. Yes, you get disappointed. That's only human. You looked forward to the company of your friend, in the above example. But should you let your whole evening be ruined because of a thought?

Some people seem to immerse themselves in a pattern of ruined plans. Like Eeyore the donkey in A.A. Milne's classic *Winnie the Pooh*, they constantly complain about how things are going wrong for them. Even when things are going well for them, they cannot trust in positive progress. They are waiting for the next ruined plan to happen upon them.

Thoughts are things. But that does not mean they are powerless: they gain power when we give them power. That is why is it so important to become aware of our thoughts. It is entirely possible to become aware of thoughts without bronzing them. And it is possible to become aware of thoughts that come from within, from the highest spiritual self, and to live in line with these thoughts.

You can consciously use thoughts to alter your biocomputer in a positive, permanent way. That biocomputer, located behind the breastbone, holds onto whatever information you feed it. If you felt pain and resentment at any time, the information went in there. When someone reminds you of that experience, the same pain and resentment resurface, even if that someone is a first-time acquaintance. Old habits of living and thinking also get stuck in the biocomputer, even without your knowing it. Some believe (myself included) that even the energy of past lives is in there, too. It may be somewhat dormant, but it is still part of your database.

The beauty of the biocomputer is that you have the ability to change your program, to redesign new software for yourself, in order to live a fulfilling life.

Achieving this is not a process of denial, or of pretense. Denial always boomerangs back at you somewhere, somehow; and pretense does not last. The process of changing your biocomputer is a complex one, but its main tenet is truth. This truth is a universal truth, based on the larger picture—the one that transcends life and death and the petty experiences of the day-to-day grind.

When you decide to find out who you really are, beneath your masks and myths, spiritual truths about your essential self will rapidly replace the old, destructive, lazy information. Deep down, the body that houses mind and soul craves a spirit-based program, one based on the principles of self-love. Not love of ego, but love of essential self. This love is unconditional, ever-constant, ever-present.

The practice of daily meditation provides a basis for opening up to truths about your self and your purpose in life. Meditation is an avenue by which you clear your channels, so to speak, doing away with all the negative thoughts that interfere with your ability to hear messages from the higher self—your best self, the one that is most closely allied with God. And messages from the higher self are being beamed all the time. It is when we have walked away from intuition, that inner knowledge that comes from within, that we feel most separate, desperate, untrusting, weak, and tired.

Children get about largely on the instinctive level. A small child does not look at the rain and say, "What gloomy weather. My day is ruined." She runs around gathering up shiny, slick raingear, an umbrella to twirl and boots to splash in. If you can remember back to being that small, you will realize that you may have lost touch with that raw sense of wonder and joy and playfulness—that first-response, or intuitive message which says "Enjoy. See the bliss in every moment. Be here. Now."

Some people get overly concerned about intuition and messages that come from within, fearing that they have not accessed their true self, their best self, but rather their delusions or fears.

It is good to feel that concern. When you do get a message—what feels like an intuitive message—it is necessary to measure it against a yardstick of goodness. If it is a true thought that originates from the higher self, it will be life-affirming, never destructive. It will be logically testable. It will make cosmic sense. A true, goodness-based thought is golden, not bronze. Every time you look at it, it shimmers in essential truth. Some believe it is carried to them in the loving, supportive arms of guardian angels; others just "know" it's right because it resonates over and over again in their hearts.

Getting into a routine of daily meditation and prayer is an essential way to gain more awareness and control over your thinking process. It's somewhat of a paradox, though, since you must strive toward non-thinking to get there. The practice of meditation takes time and will. In the beginning, it may be more worthwhile for you to begin changing your internal biocomputer for the better by focusing on simple, positive statements (affirmations) about your self. Even five minutes' worth of morning affirmations will make a huge difference. Positive words set positive thoughts in motion, yielding positive energy throughout the day. Help from the most unexpected places will come as a result of conditioning yourself into a life-affirming, self-loving frame of mind. Useful, enlightening messages will come in many different forms—such as sudden revelations, powerful dreams, or expanding relationships. Chapter 16, on Guided Meditations, contains affirmations that you can begin using now.

Thought and Change: A Tale of True Possibility

Here is a fictional example of how thoughts and awareness of one's thoughts can bring about physical, tangible change. Let us say there is a woman named Lou, who has been struggling with insecurity over her body. She is overweight and has been chronically overweight for several years. She is just beginning to comprehend that the old way of thinking—saying such things as "I am fatter than her" and

"How can anyone love a lumpy body like this?"—is not helping her. So Lou decides to reprogram her biocomputer regarding her body image. Even though she only half-believes what she is saying, Lou says affirmations daily for one solid month:

"I am comfortable with my body. I know that the life force within me was created by a higher power, a perfect power. I am a unique expression of the one perfect power. I am a perfect vessel for all that is Love, and Goodness, and Light."

During the day Lou drives to her job. She is the office manager and head secretary in a private clinic where licensed psychologists provide counseling for emotionally troubled and depressed patients. Although Lou maintains an appropriate professional distance from the patients, she basically is a very compassionate person and frequently ends up chatting with lonely patients before their appointments. After work she finds she cannot always put these people out of her mind. Lou has come to know many of them, and she worries about them from time to time.

Lou's weight does not drop away automatically as she had hoped it might through doing affirmations. However, she has become accustomed to reciting her daily affirmations. They give her a calm feeling, and her weight is staying fairly stable. She must be doing something right, she reasons. Be patient, she counsels herself.

One night Lou dreams about flying. Though she frequently remembers her dreams, this one is intense—so vivid that the feeling it inspires within her recurs throughout one entire morning. In this dream, Lou is a hawk that soars over cornfields and off the edges of mountain cliffs. She has a similar dream again, and recalls it so clearly that she wonders if it is a message about her body image problem.

Lou knows that exercise would help her lose weight and feel better about her body, but she hasn't felt sufficiently motivated to pursue it. She hopes to naturally gravitate, or be guided, toward an activity that will fulfill her body, mind and spirit. These dreams seem to suggest that she take up hang-gliding. Or flying lessons.

(What is going on here? Is this a message from the spiritual self or just a fanciful dream? First off, it would be ideal if Lou had a good counselor to guide her away from confusion. But she is trying her best on her own to become one with her messages. She steps back from the message to see what might be going on—analyzing it, imagining that her heart is opening up to whatever truth lies within the dream.)

Lou recalls that people are given both left and right sides of the brain for a purpose: one side should complement the other, and work in perfect accord. Creative activity is right-brain. The image of the hawk comes from that creative side, she reasons. Left brain does the logical questioning: Is hang-gliding an easily accessible activity that will challenge my body aerobically? The answer: Not really. Hang-gliding is probably fun and exciting as a sometime recreation, but one probably should be in good shape to even think about doing it. Flying lessons definitely do not qualify as an aerobic activity.

What, then, does the hawk signify? Lou begins to write in a journal to explain to herself how she feels when she is a hawk. She feels free. She uses the word "escape" when describing the dream sensation. She writes about the scenery, how warm the sun feels on her back, how wonderful the pines smell on the mountainside...

Intuition takes over. The word "escape" has struck a deep chord. The description of the beautiful natural scenery also stays with her. In meditation she asks for guidance, temporarily abandoning the "I love my body" statements in favor of, "I know that divine wisdom lies within, and that I will be shown exactly what to do. I release my worry about the hawk's meaning. I release all my worry, and turn it over to the all-knowing, all-powerful Creator within."

(Lou has responded to her dream in the best possible way for her, by allowing it to reveal itself naturally to her. She trusts that an answer will come in due time. Since this scenario is entirely fictitious, any number of outcomes could be devised. I will give one that comes to mind.)

It so happens that Lou decides to take a walk on her lunch break. She has not done anything like this for ages. Usually she eats at her desk, because there are patients coming in at all hours, and Lou has taken it upon herself to "be there for them." But on this particular day, all three patients scheduled to come in have called ahead, canceling their appointments.

Lou has been obsessed by a closeup image of the hawk in one particular dream, and she suddenly thinks it would be interesting to go to a nearby bookstore and look up a bird book. Maybe she would see a photograph of a hawk with these very markings. Plus, she reasons, her niece has requested a certain book for her birthday, and this would be the perfect time to purchase the present.

She walks to the store, about seven blocks away. The day is pleasant. She observes everything closely as she goes. People jog by. Women in office suits and sneakers are walking together briskly through the park. Lou gets to the store and has a great time browsing. In a book put out by the Audubon Society, she is excited to find a photograph of a hawk whose markings closely match those of her dream hawk. The bird book is on the wilderness shelf, where Lou stands transfixed. So many beautiful places she has not been to! There are books about mountains, and lakes, and hiking and backpacking.

Lou finds herself arguing in her head. Her Old Self says: "Don't even think about hiking, sweetheart! You're old and fat!"

The New Self replies: "I am a being of infinite possibilities, and besides there's something here that feels right to me!"

Old Self fights hard to stay intact, but New Self, which has become strengthened through Lou's dedicated affirmations, eventually wins the battle. Lou recognizes herself as someone who is open to change. She is no longer willing to close a door on herself. Lou purchases a copy of Colin Fletcher's now-classic book, *The Complete Walker* (originally published in 1971, the latest version, *The Complete Walker IV*, is co-authored by Chip Rollins, 2002).

She begins to walk every day at lunch breaks. Thanks to a new awareness of her thought patterns, she also recognizes her need to release all the heavy feelings of responsibility she had assumed toward the office's clients. This came to her when she caught herself referring to them as "her patients" (to herself, of course). She knows they are no more "hers" than she is "theirs."

It is not an easy process, releasing this old habit of feeling needed by them. But with each and every step she takes at lunchtime,

Lou feels better and better about herself. She is being responsible to herself. Daily she sweeps back into the office with fresh energy, and positive feelings. This energy has an effect on the whole office. People see the book about walking, which she keeps on her desk. Patients find themselves no longer sharing the details of the horrible week, but swapping stories about camping trips and mountain climbing and Girl Scouting.

Lo and behold, when Lou goes back to review her journal about the hawk dreams, she finds she has traveled a good distance toward uncovering inner truth. The hawk dreams were a perfect metaphor charting a way through all her immediate troubles. They affirmed what Lou needed to nourish her spiritual self: to connect back to nature, wilderness, and movement.

Lou could see that she needed to allow herself to be guided to her answers. She needed to escape from worrying about other people, to release any feeling of co-dependency with her office and the persons there. She needed to look with awareness at her own behavior, to consider for the first time that she had taken on other people's problems as a way to compensate for her own lack of self-worth, coupled with a feeling of general helplessness.

Escape proved not to be escape, as such. At first it felt like "I must escape," so Lou acted on it accordingly. Escape to her meant physically separating her energies from those around her, right in the middle of the day, so that she could get back to center. The dreams meant, to her, that her soul needed to get out of body, to get free from all the weight she had taken on through her job.

By and by, Lou began to walk daily, and hike with friends on weekends. Unwanted body weight naturally dropped off. But by that time Lou had already given away her scales. She was using another measuring device to tell her how she felt, an internal device. The escape message was truly an escape from unhealthy lifestyle habits. But that was the extent of the escape, because the changes working their way through Lou ended up causing her to engage in life more fully, wholly, and willingly. By reaffirming her higher self, she became grounded in a lifestyle that allowed for personal growth. She gained access to far more strength and compassion than she had ever experienced before. It was a paradox that Lou liked to think about from time to time when she was off on another nature adventure.

Every story has an ending. To end this one, let us just say that the counselors she worked for found the perfect gift for her on Secretaries Day (aka Administrative Assistants Day). They gave her a pair of binoculars. For bird-watching, of course.

Morning Thoughts Exercise

Every day for one month, grab your journal and start writing in it when you first awaken. Don't feel compelled to make beautiful sentences. Instead, let the words flow out onto the page without your judgment, in a stream-of-consciousness current. If you have had a dream and it's still fresh in your mind, write it out. If you can recall only fragments of the dream, write those out. This is a good way to find out what thoughts are on your mind well before the radio, children, TV, or your own anxious thoughts have a chance to interfere with the thought process.

Chapter 6
Overcoming Fear

When you feel fear, you say: "The Creator in me is all that I am."
—Linda Barnett

When I first began conducting workshops on migraine healing, I spent a great deal of time preparing for them, as any workshop leader should. One time I got the idea to gather together five items—five physical objects—that represented Fear to me. Fear, I recognized, was an underlying theme in my migraine history, and I wanted to share what I knew about fear. I felt certain that other migraineurs would relate to my presentation.

As I arrived at the site of the workshop, I discovered that I had left these items behind. The workshop went beautifully, anyway, but I was disturbed by the fact that I had been so forgetful. Later, in meditation, I asked my higher self why I had forgotten to bring these carefully selected objects.

As I allowed myself to ease deep into the quiet of innermost self, the answer came, manifesting in the form of a queasy, unhappy feeling. To me that meant I still harbored old fears regarding migraine. Somehow, over the years of suffering, I had convinced myself that these objects had the power to instigate pain. When I looked at them, my neck crawled and one eye started to ache.

I realized that while it was a good idea to focus on these objects, it was not yet time to bring them into the workshops. I had inner work to do on myself, to release my fear. So I put them aside in a plastic bag and did not look at them for months. I also postponed active leadership in my workshops, and instead turned to a support group full of women who were also "working on themselves." All of us were concentrating on ways to become grounded in our higher selves, and centered in our energies, through chakra study, inner child work, past-life experiences, and so forth.

Then, one day, while cleaning my study, I found that plastic bag. I picked over everything and gauged my response to them. There was no reaction whatsoever. They held no sway over my emotions. I could look at them objectively, and I could thank them for the lesson that I had learned.

These five objects mean very little to the casual observer. But to the migraine sufferer, they can symbolize a great deal.

Object #1

One was an empty bottle of Fiorinol, a painkiller commonly prescribed for headache. At one time, an empty bottle of painkillers would have sent me into a panic. More than an addiction response, my response was a fear that I would suddenly get hit with migraine and I would have too little time to try to contact my doctor and make it to a drugstore in time to deaden the excruciating pain. Furthermore, if the doctor had given out a three-time refillable prescription, and if all the refill possibilities were up, I was stuck with another dilemma—that the doctor might insist I come in for a checkup before writing out another prescription. That was a problem for two reasons: One, if I was already in pain, I needed concrete help, not a doctor's appointment which I was too sick to even schedule, much less drive to. Two, doctor visits are costly, and lack of finances was a major stress in my life.

For a long time after I began my inner healing work, I would occasionally need to take Fiorinol. Partly, that was due to my own lingering disbelief that spiritual healing pursued by myself on my own behalf would really work. Also, in healing my inner emotional wounds on the path to wellness, I found myself facing a great deal of physical pain associated with my repressed emotions. I knew that meditation could help, but I was in so much pain that I could barely walk, much less remember my affirmations. I believed that if some of the pain was first dulled by an outside agent (or painkilling drug), I could then bring myself to the point of being able to meditate. For this reason, I never suggest to migraineurs that they ditch their medicine. Drugs can play a helpful role in long-term healing, if used prudently and with awareness.

Over time, I was absolutely amazed to find that taking two Fiorinol was too much for my body to handle. (At my worst times, I was taking an unauthorized dosage of three pills every three hours. The suggested dosage is one or two pills four times a day.) Now, two Fiorinol quickly turned me into a zombie. So I cut back to just one, usually when I had my menstrual migraines, which I always felt were the most difficult. Gradually, over time, one Fiorinol began to feel like too much. That was when I saw clearly that daily meditation practice had been a fantastic boon to recovery.

If taking one pill was enough to make me into a zombie, then the drug had outworn its welcome, I decided. Nowadays, I take aspirin once in a rare while. But my first choice is to heal by accessing the physician within. I no longer run back to the house when getting in my car to make sure I have a painkiller in my pocketbook. My painkiller is right within easy reach. It is sort of like being able to breastfeed a baby. You do not have to spend twenty extra minutes getting ready to leave the house, preparing bottles and mixing formula. You just grab the baby and go. Mobile food. Likewise with a healing power developed within yourself: just pick up and go. Mobile pain relief.

Objects #2 & #3

Object number two was a Tootsie roll. Just a tiny little mini-size Tootsie roll. Object number three: an empty beer can. Until my headache incidences subsided to one or two a month, I kept away from any substance known to trigger migraine. Chocolate is listed as being a major trigger in most of the medical literature concerning migraine and food sensitivities. Of course, like most of the world, I loved chocolate. But by God, I would not touch the stuff. That's because I had had many, many headaches as a "result" of eating chocolate. I also stayed away from beer, wine, alcohol in general, cheeses, hot dogs, peanuts, avocados, fresh-yeasted breads and pastries, etc., etc.

Actually, I came to fear these foods. I hated being invited to dinner because it was a chore to answer the host's inevitable question,

"Are there any foods you don't eat?" I compiled a long list of taboo foods to hand out to friends and family. As for vending machines—well, forget it. The vending machine experience is very frustrating to a migraineur. American vending machines are typically loaded with processed cheese curls, chocolate-covered peanut bars, and potato chips laced with MSG (monosodium glutamate). For ten years I avoided Chinese restaurants, even the ones that claimed they serve no MSG.

When I began my recovery program, I continued to stay away from all of these foods. When I told Linda I had food allergies, she nodded sagely at me, saying nothing. Instead she had me focus on the practice called the Seven-Day Mental Diet (see Chapter 7). I attempted the Seven-Day Mental Diet many, many times (over many months) before I could say, "I did well this week. I did it!" Then, slowly, cautiously, after going for a good stretch of weeks without migraine, I began to experiment with forbidden foods, adding them back to my diet, one by one. I had mixed success. I had setbacks.

Ultimately, I discovered that my thoughts about foods were more powerful than any physiological response. Before I say more, though, let me make it clear that foods contain chemicals and that reactions to foods are very, very real. Psychosomatic is a word people usually hate or resent when it is used in relation to them. They feel as though they are being accused of a heinous crime: of inflicting pain on themselves to get attention, "just like a child." But all psychosomatic means is that the psyche (mind) influences the soma (body), and in the opinion of some very respected authorities, this relationship should be assigned far more importance than it currently is by conventional Western medicine.

In his book *Health and Healing* (1998), Dr. Andrew Weil writes that, in his opinion, "the best treatments are those with safe and valuable intrinsic effects that focus the belief of both doctor and patient and so function well as active placebos, unblocking innate healing by a mind-mediated mechanism while also working directly on the body. This is psychosomatic medicine at its best and good medicine by any standard of judgment, not quackery or deception.

"In fact," he continues, "the true art of medicine is the ability of a practitioner to select and present to individual patients those treatments most likely to elicit healing from within" (218).

If you have become comfortable with a no-alcohol, MSG-free, cheese-free diet, you should by all means stick with what feels good to you. In other words, if your incidence of migraines dropped dramatically after you cut certain foods out of your diet, then obviously your mind is working to free the inner healer to maintain health. (Beware, though, if you look upon these taboo foods with fear.) MSG is a major offender, so DO avoid MSG at all costs if you are a migraine sufferer, as it appears to attack the brain stem, even in the tiniest amounts.

If you still feel lousy, though—and I assume you are reading this because you still feel lousy—then now is the time to commit to finding out what the non-physical triggers are in your life. That means delving within, to conquer the old fears that have been stuffed down deep.

Why do fears get stuffed down, or swallowed, in the first place? My guess is mostly because of another fear: fear of being found out, fear of public shame, fear of what might happen if you release your fear, fear that you will lose your job, or marriage, or life. Or a deep-seated fear that no one loves you.

Sorry to say, old fears do not just fade away. They take on an energy of their own. They eat you up. They attack your health. They actually affect the way your cells behave in the body. Why? Because essentially they do not belong in your body. They are incompatible with your spiritual self. Your spiritual self is all-loving. And love is the absolute opposite of fear. Fear blocks your development as an individual. It can send you over the edge if you do not face it squarely. It is a negative energy with direct, negative effects on the physical self.

There is a saying that retrospective vision is 20:20. Whether or not that is true, I am on a personal crusade to develop 20:20 current vision. That way I know I can avoid the kinds of painful detours I took for so many years. But that means recognizing my fears as they come up. More on that later.

Regarding food sensitivities, I can laugh now about a wonderful week I once spent in Colorado Springs, visiting my brother and his wife and son. I had been working as an editor and writer for years, and I was sure that I was on the right career track. I was getting a lot of migraines—three or four a week, for several weeks in a row—and needed a vacation. I flew out to Colorado, where my brother convinced me to throw all caution to the wind for one perfectly decadent week. I ate Chinese food and drank a glass of wine. I dipped into the Oreos whenever I felt like it. I ate cheeseburgers and stayed up late and took my nephew to the playground where I stayed for hours in the blazing sun. I ate donuts and drank coffee.

Every day I waited for the headache to come. It never did. So I had myself a perfectly good time, and flew back home. Immediately upon returning to work I fell into a horrible onslaught of migraines. But that glorious week I had had was not lost on me. Because in one short week, I was able to admit for the very first time that my work situation was making me sick. The energy there was bad for me. I had tried to make it better, but there were forces, difficult and dangerous forces, going on around me that I could not overcome. The editor who had been promoted to head our division was not on the up and up. His style of managing people was deceitful and spiteful, which set up a tremendously negative energy field. Working there had become more and more nightmarish for many members of the editorial staff.

I made up my mind to leave if certain conditions were not met. They were not. I continued to get migraines on the job, but now I no longer blamed myself. I accepted the fact that I had no personal control over the matter: perhaps it was time for me to leave. Perhaps the universe had something else in mind for me. My intuition said get out. And so, five months after that fateful vacation in Colorado, I quit my job. I was not alone; others resigned too, which helped me know I was not crazy.

Fear of leaving a job is real. And leaving a job is not always the right solution. In my case, it was exactly the right thing to do.

Object #4

A small blue sheet of prescription paper, well-worn, was the fourth object. On it was written the name of my doctor, who was an internist, along with five telephone numbers. Two numbers were for his office, one was his paging service number, one was a hospital number where he could be reached after 3 P.M., and one was his home phone.

At one time I was sure that I could not go anywhere unless I knew how to reach this doctor. Actually, I am very fond of this man, who tried his best to help me. I am convinced that his personal attention and medical action helped save my life several years ago. Migraines can get you way down, and a doctor has to be awake enough, aware enough, and committed to spending a lot of his/her time with a migraineur to identify all aspects of the patient's migraine phenomenon. Each office visit was 45 minutes to an hour long. He asked many questions, and did all the appropriate lab tests.

Among the successful treatments he pursued were a course of Inderal (propanolol) to break a three-month migraine cycle, and a course of Synthroid (synthetic thyroid hormone) for an enlarged thyroid. He made himself available, which was not the usual (in my experience with physicians). He also said that counseling sometimes helps migraine patients.

I did find a fine counselor at that time. Mostly, this psychotherapist—Molly— helped me listen to the words I was saying. I had not been aware that I needed to improve my communication skills. She was the first one who said, "Listen to yourself." She taught me the counseling basics, of using sentences that begin with "I feel" and "I am hurt (when such and such happens)," etc., instead of "You should" and "Why don't you ever...?" and all those other judgment-ridden sentence structures. In this manner, Molly taught me how to open lines of communication rather than close them off. It was very useful therapy.

Getting back to the topic at hand: My fear associated with the blue piece of paper is relatively simple. I never wanted to be alone in the world, without a backup who could help me if I got a truly bad migraine. Are not all migraines bad? Of course, but some are unbelievably bad. When a truly bad migraine occurs, you fear the pain will never end, or will end in your death. To put it simply, I was afraid to walk around without these phone numbers on my person, for fear that death would be knocking at my door and I, weakling that I imagined myself to be, might be the only one at home.

Object #5

The last object was a bill, an invoice, from a major department store. As I stated early on in this book, migraine is a highly individual matter. What is fearful to one person may have little impact on another. For me, bills that get out of hand were fearful. At one time, when I was jobless and had small children to feed on very little family income, I used up all of my courage just pulling mail in from the mailbox. I remember not opening so-called window mail (bills) and ignoring the phone's insistent ring. Even people who were trying to help me could not enter this fortress of fear that I had created.

It took much inner work to unravel the multiple fears represented by one invoice. If you relate to this, please do not ignore it. Fear of bills can also be a fear of money in general. This particular inner quest took me deep into my childhood, relating to early experiences with money, and family attitudes about money. Having parents who lived through the Depression is not an insignificant point of fact. The fear that people felt at that time permeated the country's consciousness, to the extent that many people actually developed a poverty consciousness. Unwittingly, parents in my generation adopted and passed on to their children that negative energy of lack, of not having, of needing to save—even when resources were plentiful.

Money itself is not fearsome. Mostly money is a piece of paper or metal. It has value only because we assign it value; we give it value only through exchanging it for goods and services. That's why it's called currency—it's meant to flow out and then flow back in. It circulates (unless, of course, you hoard it). When used in good ways, money enables us to accomplish our purpose in this lifetime. Money is one of the means by which people express love and gratitude, whether it is for heat or clothing or counseling.

Fear of receiving money is a fairly common problem. If, for example, Carla is handed a check for her work, for example, and Carla suddenly blushes and stammers self-consciously as she takes the check, there is a problem here. Carla is the one who is uncomfortable—and she must ask herself why. Many of us, women especially, harbor a lingering fear of not being worthy. Ask yourself why you react to money the way you do. If you are not possessed of a prosperity consciousness, ask yourself why. (Be sure to read Chapter 14, "Meditating for Real-Feel Results," for help on this issue.)

There is only one way money can only make its way to you: if you open the channels for it to freely flow your way. There are many good books in metaphysical stores and mainstream bookstores alike about prosperity consciousness. Eastern philosophy suggests that when we finally are walking our path, that is, engaging in what for us is "right action," then the money that we need in order to accomplish our divine mission will be provided. It will be made manifest. And there will be no limit to the supply since the source within is characterized by unlimited abundance.

Fear Feeds on Self-Esteem

It is surprising the extent to which we allow fear to walk into our lives. It can begin to literally dominate our thought processes, and sets in motion an aura of fear around us, attracting still more fear so that fear seems to feed on itself.

Actually, the devastating thing is, fear does not feed on itself. It feeds on your self-esteem—that is, whatever little you have left. Fear acts like a parasite feeding on vital spiritual energy from you. Not only does it need this energy to live, to retain the space it has claimed inside your biocomputer, but you have given it permission to do so!

It is particularly surprising that fear gains this powerful position considering that it has nothing to do with you. Your essence, the essential unseen energy running through you, that God-force, is one of love, pure energy, light, and goodness. Fear is the exact opposite of love. In fact, it is the absence of love that allows fear to flourish.

Yet fear has no true power. We are conditioned to think that because we have had a fearful thought, it is ours to keep. But fearful thoughts, like other thoughts, are just things. *Fearful thoughts are things.* They do not have power until we give them permission. We give them permission by taking them into our bodies. That's why, when we unleash fear, we must literally exorcise it from our body's energies.

There are three major tasks ahead:

I. To get rid of the fear that has accumulated within your body, where it has been allowed to take up residence.

> Clearly fear does not belong to us. It is not part of our essential makeup, and can only hold us in bondage. The Creator-force within has no fear.

II. To inject good thoughts and good energy directly into the place once occupied by fearful energy.

> Affirmations serve an important purpose in this process of exchange. That is, when fears are being pushed out of your biocomputer (heart area) where they have been "held" for a long, long time, a vacuum of sorts—an energy vacuum—is created, which must immediately be filled by the strengthening energy of positive affirmations.

> One of the problems with traditional Western psychotherapy sessions is that, once negative emotions and experiences are brought out into the open, the patient is left feeling exposed but not necessarily whole. It's sort of like having surgery, without being sewn up after the operation. A counselor who is sensitive to how energy works generally will not only

coax out the negative thoughts (negative energy), but will always make sure the person in therapy spends time verbally affirming his/her worthiness, or aligning his/her thoughts with a higher power, before leaving the therapy session.

Tip: A useful affirmation to follow up after fear exits is: "I am a being of pure, unconditional love. Love is all that I am."

III. To keep any new fear from taking up residence in your mind and body.

There's only one way to accomplish this goal—and that's through becoming more aware of self. Self-awareness is nurtured by daily meditation, by touching base regularly, daily, with your inner guidance.

Undoing Old Fear

What can you do about this foreign invader called Fear? How can you strip it of its power, its hold on you? The Guided Meditations in Chapter 16 are designed to purge old fears. Please observe all instructions carefully. Bringing up old fears is serious business and needs careful, full attention. If you feel fear is dominating your life, seek counseling without hesitation. Counselors are trained to help you express yourself and face your fears in a safe environment. Certain support groups also serve to provide a safe environment in which to talk, share, recover and grow as a person.

Once you begin to recognize fear—and fear has many faces, hiding in the most unlikely places—it is a comfort to know, first of all, that you do not need to claim fear any more. Very simply: Do not claim fear. You do not need or want it.

But in order to purge it, you must seek it, then find it. Do not resist fear, or it will continue to be in control. Call it forth, examine it closely for what it is, then send it away lovingly. Say to it, "I do not need you any more. I claim love. I claim that I am a being of pure, divine love, and you have no place in my body. Go on. Go back to the nothingness from which you've come." You can let fear pass beyond you in this way.

Farewell to Fear

A critical question to ask yourself is: How do I feel about letting go of fear? Has fear become comfortable for me?

These may sound like strange questions at first. Please consider them carefully. This is a core area of discovery and recovery from migraine, this whole thing about fear.

I am very grateful I've had counselors to help me identify my fears, since many were deeply hidden under a pleasant facade and a capable manner. Many migraineurs are capable and they are very pleasant. They tend to organize well, they can handle a multitude of tasks, and they do this all with a smile—unless they are down with a migraine. But I say, scratch the skin of a migraineur, and you will find fear.

Ask yourself sincerely, "What good thing has fear ever done for me?" When you walk around full of excuses as to why nothing will work, you are indulging in fear. You acknowledge that fearful thoughts dictate your actions. Think back to when you were a small child, before fear got a toehold. You did not run around worrying about not getting something even before you'd asked for it! You did not stay up nights worrying about the kid who stuck out his tongue at you on the playground; you stuck your tongue back and ran off to play on the slide. Or you told mom, and she said, "I love you. Go play." So off you went.

What is the anatomy of your fear? This is a question to investigate sincerely. It's a lifelong question to ask—routinely ask—of yourself, which goes hand in hand with the soul-healing task that we face every single day.

Remember, though: Fear is nothing more than the absence of love. In some cases of inexplicable fear, where you have acquired a strong fear that has no direct cause, outside forces may be to blame.

That is, at some point fear wormed its way in while your shields were down. In a nutshell, you took on someone else's scary or terrifying experience, but it really doesn't belong to you. While some folks don't believe this can happen, I know that it can. Highly artistic and/or sensitive children and adults alike are especially prone to taking on other people's fear energies, especially if they are tired—when their normal defenses are down.

If this has happened to you, a trained psychic counselor is one person who can help you get back to the origin of this fear, as can a qualified psychiatrist, hypnotherapist. There are a few special priests out there who can also help. Accessing unconditional love and consciously directing love energy (that is, God-force) inside your heart-mind-body system when the old fear is finally exorcised is essential to achieving total, smooth recovery from this type of nebulous or "formless fear" experience.

Recovery means no recurrences: Once it is called up, spilled out, and then replaced with all-loving energy, you are clear—liberated and fully ready to move on to the next energy plane, the next soul lesson.

Some fears come about through learned behavior and bad experiences which leave you with a fear of repeating the pain at a later date. Or fear may be adopted from parents and is akin to a contagious disease. Parents who are constantly cautioning their children, and conjuring up fearful scenarios to scare their children into behaving, are reflecting their own inner fears. They do not essentially trust in the concept of divine protection and guidance, and they pass on their phobias to their offspring. As a child, you tend to trust what your parents say because they are the primary authorities in your life. It does not occur to you that your fears are actually theirs. When you finally identify a fear as coming from an outside source, you are on the road to recovery.

Fear energy tends to locate, or lodge, in the stomach or solar plexus, where the yellow chakra is located. The term yellowbelly refers to a coward, to one who is afraid. Fear manifests as stomach upset, tension headaches, and migraine response. Those who are subject to fear typically operate on the assumption that things happen to them and they act back. They have little or no directly accessible memory of the inner world manifesting externally. They have only a vague sense of being a co-Creator of their own destiny. The victim mentality grows stronger, setting up a negative energy field that seems to attract more and more fear circumstances.

Beyond the day-to-day fears there are some big fears. Have you taken the time to identify the big fears—the ones that haunt you repeatedly? Great spiritual teachers all tell us that what we fear the most will always manifest to you. Believers in reincarnation say this is for karmic reasons: That is, a fear-producing situation—either a karmic situation that you did not conquer in an earlier incarnation (lifetime), or something new that is fate-bound to happen to help you achieve transcendence—*will* come into your life again and again until you decide to view it with spiritual awareness and unconditional love. Only then can you lick your greatest fears once and for all. This theory holds that it is your job to overcome the karma if you wish to ascend to higher levels of consciousness both before and after physical death of the body. Otherwise, when you die, your spirit hangs around, waiting its turn for reincarnation, only to face that same fear situation again, just in a different setting.

Even if you do not believe in the deja vu experience, that feeling of already having been there, you might recognize a certain pattern of trouble that plagues your life. For example, I often hear people complain that they are always in the same spot with their boss, even after changing jobs. They move on to another job, because the old boss did not give them the support they needed, only to find that the new boss behaves in the same fashion. Over and over again they face this until they say, "Okay. I want to know what this is all about." Then, and only then, can they progress out of that recurring-problem mode and get on with their soul's learning-journey.

If, for example, you fear that your husband will start chasing after other women, there is some evidence suggesting that you may indeed be faced with that situation. In fact, it may hit you again and again. The fear may be triggered by an old memory from another incarnation with this person, since kindred spirits tend to find each other in the universe, for the purpose of working out old karma. That old karma, which gave rise to destruction and pain in the past between you, must be worked on with love and forgiveness this time around, or else the hatred and bitterness will simply go around again. That does not mean you need to stay with the guy if your heart tells you to go. But the conflict must be approached spiritually, delicately, and squarely. And with all the pure, unconditional Creator-like love that you can muster.

Resistance to fear is a major cause of pain. And resistance limits the soul's ability to grow and learn from an experience. Jacquelyn Small writes in her book *Transformers: The Therapists of the Future* (1984), "Dealing with the pain and fear that result in letting go of the past and opening to the present is the crux of the therapeutic process." The kind of therapist who can help you deal with fear and pain, she says, is one who is skilled at "listening, empathizing, encouraging, softening, and staying truthful."

She adds, "Blocked energy is limitation—the fear of releasing something we do not understand. And since we won't bring it out and look at it, it remains misunderstood and consequently, very powerful. Once the fearsome thing is seen and comprehended for what it really is, limitation vanishes. Neutralized through understanding, the fears are transcended. They become the force behind the positive quality hidden underneath the limitation. Negativity is merely the opposite of a positive potential, unrealized because the negative has held us under its spell" (p. 195).

What you hide about yourself generally has fear attached. The dark side of the mind, the dark past, the ghost-ridden corners of your house (body) are all places where fear has set up camp. As simple as it seems, the truth is that when you take a candle into those areas, walking boldly with the light that is your spiritual birthright, the darkness will dissipate. Being utterly truthful is the same as carrying a candle. The darkness must be exposed for what it is, not in the eyes of the law or to be judged by righteous people, but brought into the loving energy of your highest spiritual self, so that you can see clearly how it has worked against you. It takes only a little light to chase the dark. And when you begin to think of yourself as a being of light energy, the dark corners will naturally surface, and you will be able to clear yourself of fear.

In my spiritual training, Linda always emphasized that the process of releasing fears must be equally balanced with affirmations. Her standard prescription: "When you feel fear, you say: The Creator (or Great Spirit, God, Love) in me is all that I am."

I held tightly to my fears at first, finding it hard to let them go. I felt I had valid reasons for my fears, and that no one could understand me. I did recognize, however, that fear made me feel bad. It was negative energy, and I had somehow adopted a whole system of thought based more on fear than on unconditional love. Bit by bit, month by month, I examined the vise fear held me in. I practiced "turning fear around," as Linda would say.

Becoming acutely aware of thought patterns is the first step toward turning fear around. "I'm afraid I can't get that job" becomes "I am sure that if that job is on my path, then I will get it."

"I have a hell of a day ahead. I just know I won't get everything done." This is one way of expressing fear of failure. It has a way of ruining your whole day even before you've eaten breakfast. When you hear yourself say this, turn it around with: "I surrender this day to the divinity within, and I know that my higher self is in control. Everything that I need to accomplish today is already being done for me, in perfect order, in accordance with a perfect, divine plan."

That affirmation is especially good when you feel pushed by others. Do yourself a favor, and remind yourself that other people's fears are not yours to claim. All other people are doing is expressing their own fears aloud. In the writing and promotions business, clients are especially fond of saying, "We're close to deadline. Are you sure you're going to make it?" That type of statement used to trigger me into all sorts of anxiety. The adrenaline would pump and I would work crazily and the minute the job was turned in, I would spend two days with an excruciating migraine.

The word *deadline* is no longer in my vocabulary. I refuse to operate on any schedule that feels dead in any way, and I tell people that. I will set a *target date*, but I will not claim any deadline energy. I already know that I am a responsible and energetic worker, and I trust that the job will be accomplished in perfect timing. My days go beautifully when I simply stop and remind myself, "I am on perfect timing."

It is not easy to convey the beauty of this method—using the energy of positive language—in words. It must be experienced to be believed. The manifestations are myriad. People whom you needed to get in touch with will call you, not even knowing why sometimes. You find yourself saying, "I am so glad you called. I have something I need to discuss with you." All kinds of help come to the fore, simply because you have not seized up on the job. Over and over again, I have discovered that projects have a natural target date of their own.

In meditation, you can ask for fears to be revealed to you. One affirmation I use is, "Almighty Creator, I surrender to you all of my fears and I know that they will be shown to me. I know that anything unlike light and perfect unconditional love must exit my body. I know this is already being done through me, by the Creator, in accordance with divine will."

Often I simply said, "Great Spirit that made the universe, the only power and the only presence, thy will be done." The words are simple but powerful.

An old, old fear presented itself to me at a time when I least expected it. I was in the car, driving my nine-year-old to the last big swim meet of the year. She was very keyed up, and I was excited too. "Mommy," she announced when we pulled into the parking lot, "I'm going to win all three of my events today!" As she waited for me to answer, a fascinating battle was going on inside my head. Briefly, it went like this:

Fearful Me (FM): "Tell her she shouldn't get her hopes up too high. She might be horribly disappointed. It's your job as a parent to prepare her for possible failure. Be nice about it. Tell her you know she'll do her best, but that if she doesn't win, it's okay..."

Higher Self Me (HSM): "Now wait a minute here. She sounds pretty clear about winning. Who am I to burst her bubble?"

FM: "Oh sure. You would let her go up against that other girl, the one who has always beaten her in the butterfly, and not say something? You have to warn her ahead of time that it's totally unrealistic to think she can beat her today. Her chances of coming in second are decent, though. You could tell her that it's okay to come in second."

HSM: "Wait a minute. I've got it. I recognize you now. You're my dad talking. You're not me at all! I heard that stuff when I played sports in high school! You're the one who tried to spare me the pain of failure, of coming in second best. That voice of fear... But this isn't my life anymore. And I suffered enough with that failure stuff. Now I have a young child of my own here waiting to hear some encouraging words, and by God, if I have to bite my tongue off, I'm not going to warn her about anything at all. Who knows? Maybe this is the way a future Olympian talks!"

I looked back at my daughter and aloud I said, simply, "Go, baby!" We smiled at each other. Once inside, she suited up. My stomach was feeling fluttery. She came out, threw me her towel and said it again, "I'm going to win all of my events, Mom." I smiled wanly, bit my tongue hard, and aloud said again, "Go, kid!" She grinned. I wished she would quit saying that. It was going to hurt later when she got beaten in the butterfly, I thought.

I learned a huge lesson that day. About how mind and body interrelate, about how they can be so completely one that against all odds, a miracle can occur. The child won blue ribbons in all her events. Her main competitor, the girl with the fast butterfly, was two full body lengths ahead of her, but my daughter did something unbelievable, causing the whole audience to jump up and clap wildly. She kept her stroke going well down three-quarters' length of the pool, without once breaking the surface to take a breath. People around me were saying, "Isn't that girl ever going to get a breath?" Until finally, my daughter rose out of the water, took a huge breath, and plowed on. The other girl was lost in her wake. It was an amazing thing to watch. I think she took two breaths total till touching the wall.

Distinguishing between old fears and the fears others foist upon you is part of the process. Other people's fears are easier to get rid of, I think. I just say, "Hey, you don't belong to me. Get thee away. Move on, bud." Your own fears can be similarly routed, but the toughest ones probably require the help of a skilled counselor.

A wonderful side benefit of not claiming fear is that the need to obsess disappears. It is a very liberating feeling. Do not be surprised, though, if typical conversations begin to sound tiresome. I noticed that folks I normally socialized with, including family, had long made a habit out of obsessing on fear. For example, people typically get together and someone says, "So, how's school going?"

"Well, I think I'm doing okay, but you never can tell."

"What do you mean, doesn't the professor like you?"

"Sure, I guess he likes me but the main project is up ahead, so..."

"What are you worried about?"

"Well, with football season and all, I'm afraid I might not have the time to do that and also keep my job..."

And on and on. A simple question has led to a big pileup of problems that don't even exist.

When you refuse to play "pile up the problems," some people get mad and unhappy at you. All you are trying to do is stay centered, remembering that fear is a negative emotion; you're busy claiming positive emotions. But some people will accuse you of not loving them any more, or interpret your silence as being judgmental. Those are the breaks. If you fear their rejection, ask yourself why? Is it because they might not like who you are allowing yourself to be?

Keep breathing. Sooner or later, someone there will want to hear from you. The inner peace that radiates from your heart is contagious, and those people who are ready to listen to what you have to say will naturally gravitate toward you. The relationships you currently have are bound to undergo a change, even as you undergo change. Such is the nature of energy, and the nature of the universe. Things change. Within change lies hope for our future. Through change comes enlightenment: from being stuck in illness mentality, to becoming grounded in wellness.

Test Your Fear Level: A Self-Survey

Fear is negative energy. It sets up a negative energy field that may feel overwhelmingly powerful. I am not referring to "healthy fear"—like fear of having an accident if your driving companion is drunk. You do not get into a car with a drunk driver: you call a cab or you insist on driving. Nor am I talking about the fight or flight response spurred by adrenaline when you are in a dangerous situation. That mechanism of instinctual fear is kicked into gear by very real, challenging danger.

Unbeknownst to you, fear may be lurking behind many troubling life situations, emotions and health problems, especially migraine. It is powerful enough to keep tripping that adrenaline response, so that you feel surges of wanting to run away from something. Or you experience fear coursing through your body, putting your whole self on high alert. Fear comes in all ranges, from full-blown phobias to tiny, little clusters of fears that nag at you constantly.

How did fear become so powerful? Who is in control here anyway? Is it possible that you have been avoiding life's joys by an unconscious habit of accepting fear as normal?

If you suffer migraines, you probably also suffer from fearful thoughts. Even if you do not think of yourself as having fear, or having claimed fear as part of your daily life, take a week or two to test yourself—just to be sure. You cannot fight an enemy that has not yet been exposed to the light of scrutiny.

Step #1. Examine your thoughts carefully. Examine your sentences.

Just how deep has fear gotten? What kind of a toehold does fear have? What does it weigh? Is it heavy energy, daily energy, sometime energy, or out-of-the-blue energy? Listen to your sentences—the sentences you say out loud, as well as the ones that go through your head. Do this faithfully every day, for one whole week. It will be a chore, but, much like keeping a food diary when you first attempt to lose weight, this exercise will reveal what the mind seeks to cover up.

Step #2. Write down each fear as it pops up.

Rate it on a scale of 1 to 10, with 10 representing the highest level (Very Fearful, Most Scary).

Step #3. Use the following checklist to see if you relate to any of these fear categories.

For seven days, place a tally mark next to each fear category that pops up; then, at the end of the week, see what your score is.

Fears   **# of times experienced**

1. Excuses as to why you cannot do something.

2. Fears that pop into your sentences, cued by phrases like:

> "I'm afraid that..."
> "There's not a chance that..."
> "He (she) would never even consider..."
> "I don't think that..."
> "I'm not sure..."

Hedging and dodging of any kind may not sound like fears to you at first, but it important that you list them anyway.

3. Panic attacks.

4. Anxiety of any sort.

5. Severe sense of danger, with no direct reason for it. Shaking, shivers, and other signs that fear is present.

6. Thinking about someone in particular who makes you feel nervous or anxious, fluttery in the stomach, or otherwise ill at ease in your body. (Write it down.)

7. A situation you must face that feels fearful.

8. Extreme self-consciousness or sudden embarrassment.

9. Overwhelming feeling that you cannot trust people.

10. Worrying about situations, people, food, or anything else for fear that a migraine might result. (For example, worrying about getting a headache when someone sat next to you in church wearing very strong perfume.)

11. Saying "yes" when saying "no" would have been a much more realistic answer, according to your time constraints, financial capability, or do-ability.

Step #4. Make an appointment one month from today, to test and score your fears again.

Keep it up until you're satisfied with your ability to lower the fear levels in your life.

Chapter 7
Mental Diet / Mental Nourisher

Thoughts are characterized by a paradox: A thought is both nothing and everything. If we do not care about it, the thought is nothing. It does not enter into our reality. If we attach to it, the thought is quite important.

Eastern sages talk about right thinking, right action, and right livelihood. This does not mean right in terms of good/bad, right/wrong but right in relation to the inner spirit. Right thinking harks back to the original oneness with a Creator-force (the same as God, Great White Spirit, Higher Power). It is remembering deeply that you are made by the Creator, that you live within the Creation, and the Creator also lives within the Creation. This Creator is all-good, all-loving, and all-forgiving. This great force of goodness does not feel guilt, or resentment, or anger, or doubt.

Right thinking is thinking in accord with the force of goodness. It is claiming positive thoughts over negative thoughts all the time, every waking hour. Moreover, it is allowing your human mind to tap into the flow of One Mind, the mind of the all-loving God-force, so that all thinking becomes attuned with the larger cosmos.

True and lasting recovery from migraine requires extraordinary commitment. You cannot be lazy. Instead, condition yourself to embrace vigilance. Vigilance will become your best ally, yet this vigilance has nothing to do with avoiding chocolate or beer. If you are truly intent on total healing, you must at some point commit yourself to spending every waking hour in observation of your thoughts. This means you must watch over—keep vigil over—your thoughts, as if that were your sole driving purpose in life.

There is a mental exercise that can take you into total awareness of your thoughts, one that may take you weeks or months or even years to achieve. This challenge is called **The Seven-Day Mental Diet**. I attempted this so-called diet several times, sometimes with months in between, before I ultimately achieved a good measure of success.

I focus on this practice because when I was finally able to meet this challenge, I discovered that the time I needed to spend daily in undoing the migraine pattern dropped drastically from day-long work down to a 30-minute meditation in the morning, with some occasional crisis work (with a counselor) in between. Always I kept in my mind the inner knowledge that my choice to recover would lead to a tremendous empowerment.

Many times I got discouraged and felt powerless. But I kept a journal for myself, so that I could look back and watch the duration, frequency, and intensity of migraines diminish over the months of recovery. A two-day migraine, once the norm for me, became at first an 18-hour migraine, then a 10-hour one, and so on. When you are in the middle of a migraine, it is incredibly helpful to remember back to the previous headache and say, "That one only lasted eight hours. I know I am on the path of healing."

I do not know the origin of The Seven-Day Mental Diet. It is simple in principle. It calls for acute development of the awareness chakra, the so-called third eye. Here is what you do:

The goal of this exercise is to go for seven days straight without allowing a single negative thought to take root in your mind.

In this exercise, you must constantly check your thoughts, every waking moment. If a negative thought sneaks in, you are allowed to catch it quickly and throw it out by replacing it with a positive thought. However, if you go off your watch and let depression, self-pity, doubt, blame, guilt, frustration, fear, or other negative emotions dominate your thoughts, you must stop the diet then and there and begin all over again.

I never liked the word diet. It conjures up unpleasant memories of food deprivation, depression and utter failure. So I changed the name of this exercise to the Seven-Day Mental

Housecleaning. (Take your pick: You may find that the Housecleaning word suits you better than the D-word.)

There is not a whole lot more to say about this exercise. Once you try it, you will quickly see exactly where your blocks are, and you will undoubtedly be astonished by the tons of unwanted thoughts that walk up to you and try to get in. The exercise is comparable to keeping a Food Diary, which, if you have ever gone on a weight-loss diet, is a practice where you list every single food you eat for a whole week (that is, before you actually begin dieting). You have to note down each and every pat of butter, each cup of juice, even a stick of gum—everything. It is shocking at first, but very useful, very revealing. You can't hide from the truth of your eating habits once you've faithfully kept a food diary for one week. The most successful weight loss programs—where participants take off weight and keep it off—begin with keeping a food diary.

Do not be discouraged if the Seven-Day Mental House-Cleaning takes 30, 40, or 100 Day Ones in a row before you get to Day Two. Even people who regard themselves as cheerful, and present themselves as genial, amiable people find, through attempting this exercise, that they harbor negative thoughts, and unexpressed doubts and fears, beneath a happy exterior.

For me it was a great shock to have to keep starting the Seven-Day Mental House-Cleaning process over and over again, because I had always thought of myself as a very optimistic, positive sort of person. I still think of myself that way, only now my percentages are a lot better, a lot truer to my internal reality. By the time I first started a Mental House-Cleaning, migraines had bent me down so low that I barely recognized myself. I saw clearly how often I was embracing negative energy, in the guise of everyday thoughts.

How to Begin

When you are ready to begin the Seven-Day Mental Diet/ Mental House-Cleaning, try the following techniques to overcome old thought habits:

1. Ask for help from your higher self.

Each morning and at any time during the day, sit very still with your right hand on your crown (your highest spiritual center) and your left hand in the space between your breastbones (the fourth chakra, heart, or center of unconditional love). Make an affirmation of your own wording, to assure that your higher energies are in control. For example, you can say:

"I know that I am guided constantly by the light within. I of myself do nothing; the higher self is all that I am. My thoughts and my words are guided by the inner voice of my spirit, all that is good, and loving, and truthful. Anything negative that enters my mind is not of the one universal mind and is being replaced by positive, assuring words. Eternal goodness is present in my life at all times and in all ways."

2. Watch what you say out loud.

As you are watchful with your thoughts, so too must you be watchful with your words as they leave your mouth. You may feel (and sound) as if your speech is stilted, since you are probably in the habit of expressing first and thinking about it later. With practice, the words will feel less and less stilted. You will grow comfortable with your commitment to speaking the truths of eternity as opposed to illusions of your current reality.

3. When a negative thought worms its way into your head, firmly tell yourself: "Turn it around."

Write these three little words down on paper and place the message in places you see often. That way, when a negative thought begins to run through your head, you give yourself a chance to turn that thought around, toward the positive. When dark situations or disappointments arise, your brain will invariably be stretched in new, creative directions as it rewords thoughts positively.

4. Look upon hardships with love and gratitude.

People become accustomed to bemoaning the difficulties in life. Relationships are troublesome, children can be annoying, the boss is too demanding, and someone is sick or dying. These situations are hardships, yes. But now it is time to label them for what they truly are: *trials*. Your soul must face many trials in order to grow. All the struggles of your life, then, can be viewed as trials which you can face with love and compassion and forgiveness in order to grow more fully into the light of your true spiritual reality. To nourish the soul during these trials, you can replace initial reactions of depression and sadness by saying aloud: "I am aware that this is a trial I am facing in order for my soul to grow. I am grateful for this situation for I know that it comes to me in accordance with the divine plan of my life. I surrender to my higher self so that I can clearly see the lesson that is being shown to me now."

5. Surrender anxiety.

If you feel anxious about your own welfare or someone else's welfare, remember that the divinity within you, which is your true and lasting self, can feel no anxiety. "But I am concerned!" you argue. "Isn't it a good thing that I care so much about someone else, that I worry for them?" The distinction here is between worry/anxiety and caring/compassion. Anxiety generates a negative energy that turns in on itself; compassion is an outward-going, positive energy that has an uplifting effect on everyone in its vicinity—and beyond. Living in a body that claims anxiety and worry is like living in a house that has closed all the windows in on itself, for it is built with fear and sits on on shifting ground that is missing an important element: faith.

On the other hand, living in a body where compassion is nurtured and expressed is like living in a house where all the lights have been turned on, and all the windows and doors opened, inviting solutions and hope. That house is built on the solid ground of unconditional love.

The higher self does exhibit compassion. When you extend the positive energy of compassion, image-ing it as it flows out from your heart toward another, or directed inward to yourself, you are tapping into a stream of vast, incomprehensibly powerful energy. It cannot drain you, for it is a universal current. Experiencing compassion allows you to entrust your concern to a higher power, to transmute worry into love. Fear dissipates in the face of love.

Anxiety comes about when you do not have faith that the Creator is in ultimate control. Anxiety is often a signal that you carry an illusion about your own ability to make things better, or set them aright. Usually you have a deep fear that pertains to yourself, even though it is masked as worry about another person. One affirmation to say aloud for someone or a situation connected to anxiety is: "I surrender all my anxiety and concern, and all my personal relationships, to the only power, the one divine presence, knowing that divine providence is taking its course. I envision my family and friends surrounded by a great, protective white light that is the love of the Creator. I know that in the spirit, all is well all the time."

Some people have great resistance to letting go of their concerns. But when you consider the alternative, it makes far more sense to surrender those concerns. For example, if you are worried about someone who is having troubles of some kind, you are only another link in the chain of anxiety. This anxiety energy turns inward, becoming a destructive energy within your body. It has the effect of doing tremendous damage on your very cells. Recent research shows that long-term stress can lower the body's immune response, and eventually, as you continue to claim the stress for yourself, that stress pulls you toward a situation of dis-ease. No longer at harmony or peace within, you spiral into little illnesses. Finally, when your friend in need turns to you for loving support, he finds you have little energy left to share because you've been spending all your time worrying about him.

By contrast, when you recognize that your higher self is the self that can help you and others when they most need help, you attempt to do all you can to maintain your own inner peace. This can be accomplished only by rejecting tendencies toward anxiety and worry. Staying anchored in your higher self assures that all available goodness will come through your body in a clear, unobstructed fashion. You will then be the channel for beautiful energy to pass through, and this energy will carry over naturally to your loved ones, lifting them into their own higher energies, which then take over to solve whatever problems are at hand. I cannot say too strongly how important it is to give up old notions of personal power, in favor of true self-empowerment which comes only through surrender to the higher self.

6. Quit saying "I'm sorry."

If you must be apologetic about something, do so by saying, "I apologize for (thus and such)." There are very few times when we truly feel sorry about anything, but we have grown into a habit of using those two words as an excuse. The sorry feeling is tied to guilt and shame and should-have-done ways of thinking, all of which are negative thoughts that create blockages in your energy system. If you find yourself regularly saying "I'm sorry," take the time to note why, to whom, how, and when you use that expression. (If you're not sure how often you say this phrase, ask your family members or friends if they've noticed how often you say it.) One of my dearest friends first pointed out how often I was saying "I'm sorry." "What are you sorry for?" she asked. "It's not your fault. Why do you think you're responsible?" The more we discussed the issue, the more it became apparent that I was feeling completely inadequate, unfulfilled, and powerless with regard to several things going on in my life—relationships, work, children, finances. My saying "I'm sorry" to everything, inappropriately, was actually a way of calling for help—for someone to challenge me to discover what was truly making me sorry.

Go within, in meditation, to ask about the real feelings behind your sorriness. The answers may surprise you. Sometimes people who are chronically sorry are actually furious. Others are using the phrase as a weapon—both defensively and offensively. Sometimes saying "I'm sorry" is a sarcastic expression of anger; sometimes saying it too often signals depression—that you're feeling sorry for yourself and everybody and everything around you.

Many people—migraineurs especially, and women especially—take on too much responsibility and end up in the bad spot of always apologizing. They never feel adequate. Or they apologize to cover up for an inability to perform. They are seeking sympathy. They feel guilty about something, maybe even something that happened in childhood, and their sorriness transfers over into adult life.

Examine a sorry attitude closely, and with all-loving forgiveness: forgiveness for yourself, and for those people who hurt you, for they acted out of ignorance of their true nature, out of alignment with their higher self. In this fashion you can free yourself from unresolved, sorry situations.

One way out of the sorry trap is to make sure that you think twice and three times before committing your energies to anything. That is, if you are used to saying yes to every demand that comes your way, then you are setting yourself up for a sorry situation. Learning to say no may take time, but you need to do it in order to survive. Practice saying no, and realize how simple it truly is. Realize that saying no when you need to is actually a way of saying yes to your true self.

When you do make a commitment, consider that the other persons involved in the situation value their energy, just as you value your energy. When you honor your commitments, without overstressing yourself, you foster a feeling of personal integrity both with yourself and others. If, however, you make commitments and find yourself chronically unable to honor them, deeply consider a hidden meaning behind your behavior. Sometimes this points to a case of denial, where you commit to doing something out of habit, but deep down you do not care to pursue that activity (or relationship) any more. Facing the truth, and acting on inner conviction fearlessly, will set you free.

7. Turn negative statements to positive ones.

Words are far more powerful than we recognize. And achieving good communication is not as simple as we think.

How can you turn negative to positive? One way is by listening to others with care, and by speaking with careful attention to each word. Your voice, your communicative power center, is always ready to help you achieve a positive balance within—if only you allow your higher self to guide it.

One of the most helpful things psychological counselors do is teach people how to communicate effectively. They help you to cope better in life, simply by wording your sentences with care. When people are having trouble in relationships, their language is a dead giveaway: "You ought to do..." or "Why don't you..." and "I should never have..." and so on. All of these sentence structures are predicated by judgments, expectations, accusations and defenses. Re-training toward healthy communication requires that new sentence beginnings replace the old judgmental ones entirely. "I feel (happiest, hurt, disappointed, etc.) when (you do thus and such) because it feels like (you do not care for me) etc." is one example.

Or: "I am hurt when you do (thus and such)."

To open lines of communication, try "How do you feel about..." or "If I were to do (thus and such), how would you feel?"

In the Seven-Day Mental Diet/House-Cleaning, the above sentence openers will be useful to you and to others around you. Sometimes, though, the battle between positive/negative takes place in your head. For example, you may catch yourself accepting blame, in a thought such as: "Oh, I should have done that hours ago. I can't believe how stupid I was to forget." Instead of spending energy in berating yourself, turn the thought around, saying, "I know there is some reason why I was not able to do that yet. I know that I will accomplish that task in perfect time. I know that everything I am to accomplish today is already being accomplished." This assurance brings you up to your higher energies, where before you were in danger of drowning in the base energies of blame, doubt and guilt.

People will ask you how things are, or how you are. Do not stop and think about it. Never hedge by saying, "I guess everything is fine." Simply get used to saying, "I am well." *Even if you do not believe it, say it anyway.* Words have power. Others who hear you will feel better the instant you open your mouth. You will feel better, too.

Chapter 8
Words

Words have power.

In and of themselves, the words that we speak or repeat silently inside our heads carry energy. Think for a moment about certain words. Feel their energy. Watch how you react to them physically.

Love.

Pain.

Wisdom.

Light.

Anger.

Mother.

Death.

Joy.

These are some words that call up evocative images and emotions in people. They are in a language we understand, but before we assigned meaning to them, they were nothing more than mere letters strung together.

Words spoken aloud generate immeasurable energy currents that can affect the course of personal destiny. Energy comes out of literally every word that we speak.

When I heard about affirmations—that is, the practice of saying positive statements about yourself to bring about change—I admit to thinking that I was being bamboozled. I was not going to let myself turn into a mush-mouthed, sugar-talking New Age airhead. Words were just inanimate objects, in my book. They could be slung around, twisted around, misunderstood, and thrown out. I had only disdain for the notion that saying nice things about myself could cause positive growth. I certainly "knew" that speaking words to my migraine was pointless. Pain was pain.

But I was wrong. Words have power; you must not underestimate their energy. Can it be that words heal? Or, more probably, can words cause the gears of internal healing energy to rev up? Little by little, words do take hold. The energy of words that hark back to eternal truths is most powerful of all.

So why do we not use words to help us? Too simple? Too easy? We opt instead for faster-acting drugs and other quick fixes—to numb the pain of one more unbearable headache episode. But given a chance, words will go to work the moment you say them; instead of burying the pain problem, they set in motion a new chain of inner-healing events, which can both heal and prevent headaches from happening in the first place.

In understanding the concept of "Words have power," it helps to remember back to the place where words first entered our lives: in childhood. We understood their power, their energy, more fully then. Positive words encouraged us, and nurtured our growth. Negative words hurt us, and stopped us in our tracks. In order to build a defense system to protect our vulnerable soul, and maintain growth, we chanted an antidote to convince ourselves we were still okay: "Sticks and stones may break our bones, but names will never hurt us." It was a little white lie. Words can, and do, hurt.

Negative words carry negative energy. Left unchallenged, they can issue tremendous damage. If, as a child, you are repeatedly told by a parent that you are stupid, sooner or later you begin to believe that you are stupid. "You're stupid" becomes an echo whenever insecurity crops up. Even though you enjoy triumphs and successes along the way, somewhere buried in your subconscious are those damning words, "You're stupid." It takes a powerful, conscientious effort, and many affirmations of self-worth, to reverse those deep feelings of alienation and low self-esteem that were generated in childhood.

Think of the difference in the child who grew up hearing instead, "You are such a precious child. I love you." This child invariably develops a much stronger sense of self-worth and inner confidence.

When I was a young girl turning into a teenager, feeling awkward and gawky and ashamed of my bad complexion, my mother still awakened me and my sister with the same greeting she'd used for years: "Good morning, sleeping beauties." We'd shake our heads and laugh at her. "Aww, Mom, you're so corny!" But somewhere deep inside we felt good about it. Such a simple gesture on her part. To this day, I tend to wake up in a good mood. And I am sure that my mother's habitual words of childhood contributed to the comfortable, loved sensation I feel when I open my eyes each day.

So often the simplest words carry powerfully positive energy. They function like loving wings, to carry you past the treacherous psychological territories of self-doubt, alienation, and nagging thoughts of self-destruction.

Here is an example: "Life lives itself."

What does that mean, anyway? To the average healthy person, this is but a simple statement that sounds pretty logical, but nothing more.

To a migraine sufferer, or anyone struggling in pain, it could mean a lot: "I no longer need to consider dying as a way out of my pain. No matter what I do, life still lives itself. In fact, that I am still alive is evidence that I do not have to do anything to actively seek life or death. Life force is my essential makeup. It is one thing I can say for myself that I know to be true. I embrace this life-force, for without even trying, life-force is with me."

Perceiving self as made up of live energy allows a person in pain to relax inside. The words "I am life itself," spell sweet relief for the heart tormented by questions of essence and purpose. They provide grounding in life and life's processes. From acceptance of that simple statement comes a rebirth of the will to heal—which actually was never gone anyway, only hidden beneath the struggle.

Many of the affirmations that work most efficiently toward promoting healing are those that do not necessarily make sense but reveal truths beyond what we can logically comprehend. The intellect is set aside, and the heart is allowed to surface. That is, hearing "Life lives itself," the intellect cannot tell us why or how it is that life lives itself, but it does recognize that life-force exists as an energy in us. Beyond that only the heart can understand: the heart knows life-force is powerful, beyond reason, and purposeful. *Feeling* life-force, life energy, in this fashion, instead of thinking about it, helps us remember that life is a gift to us, and that we no longer need to consider running away from it.

Without a doubt, issues of death and despair come up with migraine. A migraine sufferer can feel so badly that death seems preferable. It is a strange and dangerous seduction. The words repeat inside: "I hurt! I hurt!" And the pain cycle reinforces the feeling of being a walking dead person.

The words that follow "Life lives itself" are just as powerful: "I am a unique expression of Life-force." (Or, "I am a unique expression of the Creator.") Simple to say and easy to remember, they, too, function as wings to carry us, with awareness, through the trials of daily existence. They are deceptively simple; once you begin a daily practice of saying them aloud, you become profoundly aware that you are speaking an unquestionable truth, and that Life-force reinforces itself through you. In other words, you begin to realize your connection with the divine. Divinity, you find, is not only for priests and Joan of Arcs. The potential for aligning with what is divine in the self lies within your heart, and will never leave. If you choose to foster Life-force, recognizing its power, giving thanks for it, and literally surrendering to the guidance of this higher power, you become open to all the healing your body requires.

Some say our souls have come to inhabit the human form in order to carry out a personal, divinely determined mission in relation to humankind. And for each "unique expression"—that is, each soul—the primary chore is to learn. To open to experiencing with the heart, and to look upon all others as unique expressions of the same vast loving spirit, the same Life-force that begat us all.

It is also said that if we do not learn our lessons of the heart, and perceive unity and peace within all things, then we may die with the chance that we will come back again—a soul reintroduced to earth once more, going back to school to see if we can "graduate" this time around.

This makes sense to me. I know that energy does not simply leave the body when the flesh gives out. Spirit energy has to go somewhere. Who says it all gets to a higher plane? There is much to be said for trying to get it right on this go-round. As I said to myself when my time for spiritual awakening was upon me, "Gee, if I cut out now, I might have to do this learning thing all over again. I have come a long way and I've endured a lot of pain already. I would lose a lot of ground in the grand scheme of things, so I may as well stay and accept that within me, Life lives itself."

Actually, migraine sufferers and other people in chronic pain do not really want to kill themselves so much as they are interested in killing off old, bad habits. When we walked into this incarnation, our biocomputers carried some outdated programming. So now we ask, How can we scrap old software? There's only one way. Create a new program, using words. Positive words, that resonate with the truth of the ages.

Author and healing practitioner Steven Levine wrote a book called *Healing into Life and Death* (Doubleday, 1987) which speaks to anyone recovering from years of chronic pain. He talks about what happens when a person close to us is dying; then he gets at the heart of the angst we suffer while alive.

Levine writes, "In intense grief of loss we rediscover, unmistakably this time, the grief we have always carried, the ordinary grief that inhabits and inhibits our life. Some call this ordinary grief angst. Many experience it as discomforting self-consciousness. Some experience it as jealousy, others as nationalism. But always it is accompanied by a deep sense of isolation and separation. It is the daily narrowing of perception which allows so little of life directly in. It is the envy and judgment of a lifetime, that everyday sense of loss. It is our homesickness for God."

Recognizing that angst, and how it makes you feel, represents a critical juncture in chronic pain recovery. First you must see it. Then, decide how you deal with it. If you give voice to angst, you give it power. By extension, you give power to the pain that attacks your head.

Words provide an alternative. When a migraine strikes, let these words take root in your heart:

"This is a memory of a migraine. This is a memory of a pain I once had. It is just a memory of a painful time that is now in my past."

At first, these words will feel like a lie, rather than a spiritual truth. But do not give up. Talk to the migraine pain. Declare firmly that it is but a memory. And go within—meditate—to see what messages your higher self has for you. Now is the time to consider that you are in a situation that is triggering an emotional memory, which manifests as pain. Remind yourself that you are a unique expression of an incomprehensible, all-loving Life-force.

Allow the energy of words to work for you, toward reclaiming wellness, through affirmations and guided meditations. You may not be strong enough at first to guide yourself along, and the pain may be so intense that you cannot read or remember the words that can help you alter your energy field. In that case, find a friend with a large heart who will speak the affirmation aloud and have you repeat afterwards.

And keep it simple. More words are not necessarily better when it comes to accessing the physician within. How to choose? Just trust that your angels (or your friend's angels) will naturally guide you toward the particular words or phrases you need to focus on.

One last tip: Never waste your time trying to get an intellectual grasp on healing words. Remember: You are now understanding and hearing with the heart.

Hearing with the Heart: A Calming Exercise

Think of the heart as a mighty healing power that lies like a sleeping dragon in the center of your own private temple (your body frame). Be still, and focus on your heart.   Mentally toss your Logical Self into a cage, and throw Judging Self along with it.

Now you are ready to unleash the power of the dragon. Call out the words, "I am a being of pure loving energy." Say them over and over again. Let the words resound in your heart.

Imagine the powerful healing dragon hearing the words, and rousing from slumber. As it awakens, it sends out wave upon wave of radiant light in streams of healing colors, clearing unwanted energies from the temple, allowing the crown to open up so that only the higher energies can enter, balancing, balancing, balancing...

Healing sleep follows.

Chapter 9
Me First (Right Action Will Follow)

"Me first" is not what you think it is. Me first does not mean selfish but self-full. It means: You must first be responsible to yourself, before you can truly be responsible toward anyone else.

Migraine sufferers chronically care for others before turning to fulfill their own inner needs. In that respect it makes a certain amount of sense that many more women suffer migraines than men. It is hard for a woman to put her individual needs first, especially when she has children. Children have so many needs, it is almost impossible to imagine how to put aside feeling responsible towards them even for 20 minutes a day. And yet it must be done. It must be done on blind faith, knowing intuitively that all the people in every relationship will be better off in the end.

There is an old joke that goes: "He takes a bath once a week, whether he needs one or not." I have a private joke I say to myself that goes: "I meditate daily, whether I need to or not."

Meditation, or any practice that requires going within for spiritual centering, is an absolute necessity as a mainstay of healthy living. People who meditate are shown over and over again that by being responsible to the higher self, all aspects of their life fall naturally and smoothly into place. In meditation, the constraints of the ego and the intellect are put in their proper place, and can be seen in their true perspective. That is, the ego and the intellect exist to serve, not to lead the way, or assume an illusion of control.

Here is an affirmation that calls for courage and faith. Say it aloud, and then examine honestly how you feel about it.

"I am responsible to myself. I know I can release my many roles in life and entrust them to a higher power. That higher power is all-loving and protective. I know that by being responsible to myself, I can be completely responsible to those who love and depend on me."

Did you experience a nagging question as you spoke those words? Or anger? How about fear? Initially, many migraineurs respond in that fashion. They just cannot believe that they can release responsibility for other people.

I admit to feeling anger and resentment when I first was told to consider taking care of my own business first—that I should pay attention to what my inner self needed in terms of nurturing, what my spirit needed in order to thrive. At the time, I had three small children who needed to get fed, clothed, and rounded up. I felt that only an arrogant, insensitive person could suggest that an adult's needs came first. Only someone who was free of the normal routines of childrearing and marriage could say blithely, "Just take care of yourself. Meditate. Find out what you need in order to live a harmonious life."

Meditate daily? Go to workshops and support groups and spiritual counseling? I asked myself. *Yeah, like when? In between stirring the soup, meeting the school bus, and changing diapers?* Had the migraines suddenly stopped out of the blue, I might never have taken this Me First idea seriously. But I had no choice. In my heart I knew that there was no alternative but to open up to becoming Me First. Already the migraines were screaming their own tune: Me First!

So I began to claim time for my inner work, slowly and sporadically at first. And the most interesting things began to happen. On the days when I claimed self-nurturing experiences, not only did I accomplish more, but calmness prevailed on the home front. When I took no time for my needs, it seemed like all hell broke loose and nothing happened when it was supposed to.

There will always be rocky moments at home or on the job. And when a baby cries and needs nursing, or when an emergency occurs, you have no choice but to put self aside and swing into action. However, when you have taken the time to get centered first thing in the morning, panic cannot worm its way in so easily. You are much better able to capably handle all the trials that are part of daily living.

When you are responsible to yourself, all the rest will follow.

Perhaps, though, you have become attached to your responsibility roles. Ask yourself sincerely, why do I resist giving time to myself? One problem may be that you have established a long-suffering, "see-what-a-martyr-I-am" image for yourself—wittingly or unwittingly. This will be hard to undo. Not only is there a strong possibility that you watched your mother (or another person close to you) do the same thing—always "doing for others," putting so many needs ahead of her own that she called attention and pity to herself in this fashion—and perhaps you modeled yourself after that unconsciously; but there is also the chance that you wield your power in that fashion. Martyr syndrome is built on many layers, at the bottom of which is essential self-doubt and lack of true self-worth. The martyr feels like everything is on her shoulders, which gives her a certain validation for existence.

The fact is, such validation is horribly shaky. Martyrdom is injurious to both psyche (mind) and soma (body). It leads to serious trouble within marriage and all other relationships, including work relationships, and perpetuates a role model that children (especially girls) emulate as a matter of course. Moreover, no true power exists in martyrdom. There is only an illusion of power.

Migraine sufferers know that headaches often increase in frequency as frustration and anger increase in intensity. That is because the spirit is crying to be heard. It is giving you messages that you are too blocked to hear. Messages you have no way of accessing unless you practice opening up for them, by listening for inner messages every day.

If the messages cannot get through, pain will be the primary symptom of your spirit's malaise. Eventually, you will get pain strong enough to cause you to stop, lie down, and pay attention to yourself. Only by now, with all this pain, you cannot really love what you are since you're so busy hating the pain.

It is a bad cycle. There is no way out except to change basic behavior patterns so that the higher self is nourished above all else. Anything less is just another short-term fix.

If somewhere inside you are still insisting that you have no time to take care of yourself, look hard at that insistence/resistance. Consider for a moment that long ago, in childhood, you began to define yourself in relation to other people. That is, rather than develop a strong self-image based on a pure love for your own good self, you looked to others for validation and support. You came to think that taking time for yourself is indulgent. You did not allow yourself to love who you were exactly as you were at every given moment of your life. You became caught up in what you could become, or what others needed you for. Finally, you grew away from true self in a desperate attempt to be labeled "good girl" or "good boy."

People go on for years feeling this way. But no way does this behavior go unnoticed by the body. The energy of self-denial blocks good health. At some point you may come to realize that you simply cannot deny yourself spiritual nourishment forever. And when I say spiritual nourishment I do not mean attending church or temple. I refer to going within for the answers that lie inside.

In the large picture, there is only so much time allotted you for your stay here in the body. In the even larger picture, there really is very little meaning to time. In each moment there is contained all of the past and all of the future. Time itself, along with clocks and calendars, is a construct of humans. Within each moment, then, lies the potential for ultimate self-realization. The inner harmony that results from self-discovery cannot be put off until a better time, precisely because there is no better time. There is only the moment as completely as you can know it.

Claim this moment. Claim time for yourself. Do so confidently knowing that everyone will ultimately be better off for your action.

The people who truly love you will not mind. They will appreciate you more. And those people who have gotten used to using you will be upset, dubious or resentful, but remember: they cannot be free either until they become responsible to themselves.

Affirmation Exercise: Claim What You Need

Beginning today, announce to yourself that you are claiming time for yourself. Begin actively to claim all that you need to become a whole person.

Place the right hand on your crown, and the left hand over your heart area. Using the words, "I claim..." declare all of those things that you want for yourself.

Claim meditation time.

Claim solitude if that is what you wish.

Claim time with your loved ones.

Claim good health.

Claim the money you need to live, knowing that the Creator within is at once the source and the substance of all your needs. Claim all kinds of goodness for yourself.

Claim "I know that my higher self is all that I am."

Anytime you make a claim for yourself, always be grateful when the goodness starts rolling in. Never let a day pass but that you give thanks to the higher power for all that you have. Hold one hand over the heart area and state simply, "I am grateful."

Small Mercies

Once you begin actively claiming your needs, small mercies will mark the path along the way. For each person, these mercies manifest differently. For example, imagine the scenario of a woman named Susan. Let us say Susan has claimed a quiet meditation time for herself, trusting that she will be shown exactly when by a higher power. She repeats her affirmations as often as she remembers to, usually when she is on the verge of being totally frazzled.

One morning, she finds herself awakening at 5 A.M. *Wow. Too early*, she says to herself. But going back to sleep is impossible. Suddenly, the question enters her mind, "Is this to be my meditation time?" She reasons it out. Since the whole house is quiet and restful, and since the family usually starts rocking and rolling by 6:30, then this could well be meditation time. Instead of grousing about, she says simply, "I am grateful."

It is the beginning of her early-morning meditation routine.

Susan wants to go away on a women-only spiritual retreat in the mountains. But she knows her finances won't cover the whole fee.

She feels more than a little silly, claiming that she can go to this retreat, but nonetheless her will to go is very strong. In meditation she keeps visualizing herself in the mountains, so she devises a powerful affirmation: "I am already at this retreat, in accordance with a divine plan. I claim that I already have all that I need for finances, and surrender all my concerns to my higher self." She mails in her registration form.

Growing panicky as the retreat weekend approaches, Susan begins to wonder if her desire to get away has led her into delusion. No extra money has dropped in her mailbox. No one has offered to lend enough money to help her. Slightly discouraged, she then switches her affirmation to say, "The higher self is all that I am. Only the higher energies can work through me. I surrender this trip to the Only Presence and the Only Power, which works through me at all times. If I am meant to go, so be it. If not, I know there is a reason why, a reason known by One Mind. I have all that I need. And I am grateful."

Two days later, as Susan is reading the paper, she does not know why but she suddenly decides to drop the news and pick up the pamphlet advertising the women's retreat. She feels suddenly compelled to study the pamphlet carefully. There is a sentence in the description of the retreat which had bypassed her entirely. It is just one sentence, but it is an important one. It says, "Participants willing to work at mealtimes are eligible for fee reduction."

But wasn't it too late to sign up for that? With her heart pounding, she calls one of the workshop facilitators.

"Good timing," she is told over the phone. "One of our kitchen crew just called to cancel. We were just hoping we wouldn't have to do too much cooking ourselves. Do you want partial work or fulltime meal duty?"

Susan cannot believe her luck. It is the break she's been hoping for. It is not how she imagined that she would pay for the retreat, but it suits her needs perfectly.

The break she received had a timing and a rhythm all its own. Perfect timing. Had she called a day earlier or a day later, she might not have had the opportunity that fell into her lap. The best thing

Susan did for herself was relax about it—to announce that she was letting it go, turning over the situation to her higher self. It's like saying, "Okay, Higher Self, you make the arrangements. I'll go along with whatever you come up with."

All of us have heard of cases where couples, desirous of having children, try for years to get pregnant without success—until they finally quit worrying about it, give up, and prepare to adopt. Then, out of the blue, their child is conceived.

There is such a thing as perfect timing. Perfect timing can be likened to a pure and mighty river that is flowing constantly, powerfully. When you meditate, you can feel your body's energies open into this flow, and you know that you are exactly where you are supposed to be. You merge with the river, and flow with it.

When you are scattered mentally, or frazzled or anxious or attempting to control everybody and everything around you, you basically are launching your body on its own detour off the main river. It will travel along in eddies and streams, bumped by sticks and scraped up by the rocks below, till eventually it finds itself stuck in a lagoon or a swamp somewhere, floundering and in pain, cursing about how nothing is going right, how the timing is off, how rotten life is treating it.

Fortunately for us—and this is the beauty of being a human being—the way home to the main river is never far away. All that is required is that we still ourselves long enough to feel the current. Submit to the current. When we ease our body/mind/soul into the main current, this mighty river of energy, we lose ourselves and gain ourselves at the same time. We perceive perfect timing. We know deeply that there is a time and purpose to everything—even for our detours into pain and suffering. Finding perfect timing is not a completely passive process, but it's nowhere near as active as we figure.

When you make the commitment to nurture your spirit, to still yourself and feel one with the mighty river at the start of each day, your health will begin to turn around as a matter of course. You start to reclaim a natural awareness of what your spirit needs to sustain itself and to foster the growth of your soul.

At one point, in this period of recovery from migraine, sit down and make a list or drawings of what kinds of things feel good to you. Write another list of what feels bad to you, or uncomfortable. Reconnect with desires that you have squelched, or pushed down. Likewise, list all your disappointments. Be brutally honest. Hide nothing.

Do not allow others to encroach on the time you have set aside for nurturing your spirit. If you have small children, you may need to enlist help from your spouse or a friend so that your quiet time is ensured. Insist upon it, as if your life depends on it—which it may.

By the phone, whether at work or home, keep the following reminder written on a piece of paper for those times when people catch you off guard and you find yourself overloading your calendar:

I have a previous commitment.

Say it often. The sentence gets easier and easier to say with practice. Should people press you, asking, "What commitment do you have?" you can always let them know, "It's to myself."

Chapter 10
Anger

"Anger is the stepchild of fear." —Linda Barnett

Assuming you are keeping a journal about this healing phase of your life, by now you should have devoted space and time to listing out what you do feel comfortable about in your life, or about yourself, and what you *don't* feel comfortable about. The former list is about ESSENCE; the latter list is about STRain on your ESSence—or stress. (If you have not yet taken the time to explore those topics, do so now. It is an important step in the process of identifying your core self. Some people write down a short, sketchy list when they first begin a journal, and then find themselves adding to the list, and even changing some original answers as the self-exploration process continues.)

Migraine sufferers generally agree that the Stress List is an important list, but they commonly dismiss its importance by saying, "So what? Everybody can't be happy all the time. Everyone faces things they're not happy about."

This attitude represents a fundamental misconception, which is that migraine sufferers are just like the general lot of humankind, only they "take it more personally." Unknowingly, migraineurs take on the yoke that others around them have placed on them. "Others" are the general populace, who do not take the migraine problem very seriously—not because they are callous so much as they simply cannot comprehend it. They are the ones who say, "Just take an aspirin."

And "others" are all those lucky folks who have "never had a headache." We have all met them. And our usual response to meeting up with people like that? If truth be told, we are torn between wanting to kiss their feet or hurt their face.

Torn between reverence and violence. Though we say it in jest, the response is not a quiet one that goes away. Underneath the feeling is a desperate cry, "Why me?" And there is anger. There is a wanting to blame. And deep down, there is usually a feeling of being forsaken.

Who is forsaken, and by whom?

And what part does anger play?

It does no good for migraineurs to lump themselves in with the general populace. People who get migraines cannot measure themselves against others and come up with a good feeling about themselves, especially if they continually aspire to become one of the "others." On the other hand, it does no good to continually excuse oneself from actively living life on account of the pain.

Somewhere in here lies a new definition of migraine-prone people. Migraine-prone people are sensitive—supersensitive. Obviously, for whatever reasons, migraine-prone people take their stresses seriously. Their essential self cannot tolerate too many entries in that second list referred to earlier—the list of things, people, routines, or situations that make them feel uncomfortable.

Each and every item on that list weighs against migraine sufferers, effectively landing another strike against the higher self. That means their calling in life is threatened. The mission that they came here for is in jeopardy, unless they work to confront the offending items off their list—one by one by one.

Typically, migraine sufferers avoid confrontation. "I can handle it," or "I'll find a way to get around it," they say. Or worse: they tell themselves "It [this conflict] will go away on its own accord."

This is a tough subject to make generalizations about. But I think it is entirely possible that the stress list is a list that migraineurs are angry at. That is, not only are we deeply uncomfortable about stress, we resent the people, situations, and events that have caused us to feel that way. And since we allowed the list to grow longer, year in and year out, usually by not speaking out against the stresses as they were happening to us, we are deeply angry at ourselves for not knowing how to take action against stress.

A long time ago someone said to me, "My therapist says that migraine is the mask of rage." Perhaps it is true, and perhaps it isn't. All that really matters is, if anger is present, total healing is not possible. And, the reverse side of the coin: if anger is uncovered, healing begins.

Why is that? "Anger," Linda Barnett says, "is the stepchild of fear." If you stop to think about it, every situation involving anger has fear at its root. For example, the sentence: "I am angry at her" translates—on the subconscious level—into "I am afraid she will turn her back on me and that she will not love me any more." Or, "I wish I could tell my boss how angry he makes me" carries an unstated, additional fear message: "...but if I did, he might not see things my way and I could lose my job."

Expressing anger then involves risk—risking relationships, entering into the unknown, asking for change. Scary stuff. But it is not something we can choose to ignore. Anger plays too large a part in illness.

Exercise: Write It in Red

To examine what role anger plays in your body's state of dis-ease, make a new journal list with the heading, "What makes me angry." Write it in red—for you are seeing red when anger energy is present. Red, incidentally, is the energy center that corresponds with fight or flight—the adrenaline response to stress, or put simply, the Anger-Fear response. Start on a left-hand page and leave the facing (right-hand) pages blank. Let the list become a long-term list which you do not feel compelled to finish in one day.

Each time after you have finished listing the angry items, list what fear could possibly lie underneath each item, on the facing right-hand page. If you cannot see the fear at first, you may need a therapist to help you dig it out. But exist it does.

Why the Big Focus on Anger?

Doing the above exercise is critical work for healing, because fear—being the 180-degree opposite of love—blocks the work of your physician within. Loving energy always heals; whereas fearful energy turns in on itself, and can be reversed only by replacing it with its opposite—pure, unconditional love. Repressed anger is particularly destructive, because it has nowhere to go, but to cycle back down into your self, and fester, and smolder, piling itself up in a great toxic heap. Its energy is poison to the spiritual self. Its effect is to stunt the growth of your soul, and it manifests in any number of unpleasant ways—migraine included.

If you are a typical migraine sufferer, you probably do not want to know too much about your anger while a migraine is coming on. You tell yourself that you will make your Anger:Fear list in the BEING journal *after* you are feeling better—perhaps in between headaches. Or after church, when you can take a softer attitude toward anger. It might even be that you do not see any need to make the list at all, and you are about to decide that this exercise is a waste of time.

But I say, give it a shot. After all, we human beings all face situations that make our blood boil, or get us riled, or inhibit us to the point where we are afraid to freely be who we are. The angriest people around are those who say, "I can't really say I'm angry about anything." Typically, they are women, and they have been engaging in a long pattern of putting self second behind everyone else's needs. They have pushed their feelings so far down that there is no getting at them—and to explore those feelings would fundamentally unglue them, or so they fear. Or, they are unconsciously aware that bringing up angry feelings might change their life situations, or would meet with severe disapproval by their loved ones, and so they keep quiet to preserve the status quo. The most troubling consequence of this behavior is that the migraineur convinces herself that it is okay for her to be sick—so long as the rest of the family is able to function well. In other words, she martyrs herself by compromising her needs so severely that her own life is thrown into jeopardy.

Certainly that was not her intended result. When the headaches get so harsh that she is disabled more than 30 percent of the time, the people around her begin to exhibit signs of not coping and she is thrown into a further frenzy of trying to over-function for the sake of everyone else on her "good days," when the headaches are at bay. She enters a period of seesawing between good days and bad days, and gradually loses a sense of control in her own life. That in itself is frightening—and fear feeds upon fear to make her life a living hell.

If you suspect that anger lies down below, but the very thought of looking at it, or listing it, is unsettling, by all means take the advice of the experts: get counseling and get it fast, before your self has been completely negated. Tell someone you love that you need their help. Ask him or her to find a counselor and make the appointment for you. It's a long road up from being down, but an experienced psychotherapist or other counselor can help you achieve miracles, working in concert with your own inner-healing mechanisms. There is much work to be done, and you cannot accomplish much alone; you must seek help and remain committed to following through until you become capable of recognizing anger when it occurs. The next step is to learn skills of expressing and coping with anger, also an arena that counselors specialize in.

And if you are from the old school of self-sufficiency, consider yourself graduated the moment you choose to let others help you. It is no disgrace to seek counseling. Counseling is not "for crazy people." Those kinds of inner statements are someone else's tapes— perhaps your father's or your spouse's—running in the back of your head. Create your own tapes now—tapes that say you are bold and that you dare to live and confront life head on. That you are willing to help yourself to the many techniques professional counselors can teach you regarding effective communication (saying what you mean without fear), how to deal with emotional pain, and what to do about those things/situations/people that are on your stress list.

To see if anger lies at the root of migraine, explore the feeling as thoroughly as you dare. Open yourself to doing whatever it takes— usually a combination of journal writing, counseling, confronting situations and people with your feelings, making attempts to resolve festering conflicts, and generally resolving to make changes in all of those areas in your life that make you feel uncomfortable. And, if you cannot easily distinguish between what feels comfortable or uncomfortable, put the situation to a simple test: Does this make me feel good? Or does this make me feel bad?

As you work out areas of anger, keep in mind that you cannot control others and you cannot control events around you. The best you can do is work to identify your feelings of anger, bring them up with all their fury, surrender them over to the higher self, and then actively forgive yourself for holding onto the anger.

At the end of this chapter is a powerful meditation exercise on forgiveness. Some readers may wish to skip ahead and get deeply engaged in forgiveness before returning to read the rest of this chapter.

Anger as Villain

Just as anger can make your blood boil and raise your blood pressure, it can be the very villain that triggers your migraine. Anger in all its forms and degrees—frustration, unresolved situations, unexpressed feelings, and feeling thwarted at being who you are—turns in on itself in a big loop of energy. It blocks the higher self from taking over and guiding you harmoniously throughout the day.

Often you are not even aware that you have become frustrated about something. And sometimes a seemingly innocent exchange or encounter can trigger an unpleasant event involving old, unresolved anger from your past, or your childhood.

For example, let us conjure up a migraine sufferer named Karen. One day at work, Karen's boss yells at another employee, an older woman whom Karen likes and respects. Though he is not cursing, the boss says some pretty unkind words like, "How could you do such a stupid thing?" and "You seem to enjoy letting me down, don't you?"

After the scene, Karen winds up with a splitting headache. Amazingly (to Karen), her friend is not taking it too hard. She simply shrugs her shoulders and says, "He'll get over it."

The friend finishes out the day at work. But Karen ends up going home early. Her headache has turned into a full-blown migraine.

In the quiet of her bedroom, she asks herself: Why? So I'm too sensitive. But is there something more to it? She knows that something about the encounter between her boss and her friend unsettled her. But she cannot quite put her finger on it. She scribbles on a piece of paper near the bed. "Show me what this is all about. Show me." The words are directed at her higher self.

Nothing comes to her. So she closes her eyes, trying to escape the pain in sleep. In her dreams she sees not her boss but her father. He is drunk, and he is talking. He is heaping abuse upon abuse at Karen's mother, who sits like a monument at the kitchen table, unmoving. She seems to be waiting for him to finish talking and stumble off to bed. But he goes on and on and on...

Karen wakes up, agitated and in pain. But she has vowed to release her anger into her journal. "I'm mad at myself for not defending my friend," she writes. "I feel like I am weak because I did not say something..." Then, "It reminds me of the times I heard Daddy yelling at Mommy, saying those horrible things, and I never did anything to help her." As Karen writes on, she feels a shift in the energy of her anger. She feels, rather than reasons, that she is "onto something."

She continues, "I was angry at Daddy for being so cruel. I was angry at her for taking it. I am angry that it happened over and over again, and I felt so helpless. Trapped. I am angry at both of them for letting that enter my life. I was a child...Didn't they know I could hear them? I'm angry at them, and angry because I think I have allowed my mother's response to become my response as an adult."

Karen cries bitterly as the emotional pain of her alcoholic household floods over her. The migraine throbs and aches, and she runs to the bathroom to throw up.

When she crawls back into bed, she prays, "Please, if there are angels watching over me, remind me that I can get over this anger. I don't want to be angry at my parents any more. I don't want to be angry at myself. I was only a child. I am still a child inside. Help me forgive myself, and forgive my parents."

The next day, on re-reading her journal, Karen decides she has some very old, complicated, difficult issues to deal with. Making contact with her old anger encourages her to do something she had long been putting off: she decides to seek counseling. It is not even so much the depth of the anger that scares her into going; it is the notion that she might be unwittingly passing on the same behavior patterns to her own daughter. And she definitely does not want her daughter to go through what she is going through now.

When a migraine first starts making itself felt, stop whatever you are doing and ask, *"Is there any anger lurking? Am I frustrated or angry about something? Have I been trying to control someone else, and am disappointed because he or she is not responding the way I want?"*

Turn to your journal and get it all out. If anger is a significant factor in the migraine, you probably will notice that simply writing about the anger and how you feel can not only lessen the migraine's intensity, but it can actually abort the attack. It usually will not be an instantaneous relief, but rather a steady lifting and changing of the weather. By opening to your bottled up feelings, you not only break the cycle of repressing those feelings, you actively open energy centers in critical areas of the body, allowing fresh healing currents in.

Another angle to try is to directly speak with people who have pushed your buttons, and stimulated the anger response. Or you can write a letter expressing how you feel. Much has been written on anger and how to express anger appropriately, and yet it seems we still need more lessons on conflict resolution. Obviously, the world would be a far more peaceful place if we were such experts on anger. In fact, we have tools at our command—words—which we can use every day to build bridges with other people. One of the basic sentences counselors teach us to use is "I feel _____(angry/hurt/confused, etc.) when you behave in thus and such a fashion."

No progress is made if you dwell on the anger and allow it to rule. Finding ways of getting back at people is not the answer, if healing is your goal. Healing the emotional wound is what you want to accomplish, before the body can follow suit. This healing is not accomplished through sympathy, self-pity, or denying anger, but by a process of consciously embracing the energy that "All is Love." In perceiving that, ultimately, all of us really want to love and be loved, and viewing every experience as an opportunity for the soul to heal itself, we free ourselves to move upward onto a new plane. Healing inner wounds is deeply effective: once you have gone within to embrace yourself and the people who made you angry, you need not expend energy doing that again. The energy is so powerful, it wipes out old blockages once and for all.

Techniques that are useful in purging old emotional energy include regression therapy, hypnosis/hypnotherapy, chakra balancing, inner child meditations, intuitive massage, and others. I would be remiss not to mention the very important work of John Bradshaw (available on tapes, DVDs, and in his books), which is especially useful for those who have substance abuse in their family history. Some relevant titles include *Bradshaw On: The Family*, and *Healing the Shame That Binds You.*

A few last words about anger. It is not easy to do anything while you are in migraine's torturous grip. It takes will, determination, and great courage, to pick up a pen—or call a friend in to listen, if that is your preferred method—and explore what could possibly be making you angry, frustrated, or uneasy emotionally. But the rewards of "listing your anger" could be potentially so great that you cannot afford to ignore this technique. And after all, it is just a technique. You do not have to think it through, work out the situation, or replay it a hundred different ways in your head. All you need to do is seek out the anger, just as thoroughly as looking for any other migraine trigger.

Also, come back to this chapter again after some time has passed. These last paragraphs will make more sense then.

Chances are good that you are also angry at being sick. You are angry at all the missed engagements. All the times you wanted to be somewhere, but were sidelined by a migraine. The times you wanted to give of yourself to your children or spouse or friends, but were stopped.

Beware of that particular anger, for it has nowhere to go but in on itself. The best thing you can do is forgive yourself for feeling that way, and quit being so hard on yourself. I think there is a key answer in worrying about not "being there for" someone else. It is time to consider that the sidelining feature of migraine is actually a good thing, a cry from your spirit, demanding that you begin tending your own campfire. It is time to start loving yourself from within each and every day.

Becoming practiced at seeing anger in yourself is a useful lifetime skill. You learn the anatomy of anger by studying it first in yourself. Attuned to what bothers you, you become more and more capable of speaking out whenever something disturbing happens—so that it never even gets to your Anger List. Instead of waiting for it to get trapped in your body, you get honest right away.

Once you have become aware of your responses, the bonus is that you become better able to identify signs of anger in loved ones. What's hard to face is that our loved ones are also angry at us. They may think they are angry about the illness—migraine—and how it affects you and them, but they are also probably angry at us. They may fear we are controlling the scene via headaches, or that we may develop a stroke, and die, leaving them alone. Our vulnerability invariably makes everyone around us consider their own mortality. They may have a repressed death anxiety that has become uncomfortably associated with us, our very persons. Overcoming migraine's effects truly takes a lot of healing, for the whole family.

Feeling guilty about being sick and taking it on our shoulders does nothing but hinder true, long-term healing. To get around that, we must mentally envision our heart area opening to embrace all the people who care about us, and remember: "Everyone is in recovery, not just me."

Meditation: How to Forgive

Find a quiet place to sit or lie down. After you have closed your eyes and taken some long, deep, cleansing breaths, say aloud, "I forgive myself...(for getting angry, for blowing up at someone, for feeling completely frustrated at someone's behavior, etc.)" Repeat the three words "I forgive myself" until you begin to really believe it. There is tremendous power in this simple statement.

If the situation warrants, forgive individuals who are involved in making you feel angry. Forgiving others does not mean you accept or condone their poor behavior; it means you forgive them their ignorance which resulted in hurting you. Even if they knew what they were doing when they hurt you, you can consider them ignorant—in matters of the spirit, that is. You can say to them (first in meditation, and later in person, if you feel you can): "I do not have to like your behavior; but I do love you." Or, "I see in you the same light that I see in me. Nonetheless, I do not choose to tolerate any behavior on your part that shuts my light down."

In this fashion, you release these people from having any furher power over your life. You let them go; and they let you go, energetically speaking.

For most of us, receiving a sense of complete, total, loving forgiveness isn't something that happens overnight, as the result of one forgiveness meditation or prayer. This is especially true when you're working on forgiving someone for a large, aching hurt. However, if you consistently forgive others in meditation, and always take time to forgive yourself for feeling badly or making mistakes, you will eventually achieve total forgiveness. It may take two days or two years, but trust this process. Here's how it works: With each concentrated prayer of forgiveness, you will feel your own walls of resistance, anger, and hatred crumbling until one day, in a clear and joyful moment, you will know that love has completely replaced your anger. You will be able to feel this shift physically—like a rush of clear pure water coursing through your body from your head to your toes. From that point on, your forgiveness for that particular situation will be in your past, never to recur.

People who say the Lord's Prayer on a daily basis are regularly setting this power to play since forgiving self and others is an essential part of this traditional prayer. ("Forgive us our trespasses, as we forgive others who trespass against us" or "Forgive us our debts as we forgive our debtors.")

Forgiveness is a critical part of any spiritual practice. If you call for forgiveness daily, its power will change your entire life.

PART THREE

PATHWAYS TO WHOLENESS
Releasing the Message of Migraine

Deep within, there is a message in the migraine, deep beyond the intellect, buried beneath the pain itself, in a place where no pain exists or has ever existed.

Migraine thinking is desperate and wild. In the throes of an attack, words crowd into your head, or jumble together into a seemingly indecipherable mass of images and notions. Ideas and scenarios push relentlessly, till your head feels stuffed, as though you were suddenly the complete repository of a vast collection of every film ever made, from everyone's corny home movies to sweeping Academy Award-winning epics. Confused amid the flood of bizarre thoughts and worries and machinations of the mind, you also are overwhelmingly aware of the pain, and your search for relief begins in earnest.

Trying to block out the pain becomes your main priority. You grope around for dark clothing to drape over your eyes, to keep out the light that seems to stab into your brain. You consider soaking your whole head in a bucket of ice. You envision yourself as a soldier on a bloody battleground in a vicious war. You wander into the bathroom, and stare into the mirror to see if you can still recognize yourself.

You wonder who turned on this switch, who thrust you into this time-distorted prison of pain and pounding. Is there someone, some thing, some action to blame? And what of the thousands of thoughts that course maddeningly through your head? Can't you shut them down somehow?

Often, the first thing that comes to mind is a drug. Taking a painkiller can have a calming effect, slowing down the barrage in your brain. Painkillers bring you to sleep, to escape, at least momentarily. But so often, even after sleeping, the head still throbs. You take another dose, hoping to kill off the attack once and for all.

121

And yet the sleep is not deep, but shallow, with the same jumble of thoughts mashed into the brain, straining your head to capacity. You wish you could turn off the switch, and bring all this to a screeching halt, or at least to a pace that you can manage.

Assuming you are not completely drugged out, eventually there comes that rare moment of clarity, though, breaking through the pain. Something that is bothering you comes to the fore. Focusing on it, you realize that your mind is trying to clue you in on something important, some stressful elements or elements, some area of your life where you are desperately fighting for control, without tangible effects. Somewhere in there is a voice of truth crying to emerge.

The intellect struggles to stay in command. "You must think logically, and figure this out," says this voice. It is such a familiar voice that you mistake it to be truth. Yet that voice of the intellect turns out to be a ploy: worse than a distraction, it is a formidable roadblock.

Deep within, there is a message in the migraine, deep beyond the intellect, buried beneath the pain itself, in a place where no pain exists or has ever existed. This message is always psychic, intuitive in nature. That is, the message lies not in the topsoil of the logical, rational mind, but in the bedrock of the soul's foundation.

There are basically three main categories of messages within migraine experiences. The first type, which is very common, signals a fundamental anomaly within the body system, serving to point out where you have compromised your soul's growth. Typically, it is related to stress and unresolved conflicts. Negative energies build up in the body to a point of ultimate crisis. Guilt, fear, difficulties in relationships and communicating with others, frustration, self-doubt, anger and other emotional problems are key elements emerging here.

The second type of migraine message deals with your future direction. This message, which you may see in a vision or hear as words spoken to you through your innermost spirit, gives you specific instructions on how to solve your current problems and accomplish your personal mission in this lifetime. There is, underlying that message, a deep, secure sense of knowledge that acting on your inner vision will bring release and bliss to your life. It is a message that you open up to, by consciously or unconsciously reaching through all the layers of your persona, aiming at individual essence itself.

The third type of message is a channeled message from a force that feels like it is much greater than your self, like it is being beamed your way—and all you can do is try to record or decipher it as it comes in. The migraineur with this experience is able to tune into a wavelength that reveals the unseen forces that govern the universe. Born of this experience are revelations, creative visions, artistic projects, scientific breakthroughs, inner knowledge about one's destiny, clairvoyance, outer-galactic wisdom, music that has never been heard before, words of the prophets, memories of other lifetimes, and so on.

Releasing into this experience is very scary for most people. They fear they are going mad—mostly because our society does not teach us how to deal with revelatory visions, nor does it place much validity in visionary experience. Visionary experience is honored— but only as it pertains to saints and prophets and not-very-real people in the far-off historical past, where we are distanced from the actual players. In America today, fortunately for us, there is an increasing acceptance and exploration into visionary events and their significance in mental and physical health. But our predominant social code is generally opposed to fostering revelation experience. One has to undergo a near-death experience to gain any degree of credibility in this area. And people who have had visions or who have traveled out of body during near-death are not considered mad at all; rather they are seen to have reentered the physical world with a new stability, sense of place, and reverence for others. They have experienced cosmic unity, and thus are even looked up to by others who have not yet experienced the white light signaling an all-loving presence, or God.

It is comforting to know, though, that *once a spiritual message is safely transmitted through the person with migraine, the migraine not only disappears but the migraineur is left perfectly intact and feeling sane.* It is possible that regarding the psychic message as abnormal is what leads people to exhibit abnormal behavior.

Migraineurs literally talk themselves into thinking they are abnormal by comparing themselves with the general population.

However, migraine people are sensitive folks. And it is absolutely normal for sensitive people to feel and hear the world in a very sensitive way. If we recognize that there are all kinds of wavelengths out there, such as those caught by satellite dishes, we can consider that certain cosmic transmissions are "caught" by migraineurs and other sensitive people. For example, it is entirely possible for a migraineur to pick up on someone else's migraine pain, especially if the person is a family member or someone close. The migraineur is very much a transmitter in the fullest sense of the word. And to accept psychic messages with grace and love, in the manner that speaks of accepting the higher self, is to perform a great service to one's self. The soul's development depends on divine messages, what it instinctively knows to be in tune with cosmic order.

Of course, more than one type of message may come through at the same time. For example, when you uncover a problem related to stress (the first type of message), that blockage then dissipates, which opens the mind to a solution, or an insight (the second type of message), as to how you can proceed to eliminate the problem.

Always, always, always a message of the spirit is circling around, in a form of energy. This message is yearning to be heard. It is so insistent that it has brought you to the point of pain just so you will finally give it the attention it deserves. Your job, therefore, is to find ways to muster up the courage and faith to know that you are being called upon to dig beneath the surface, to smash through the barriers set up by the intellect, to begin decoding what native Americans term your Original Instructions, which dictate the very course of your soul's evolution and your life's journey.

In a nutshell, your Original Instructions refers to the body of information concerning your actual essence. You carry these instructions with you from birth. This is the information that tells you the reason for your being here at all. It is encoded within your being, and accessed through the heart area. People instinctively know that the heart area is vitally important, but they commonly misunderstand "heart," mistakenly assuming that the heartstrings, or emotions, govern destiny. Focusing on the heart area is actually a way in which you can consciously work to unlock vital data so that you will act in accordance with your individual purpose as it was set up long before your birth.

The prerequisite to decoding your own instructions necessarily involves banishing the overactive intellect to its proper place. The logical aspect of mind is a valuable tool, no more. It is not a be-all and end-all. It cannot even begin to comprehend the vastness of the universe or all that God-force is. It has severe limitations. It helps you function in the real world, but it is not its own reality. It tries to convince you that the outside world impacts on you, and that you must react to outside forces of environment, society, and other people's energies. It actively dismisses any idea that reality functions in the exact opposite manner: where the internal world of God-spirit makes itself manifest in the external world.

And so, in the treatment of migraine, the best way to get at inner cause, the message that shines underneath the intellect, is to go into meditation and declare firmly, with hand over heart for full effect, "I surrender my intellect to the loving arms of the universe. I know that the true reasons for my despair and pain are being revealed to me through the higher self. I know that my Original Instructions are being revealed to me at this time. I am free to hear the voice of my higher self. I know that in the spirit there is no pain."

When you get a migraine, enter into a meditative state as soon as possible. As you sit or lie quietly, watch your thoughts and see them for what they are. If you hear yourself saying, "I should never have eaten that fondue," consider that you cannot be hearing the higher self, because the higher self cannot blame, nor does it feel pain nor does it submit to pain. It is that part of you that is one with unconditional love, and as such is not able to suffer or lament. The higher self must be allowed to come to the fore with its answers by talking the logical mind into submission. "I open myself to my higher energies, and all that is good, and wise, and true" is one affirmation you can use to get into that awesome space where messages of the spirit spring forth.

If you still find yourself wrestling with your rational self, affirm, "There is but One Mind, which is perfect and all-knowing. I choose to believe that my mind and the One Mind of the Creator are the same. I relax and let go of all control, for my destiny is in the hands of the One Presence, and the One Divine Energy."

The beauty of recognizing that there is a message in the migraine is that, with practice, the migraine experience always becomes a learning experience, where essential truths about your essence and your needs and your purpose are revealed. And once you direct your struggle to relaxing and letting go of old notions of control (that is, the illusion that your mind controls your life and others), migraines begin to decline. First they decrease in intensity, frequency, and duration. Eventually, there will be recognizable miracles in your life.

When you get a headache, and pay attention to its spiritual message instead of focusing on outside causes, you will find that the headache lifts off of its own accord. You yourself will act as an agent of healing, simply by opening to the message within. Beyond that, your own healing powers act upon you in grand, unseen ways, bringing your body back into wholeness.

Migraine signals an imbalance. There is something out of line, something out of whack, something blocking your internal messages. It is unbelievable how swiftly a migraine disappears, once the migraine message is released. Writing in a journal (or on any paper handy at all) is one way to unleash the messages. Allowing your voice to talk out the sounds that come to you mid-migraine is another way. Do not worry if the words are unintelligible. Give them voice. Or paint what you see and feel. Tell a friend what you see in your mind's eye, if you have someone helping you. The more you release migraine messages the more you come to trust the process of doing anything you can to get at that message. You will be shown over and over again that the message carries with it a total relief from pain. Without drugs.

It makes sense that when you get blocked up, usually by not paying attention to spiritual needs or by resisting change in your life, a headache results. The dis-ease of not being in harmony with the cosmos produces symptoms of migraine. Instead of lamenting your propensity to suffering, remind yourself constantly that your individual path is important enough to warrant great pain if that is the only way you will be forced into putting aside the outside world in favor of listening to the inner world of the spirit.

In other words, if we are so blocked that we can no longer hear our own instructions or directions on how to walk our path, then it follows that we are also too blocked to allow the "physician within" to heal the pain.

The migraineur's body-mind-soul system can be likened to a telephone system. When the electric lines are jammed up (often with unresolved emotions such as anger or fear or worry), the system eventually breaks down or short-circuits. The migraine sets in, causing the whole network to collapse. The migraine signals that a message of great import, a message within the system itself, needs to be heard. It's coming in on a special hotline. Once you commit your energies to unjamming the lines so that you can pick up that incoming call, the next thing to do is record the message itself so that you will not forget it.

Make a commitment to pay attention to this message, to explore its impact on how you live your life. At that point, all the lines become cleared for healing energies to flow in. The physician within can dial your number direct, and you become well. More than that, you become deeply well, not just temporarily relieved.

The migraines may continue to plague you for awhile, until you gain practice in keeping your energy circuits clear. Eventually, when a migraine strikes, you recognize that you must literally force yourself to clear unwanted energies from your system. You know that a cleansing process is about to take place, and do all you can to access the message of the heart.

How can you tell that what you hear in your head is a message of the heart? The best way to be sure you are listening to a divine, inner voice rather than a mere loose thought that is floating around, is to commit to the practice of listening to the higher self. Meditation is the single most effective way to grow familiar with the inner voice. Not any old meditation style, but a specific style incorporating truths and thoughts about truth into the meditation itself. The chapter "Meditating for Real-Feel Results" is devoted to this style of meditating.

Another aid to keeping your lines clear is to devote attention to your dreams on a day-to-day basis. Keep a dream journal or sketchbook. Pick it up the minute you awaken with a dream image from the night before. In migraine prevention and treatment, sleep plays a big role. Partly that is because the body sometimes has to take you out of the conscious realm, completely relegating the intellectual side to a posture of weakness. Only then can your subconscious function on your behalf, sending you messages that push you along the healing path. Whether in mid-migraine or during painfree times, dreams serve a purpose.

Sometimes you dream of doing things that are entirely inappropriate in the physical world. That kind of dream serves to move along certain karmic situations, confronting people who have come into your life specifically to heal old hurts from this lifetime or from past lives. It's safe, precisely because the situation is handled in the dream realm. Without doing anything more than sleeping, your body-mind-soul system is working out things in the dream state. At other times your dreams contain direct messages to help you understand what is going on around you, to give you perspective on where you are in your own development, and to guide you toward your purpose in life. Write them down. Get in touch with your subconscious.

If you are having trouble recalling your dreams, call on your higher self to help you remember your dreams. Before falling asleep, place one hand on the crown and say, "I know that I am receiving help in recalling my dreams. I am now claiming all the help available to me in remembering and understanding my dreams. I am grateful."

Migraine sufferers typically require long hours of sleep mode before they emerge from their darkened, quiet bedrooms bedraggled but finally free from pain. Why is that? In the absence of an understanding regarding the body as a total energy system, people simply act on instinct and climb into bed when migraine strikes. What they are not aware of is that sleep allows higher beings, or angelic healing energies, to work on clearing the body's channels without interruption. As the conscious mind shuts down, unseen forces take over. They work to untangle the mixed signals that caused the body to grow overtired in the first place. Waves of healing light frequencies are directed at the corresponding energy centers:

- red for the anorectal region (fight or flight response);
- orange for the genitals (sexuality and creativity center);
- yellow for the solar plexus (the seat of the emotions);
- green for the heart (the love zone);
- blue for the throat (communication and speech center);
- indigo for the forehead (third eye, or intuition); and
- purple for the crown (highest spirituality center).

With this energy bombardment, the seven main centers listed above, which whirl in circles, become literally unraveled, or untangled, in a massive clearing action. It is a gradual process, one which you can initiate yourself simply by meditating on specific colors.

Migraine is then a cleansing process, and the clearing action is total. Throwing up is an extension of the process, along with diarrhea which sometimes accompanies migraine. Women who tend to get migraines during menstruation experience an extreme purification. Having the wherewithal to say to yourself, "I am going through a clearance" can ease the whole process somehow. Suddenly there is a goodness you can grab onto—a knowledge that migraine is like the hurricane that cleared out all the old brush so new plants could grow.

When you close the drapes and shut out the external world, you hasten the cleansing work. When you drink water (migraine sufferers are likely to shun flavored drinks when they're in pain), you speed the process by routing toxins from the system. Interestingly, from ancient times, the herbal teas prescribed for migraine tend to contain a cleansing property. (See Chapter 17.)

When you stop to think about it, what you are doing in migraine mode is cocooning up. Slowing down. Migraine is a message in itself—a direct *command* to pay attention to how the body is affected by all energy that enters it (emotional, psychological, physical, and psychic energy) and to go back to the innermost spiritual wellspring for the bountiful cosmic energy that is needed for rejuvenation.

Taking that one step further, it makes good sense that if the migraine-prone person chooses to go within on a daily basis, before channels have a chance to become too jammed, she or he can more promptly access those important messages without suffering. The spiritual energy that got painfully, destructively manifested as migraine pain before, would now enter through the crown (the top of the head) unencumbered. The message would be received via intuition or vision, and recorded. The result: a state of wellness, balance, and health. Finally, a method of preventing migraine is possible.

There is always the chance that the message in the migraine carries a heavy energy. For example, you may at some point hear a message to leave a highly stressful job,. terminate a relationship, or face some kind of trial you have been avoiding. Facing one's inner truth is not an easy exercise. And yet, if the same message appears again and again, there will be no escape from it. If you suspect that your message will cause you a great deal of personal trauma, do not hesitate to seek a psychotherapist or other counselor. You need support in this time of struggle; going it alone is not a viable solution.

Above all, it is important to remember that a message from the heart will never be destructive to life. A voice that tells you to harm yourself or others is not from the higher self. The higher self is always life-affirming. Always loving, coming from a place of pure, unconditional love. It is an energy born of the light, not darkness.

Migraine experience is a pathway to hearing the innermost voice of the spirit, to bring you into the best of what you are. To understand migraine as anything less than a critical message is to ignore the cry of your spirit. When you get migraine, you must remind yourself, through the pain, that there is always a message. There is a call on your red telephone, the hotline to permanent healing. Pick it up. Answer. Listen well.

Commit to Hearing Your Migraine

Make a sign for yourself, and place it where you'll see it the next time you get a migraine. It should reflect your commitment to understanding migraines, and your willingness to listen to what migraine is telling you—not to shut it out or merely close it down with painkilling drugs. This sign might read:

> "I am willing to listen to my migraine."
>
> *OR*
>
> "There is always a message in migraine. Help me, Almighty Creator, to open to this message so that I no longer have to live in pain."

Chapter 11
Letting Go

How is it that anyone comes to wear a heavy cloak of pain? Even on a "good" day, many migraine sufferers still feel the heavy cloak, weighing their thoughts, tempering their everyday pleasures with the threat of pain to come. Intuitively, we know that letting go of the pain is part of the process in getting well.

Letting go is one of the hardest things to do. And yet, in one of the most profound of all paradoxes, choosing to let go speeds us along the road to revelation, and health.

Earlier, in PART I, was an exercise for "casting off garments." Now, many chapters later, it is time to go back to that prescriptive exercise, to cast off more garments (through writing in your BEING Journal) so as to un-do the self that is characterized by pain, and then turn to the task of re-making your person in the image of your higher self. In this process you'll be letting go of "I" and think of yourself as "I am." You'll strip away the roles that have defined you, and allow your innermost core of goodness to burn through first, so that all the rest of you can align with that higher self. Your personality, your ego, your mind, your body—all fall in line eventually when the "I am" uncovers itself, declares its purity, demands to be taken seriously, and finally assumes its rightful role as essential self.

From time to time, especially early on in the process of uncovering essential self, you will feel completely whole one minute and scattered, or out of balance, the next. In the process of becoming your own best friend, you are bound to experience such swings. Partly that is because you have long allowed the outside world, and other people, to define your self. You gave over your power—perhaps because you feared rejection—and the end result was that you felt powerless. You only felt integrated on some days—the "good" days.

Everyone has days when everything seems to click, and people like who you are, and you like who you are and how you're being perceived. Now, through letting go, and reclaiming who you truly are, you can open the door for that alignment to occur more and more often, until integration of personality-soul-mind is a fundamental aspect of your identity. After all, we did not come here split apart; but we got split along the way. Our inner spirit got crushed by the circumstances of human existence. If liberation from pain is a goal, then it is our task to do everything possible to remember back to that initial one-ness that we were born into. Letting go of our notions, or casting off the garments of identity, is machinery necessary to rewind the tape back.

Personal myth deconstruction can take weeks or years to pursue. You may hold on tightly, fighting every step of the way, before eventually letting go. Mentally let go of the background that dictates who you are; let go of the jobs and schooling and even overseas travel which qualifies—in your mind—what you are. Mentally release your roles as they relate to other people, in order to see yourself standing alone.

A two-step process unfolded for me as garments dropped away. These lessons in essence came about through a combination of self-searching, meditation, reading, writing, workshops, and private counseling sessions. I share them now:

1. Who am I? I know myself as the child of my parents. My mother has taught me many things. She had expectations and hopes for me... And I am my father's child. He taught me many things. He had expectations of what I might become.

But that is not what I am. It is not what drives me inside. That is what I learned. What I learned was good, and I am grateful to my parents. My parents are my first teachers, two souls in two bodies who united in marriage and had children... I was a soul out there, waiting to be born, and I chose—and it was chosen for me—to come to these
two people so that I could learn from them and they could learn from me...

2. I am a sister, and as a sister I am aunt to my siblings' children. I have siblings who love me and care about me. They have hopes and

expectations for me. We share the same parents. We know our ties are deep and strong.

But it does not matter if I have not lived up to their expectations, or notions of what they would like me to become, because they are not me and I am not them. I am a unique expression of an all-knowing, all-powerful Presence... Like me, each sibling was a soul who chose to come to our parents in this lifetime, to learn from them and to learn from me. I am free from my siblings and they are free from me. We support each other but neither blood nor history can bind us in the end. We each find our paths alone; we have a unique mission to accomplish.

3. I have an education/training that qualifies me to perform certain tasks better than a person who is unskilled. I can help people by doing these things. I will list all my schooling and training now, and I will list all those jobs I am capable of doing. I am grateful that I can do so many things.

But I do not have to do everything I was trained to do, even if I spent many years or many dollars along the way. I can put these jobs in order of priority. The work at the top is the one I enjoy the most and feel good about. It may not be the one that earns me the most money, but it is what I feel right doing. The rest of the activities are jackets and sweaters that I can put away in the closet. When I find I need them, I will allow them to slip on, as garments that fit naturally and effortlessly into my life work, without losing sight of their proper place. If I do not feel that any of these activities resonate with purpose within my heart, I will accept that there is more to discover about my essential path here on earth, for I know that I have a purpose here on earth.

4. I have close and loving relationships with people. They care about me and I care about them. They depend on me, and I depend on them. They give me suggestions about my life. They try to help me figure out what to do next. They have learned things from me, and I have learned from them.

But I will release my relationships with them for now, realizing that they cannot live my life for me and I cannot live my life for them. I am a unique, individual expression. Only I can know who I am and what I want. I cannot worry about the opinions of others. I know that those who truly love me will continue to love me as I become myself more and more. True love is open, unconditional. No matter what path I follow, if it is good and true, then my loved ones will still love me.

5. I am attached to certain locations and I am used to having certain things around me. I am used to presenting myself in a certain way to other people, wearing clothes that suit the occasion and fit my station in life...

But I must question how I came to live here. Was it my choice, a choice from my heart? Does not my spirit go wherever I go? If I leave, I still breathe and feel my heart beating... I ask how much of me is in that vase on the dining room table. If the vase were gone, I would still be here. I can release these things for ownership is truly temporary, a fleeting illusion. I do not own any thing forever into eternity.

Things are mine but they are not "of me." My clothes fit me. But do they reflect who I am? If I could design clothes to suit my soul, what would they look like? At any rate, clothes are but the covering for my body, to keep the flesh from growing cold and endangering organs inside...

6. I have a body. Everyone else I know has a body. My body is the home of my blood and my brain and my heart and other organs.

But my body is not who I am. I am something more than a collection of organs and bones. I have a force that qualifies me as alive. I am filled with life-force, an energy that I cannot touch or wear on my body. It is a force that does not originate in the material world, but comes from the spirit. This spirit feels as if it is beyond comprehension, beyond words and thoughts. It is governed by something other than myself: I do not consciously design and program my dreams at night. Life-force is with me despite the horrible pain I have been through.

When I come through great pain, such as migraine, and I look around at my world, all is fresh. The day after migraine, the natural world is intensely beautiful. Though I am tired and wan, leaves shimmer. Flowers amaze me with their color and form. Fed only by water and sun, trees tower. Children's laughter sounds like music again. I am grateful to be alive. I know in my heart that I was kept alive by life-energy constantly created within me, and that this energy is one and the same as the Creation itself. I identify with this Creation Energy. It is truly my essence. I am one with life-force. I release into life-force and allow it to guide me to my divine purpose.

I am a being of pure energy, living within a human body. I have come here so that my soul can learn many lessons. I am here to learn how my soul can merge with higher self, my most spiritual self, and I know that my personality must align too in accordance with a vast, divine plan.

"We are not human beings having a spiritual experience. We are spiritual beings having a human experience."

I am not sure who first said this, but that statement rings true to me. It is a reminder of the proper order of things. The body does not put on the garment of spiritual force. The force, pure spiritual energy, exists first; then the body, then the "garments" worn through life.

In *Transformers: The Therapists of the Future,* Jacquelyn Small says that the energy of the Higher Mind "contemplates, then expresses itself in two modes, an active one of authentic Self-expression, and a passive one of comprehension. It is the level where we begin to do our Being, rather than taking on roles and identities that are unnatural for us." Small refers to this as an "intrinsic value system" which "draws its approval from the Higher Self, no longer needing so much endorsement from the outside world" (*Transformers,* pp. 104-5).

She adds that once we identify what we intrinsically value, making that decision all by ourselves, it is a short step toward seeing that manifested in the physical world. Small writes:

> No longer are we controlled by an external 'should system;' our 'shoulds' now represent a natural urge coming from deep inside us, expressing our essential nature. We begin to express our unique purpose in life, utilizing our bodies, our emotions and our mental life in service to the Higher Self. It takes no energy to do our Being...flowing effortlessly toward the activities in life that are intrinsically right for us...(When) we do the work of the God-self, we will find it to be the place where we are the most comfortable and the most at home... The struggle has been in letting go of the images and expressions that did not fit, or the ones we've outgrown. (Excerpted from *Transformers*, p. 105.)

But what about all the rest of the things that we are? But what about all the other personalities that we see in ourselves? Are they not true?

Reverend Linda Barnett said something interesting about that. She said that we— our bodies—do not house just one personality acting the same way all the time. We have energies, unseen entities, that function through us. Choosing to walk the path of the higher self means choosing to invite in those energies that will act through you in accordance with a divine will, toward a higher purpose.

"You have multi-selves. We all do," she says. "We open our channels to let certain selves act, using our bodies. That is why we can get so lost. In not knowing how to ally ourselves with our spiritual center—the self that we most need to keep functioning, to keep active—is abandoned. Temporarily, that most important self (the higher self) is relegated to a position of unimportance. As a result, we lose balance. We lose health."

The body is but a shell, according to Linda. "The body is a vessel that contains light and love and divinity and all the force of universal creation. We have male energies and female energies. We can learn about all of this through meditation and inner work."

In understanding essence, and essential self, it helps to think back to our childhood, before we have become filled with other people's notions of what the world is all about, and who we are. When we are small children, we do not spend time wondering who to be. We are open, directly connected with the natural world, being fully what we are.

In my childhood, I remember running along and then, suddenly, flying. I have never forgotten that feeling. Was I really flying? It is hard to tell, since no one else was there. But the experience is so vivid in my mind that I feel sure I was flying in some fashion, possibly in an out-of-body event. It was a fantastic feeling. I also remember that I did a lot of writing. Writing stories from start to finish. And reading. I did a lot of reading.

Going back into childhood memories is crucial in helping you find essence. Devote a block of time to thinking about what you did as a child. Not what you were forced to do, but what came naturally to you. Therein lies another key to your essential self, which will lead you to the keys that unlock the door of your migraine prison.

If you have trouble remembering back to childhood, meditation and hypnosis are two ways of accessing the early, spirit-aligned self that manifested in childhood. Ideally, you should try to take yourself back to a time before you experienced any major self-consciousness.

Interestingly, one of the nicest side effects of finding my essence was dissolution of the intense self-consciousness that had plagued me for years. It made sense: Once inner truth is known, there is really nothing to be embarrassed about anymore. The Buddha (divinity within) is never embarrassed.

Discovering essence is not an intellectual exercise. Essence must be experienced to be known: that is, the search for essence will be experienced by your entire body on all levels—physically, psychically, mentally, and in the energy waves (aura) emanating from and surrounding the body.

Experiencing essence is feeling and knowing deeply an original oneness with all that is light, all that is good, and all that is meant to be. It has been called revelation, peak experience, and many other things. People who have near-death experiences know much about what essence is.

Most of us feel separated, fragmented, disconnected from our beginnings. We yearn to feel whole.

The revelation experience is not as far afield as we assume. It is always within our potential. Life-force, and all the beauty and power that is inherent in the act of creation, is our spiritual birthright. It is ours for the claiming. But it is up to each individual to let go of outmoded, destructive concepts of herself/himself in order to actively encourage alignment of personality, soul, and spirit. When you choose to find your true essence—not just desire but actively choose and surrender yourself to that choice, wherever it may lead —all the energy of the cosmos is with you. More than half the battle is won.

Repeat the Garment Exercise with a Focus on Childhood

Turn back to the journaling exercise at the end of PART I. Read what you wrote before; then repeat the exercise, adding roles you may not have remembered to uncover the first time you did the exercise. Concentrate on rôles that you assumed in childhood. For example:

I am...

the daughter or son of _____;

a sibling to _____ and in relation to each sibling I behaved _____;

or

the only child (describe its impact on your life at home and in relation to cousins, etc.);

the grandchild of _____ (examine how you felt in relation to each individual grandparent);

the pupil of _____(teacher's name) in grade school;

[any other role you assumed in childhood that played a major part in your early experiences].

After writing down each role and describing anything that comes to your mind about each role, follow up with a challenge to the role. Start it off with the simple word "But." For example:

Role: "**I am...** the granddaughter of Joseph A. Jones. My grandpa said I looked just like his sister. I remember feeling that I would probably grow up to be just like his sister (my Great Aunt Theresa), too. That scared me a little, because she always stayed inside, and I loved to go fishing with my father and be outside."

Challenge: "**But...** I am not Great-Aunt Theresa and never will be. Maybe my grandpa saw a resemblance and that made him happy, but it made me feel like he wasn't seeing who I was. Theresa is Theresa, and I am myself, and we don't have to be mixed together any more."

Recall Earliest Memories of Feeling Whole

Sit comfortably in a chair or lie down on a bed. Breathing in and out deeply, allow your mind to wander back to a point in childhood where you felt completely open, happy, and whole—connected with nature, surrounded by loving family, feeling joyful with a pet dog or cat, or any snippet of experience where you felt just plain fine.

Enjoy reliving the experience. After you have been bathed in the glow of that happy memory once again, open your eyes and write it down in your BEING Journal. If you had several moments to recall, write each one down. Try to recall smells, the weather that day, and other details of the experience.

Repeat this meditation as often as you like, until you have uncovered points in your childhood timeline that help you recall that once upon a time, you felt okay with the world.

Note: If you cannot recall any experience that fits the bill, please consider seeing a counselor, certified hypnotherapist, psychiatrist, or other qualified mental health practitioner to help you re-find your sense of being a pure child.

Chapter 12
Honoring the Body Temple

What is obvious is not always plain to see.

The impact that the outside world has on your body is obvious when you work outside in the garden. As you loosen the earth and plant a flowerbed, you get dirt on your hands and on your knees and all over your shoes. Green juice from the weeds you pull oozes out and stains your knees. Sap from the branches you're clearing gets stuck on your fingertips and palms. After digging, tiny bits of gravel and sand are sprinkled on the top of your scalp, making your hair feel gritty.

You notice how dirty you've become as you turn to go inside, and you dust yourself off, place the muddy shoes at the back door, and then prepare to shower. The water has a wonderfully soothing effect. Afterwards, you feel incredibly refreshed as you change into clean clothes. The garden never looked better, you think, as you gaze outside.

Now here is another scenario: You are at your job, and it is a challenging day, to say the least. You dig into a project that needs a lot of your close attention. You sit in a master planning session where you and others scrap old plans that aren't working out, and then plant new ideas in their place. You work closely with others, hearing their thoughts, liking some of what you hear and disagreeing with other parts. Over lunch and coffee, people share personal jokes or stories, worries, hopes, and complaints.

At the end of work, you drive by the daycare center, listening to the sweet call of what seems like a thousand screaming voices, "Sherry! David! Your mother's here!" And you get the kids in the car, strap them up, face a line of cars heading home in the rush, and turn on the radio to catch some of the news around the world.

Chances are you know where this story is leading. Unlike the situation where you have just come in from the garden, you probably don't walk in the house and evaluate your body to see what "dirt" you accumulated simply by being in contact with a myriad of other energies. Yet when you think about it, it makes no sense to assume that your body is unaffected by the demands of your day.

There's a saying we use when we cannot stop thinking about something: "I just can't shake the feeling..." is a phrase we all understand. We use it when we become aware that some problem or some person has "gotten under our skin." In other words, there is such a thing as "psychic dust" which literally does settle on our bodies, and does need our attention at the end of every office day, at the end of any difficult encounter, and especially after being in an environment that involves many persons, many energies. Invisible as this "dust" is to many people, it is visible to some extrasensory folks and at the very least, is probably already palpable to you to some extent.

I had a friend who worked in the operating room of a major hospital. She saw death and was in the presence of illness every working moment. Her apartment was her refuge, yet she could not understand why it was so hard for her to just relax and mellow out upon returning home. Although taking a shower right away helped, it was not enough. She was still carrying around psychic dirt. It was not until she put together a full ritual of physical and spiritual cleansing that she was able to achieve balance.

The body, it is often said, is a temple. A house for your soul. It is the vessel that holds your light. To an extent, affirmations and meditation help cleanse and balance the body so that your spirit can glow ever stronger. There are people who focus only on the body and the body's pain or pleasure, who tend to clean the body only when physical dirt is observed. Then there are people who focus only on the metaphysical, caught in the realm of mind, thought and otherworldliness, forgetting that the body needs honoring. An imbalance—or more correctly, a splintering, occurs.

If migraine plagues you, it is time to consider applying basic principles of psychic protection to not only care for your body more effectively, but to create a strong, positive energy field that can serve to ward off migraine attacks.

Our ancestors—from every ethnic tradition—knew of many practices to "clear" unwanted, unseen energies from their bodies. Many traditions still observe rituals for cleansing both body and home. So far away from our traditions are we, however, that we would sooner put on deodorant sold to us by a smiling girl on TV than take a healing bath using herbs of well-respected, ancient healing properties. The culture of materialism has not only robbed us of our respect for the old traditions, it has filled us with disdain for them. Personally, I am glad to see that trend reversing, and take heart as I put forth some tried and true, simple, and reasonably inexpensive ways of balancing and cleansing the body when it has been stressed in the course of the day.

"House"-cleaning: Four Steps to a Clear Body

1. Upon arriving home...

When you come home, take 5 or 10 minutes to sit down, right away. Do not put on the TV or a record. Just sit. Dust yourself off with your hands, gently, over the shoulders, chest, arms, head, and so on. Imagine you are dusting off the worries and cares. Shake out your hands, and flick your fingers. Take the time to just breathe in and breathe out.

Fill a mixing bowl with warm water, and drop in just one or two drops of a pure essential oil, such as musk or sandalwood or lavender. (Or, you can use 1/2 teaspoon of salt.) Dipping your hands in the water, say to yourself, "I release. I let go." When you pull your hands out, and wipe them dry, the scent of the oil will stay on, reminding you as you go about your business that you have "let go" and are trusting in the divine flow of the cosmos. Encourage others in the household to also use your blessing bowl.

For a soothing bath, one that serves to neutralize stress and negative energies, toss 1/2 cup of baking soda into warm bath water. (Adding a few drops of essential oil is optional.) This treatment is an absolute all-around standard for psychically sensitive people. Baking soda is one commodity I am never without.

2. Stretch and move your body daily.

While you are doubtless already aware that you must do some kind of aerobic exercise three times a week to maintain the most basic level of fitness, you may not know that the body also needs a mild stretch session at least once a day. Depending on what you do for a living, or how you spend most of your time, your body will need stretching in a particular area more than others—and you are the best judge of that.

Try this basic stretch, taken from an amalgam of yoga, modern dance, and the martial art aikido:

Daily Stretch

Begin by sitting in a chair, with closed eyes. Lift your eyebrows high, then drop them. Scrunch up your nose, then relax it. Tighten your mouth into a little ball, then open it as wide as it will go, and relax. Placing your hands on your face, gently massage everywhere: cheekbones, nose, jaw, mouth, and around the eyes, forehead, and temples. Feel your ears. Feel the back of your neck.

Next, drop your hands straight down and let your neck fall slowly forward. (At no time should there be pain, just a gentle stretching.) Breathe in and out, then return your head to center. Next, open your eyes and look up at the ceiling, taking a deep breath in and out. Return your head to center. Look to the right, breathing deeply, and then look to the left.

Stand up and away from your chair. Reach high overhead with first the right arm, then the left arm, four times each; then repeat stretching the arms to the side. Bringing your arms to center, grasp them together and in front of your pelvis. With both hands clasped, make a slow, wide circle out to the side, then up over your head, over to the other side, and then sweep down toward the floor (without bending your legs). Continue on in a large, 360-degree circle, slowly, remembering to breathe. Repeat in the opposite direction.

Coming back to center, with your hands still together, concentrate on your lower belly, and in your mind's eye, visualize your body's center as located directly behind your navel. Close your eyes and concentrate on this center. Feel the center as a heavy, shiny, ball bearing that is always in place, never disturbed. After standing for several seconds in this position without losing your balance, open your eyes, spread open your palms, breathe in, and breathe out.

Now is a good time to affirm:

"It's another beautiful day. I know why I am here in the world, I know I have a divine and good purpose, and no one is going to rattle me. I have faith in my self, and I give thanks for my body. My body truly is my temple."

3. After observing a pattern of body discontent...

Sometimes it is all you can do just to watch your body's own patterns, and respond accordingly. What is right and harmony-filled for your body will eventually be apparent to you, its owner. You may, for instance, use a certain computer with no problems, but after using a computer with a different monitor—one with those very fast flickering lights—you wind up fighting off a migraine response.

Or you may find (through therapy or meditation) that you've been doing a job that you virtually hate to do—because you got stuck doing it, your father/mother/spouse pushed you toward it, or you were reasonably good at it. Your body tells you in no uncertain terms:

"When I do this, I feel bad. When I do the other thing (something you truly love doing) I feel good, and I suffer far fewer migraines."

If you have suffered long enough, if it's something in your physical environment that's hurting you, you'll probably start thinking about what you can do to achieve a less painful lifestyle. Whatever it is you finally decide to do, in responding to your body's comfort dictates, be committed to helping your body through the transition. Whatever the trauma, whatever the change, it is never felt solely on the emotional or psychological level. Every experience impacts on your body. Each time you cry inside, your body cries somehow. Each time you rejoice, your body rejoices in a physical experience of some quality. Spiritual revelation and awakening is felt on the cellular level.

You may try to avoid this phenomenon, but it is absolutely unavoidable: mind, body and soul are intertwined, and there's no getting around it. It makes far more sense to accept that this is so, basically changing your mind toward it.

Nurture the vessel then as much as you nurture the psyche: for every counseling session with a psychotherapist, schedule a massage (whether it's done by your partner or a professional masseuse). Every time you release an old hurt, fill the void with a big dose of highly positive, highly spiritual energy—accompanied by a hug. Find the bodywork that suits you best. An array of bioenergetic therapies exist: reflexology, intuitive foot massage, hand massage, reiki healing, aura scanning, and much, much more.

4. Balance your body at home.

If all this is new to you, or if you have a shy, conservative nature, the instructions for intuitive foot massage in the upcoming chapter "Rx for Pain" will allow you to stay at home and do bodywork at home. Find a friend or enlist a partner with whom you can swap regular foot massages. Regular foot massages—that is, daily, every other day, or weekly—help to ward off imbalances that result in the migraine response. And if you have a migraine, having someone massage your feet works like a charm in calling up the body's healing militia.

How is that? Well, in the midst of migraine, it is often the case that your head is too sore to receive touch. The feet, however, are eminently touchable, being so far from the site of pain. Also, the sole of the foot contains hundreds of points which, when stimulated, travel along healing lines or meridians, of energy, in the body, balancing every organ and every nerve system. Foot massage works by relaxing you to the point where your own healing energies take over; the intellect is quieted, and relegated to a lesser position; the electrical impulses at odds within the body are altered; and a healing sleep gradually descends.

The healer can see or call up healing light while working on the feet—mainly purple or pink or green—and can direct that light on your behalf. If you are awake and have the wherewithal to concentrate on healing colors while being given a foot massage, the healing work is enhanced. Seeing light is too much for your head area, but nonetheless, you are dealing with light. If that is hard to imagine, consider laser beams and the fact that we now carry out gallstone operations with these intense light sources, and that we are only beginning to understand how very powerful light healing, or healing with light is. Definitely, it is the wave of the future. And you can access it yourself.

It's not been unavailable to us. It's been done through the ages, and at this point in time, it seems evident that we are experiencing ever-stronger consciousness shifts that enable humanity to appreciate not only that which is strictly scientific but also potent, unseen healing forces at work. In this new age, there is an old Chinese saying that is sinking slowly into our Western consciousness: "Some things can be sensed and not explained." So it is with becoming attuned to the unseen needs and care of the body, temple of the human soul.

Chapter 13
Calling Up the Light, the Love That Heals

Love heals. The light born of love heals. If someone were to ask me which chapter contained the master key to healing, I would have to answer that this is it. You may skip over the others but not this.

There dwells within us a capacity to love freely and without conditions. But many of us live our whole lives tasting only the tiniest percentage of our innate capacity for love. Every so often we surprise ourselves with a pure love that flows out of nowhere: when we forgive someone who has behaved abominably toward us, or when we put aside doing something that means a lot to us in order to help someone else whose life is falling apart. When we tap into this love feeling, all worry dissolves. A feeling of deep calm descends, warming us, spilling over into the air around us. We know we are doing the "right" thing.

How we feel about love is affected by our parents, our society, the way we see people dealing with other people (role models), our culture, the media, and our religious orientation. Experiences with love have important consequences for how we behave, how we receive love, and how we give love to others. We break love down into categories: love for a child, love for a friend, sexual love, self-love. We hear about love on the radio, on TV, in ads and in movies. It is a universal best-selling theme.

The love that heals is greater than any of the love categories put together. It is all-encompassing. Desire has nothing to do with it. No one can take it away from you. And it is not dependent on how you behave. This love exists all the time, in all ways, in all things. It does not judge. It does not hurt. It is all that you are, regardless of the way you live your life. When you recognize and foster it, life becomes infinitely easier and richer. This chapter is all about calling up the love that will heal you.

Love manifests as light energy. If we could only look past flesh and bones, seeing with the eyes of the sages such as the Christ and Buddha and all the master teachers and enlightened ones through the ages, we could look at different people and see at a glance the love energy that burns with light in each body. In some the flame is flickering low, like a pilot light on the stove. This low flame is not due to imminent death, so much as it signifies a spiritual dearth or ignorance of one's true relationship with God. In other people, the glow of love energy burns steady and strong. It is non-threatening, totally safe, compassionate. The light spills out beyond the borders of such a person. It warms others. People laugh easily in the company of such special people, and gain solace from being in their presence.

When you meet someone with pure love radiating out from her/him, it is common to say to yourself, "Wow. Look how happy she is. Look how easy it is for her to share love. When they gave out hearts, she was first in line." Typically, you attribute that big, big love to heredity or chance. You think it is a natural gift, something you were not born with. Actually, though, you are recognizing something temporarily lost inside yourself. You are remembering a fantastic feeling that has been smothered or stuffed way down in your body frame. In fact, you could not have responded to that person positively had you not been possessed of the very same capacity for love. In a way, you were looking into a mirror of your own love. In the presence of loving energy, your own flame within ignited into the bonfire that it is meant to be all the time.

"I'm a very loving person, but I can't seem to share that with other people." This is a common complaint, and it is a painful dilemma. Being unable to express the love you feel hurts your whole body. Migraine sufferers throw themselves headlong into pain over this angst. And because love energy is vital to healing, this particular problem cannot be ignored or wished away. Eventually, you must analyze your love energy and figure out why, how, when, and where it gets blocked.

In the chapter called "Me First," the main message was "Be responsible to yourself." The chapter on "Essence" focused on stripping down to the bare basics of self, beyond parents, husbands, schooling, job, and roles. In "Fear" the topic was getting at the fear that binds, and realizing that fear is nothing more than the absence of love. All of these relate directly to this chapter on love—because you cannot truly love others until you first perceive that you love yourself.

Ask yourself sincerely, *Do I love myself? Do I really feel I possess the capacity to love with total compassion? Am I selling myself short on love?* In exploring these questions, begin to keep lists for yourself in your journal, to help identify what it is you like about yourself. Tell yourself that these lists are only for you, that you are loving yourself by paying attention to who you are. If you would also like to keep a list of things you do not like about yourself, go ahead. That should prove interesting when you look back over it later.

Just for the record, I personally discovered that the things I did not like about myself fell into two categories: (1.) things that I perceived as characteristics my parents and others did not like about me; and (2.) things that keep falling by the wayside one by one as I grow more and more spiritually awakened. Eventually, I decided I did not really have a choice at all regarding love of self. Love was there already. Love is an integral characteristic of essence, therefore, my job is simply to remind myself of my true love nature, and be grateful all the time that I am made of the stuff and substance called love.

You will find meditating on the phrase "I am a being of pure love" is unbelievably powerful. It sounds too simple to be true, so you will just have to take my word for it. The process may take a long time for it to make noticeable waves, maybe even months or years, but that is due to the fact that you are undergoing a careful deconstruction (tearing down) of old thought patterns that told you about your worthlessness, your inner hate, your inadequacy. If you were to turn into a full-fledged being of love in one night, the shock on your body would be positively overwhelming. It might even kill you. Your guides, who help you make the transition to a being of love, take care that your system will not be shocked too greatly. And little by little, progressing at your own pace, the human mind deconditions itself. Your biocomputer, located in the heart area, ejects the old software (which wasn't working well for you in the first place) and begins to operate on the underlying program based on your essential self, your spiritual self, uniting self with pure love. Pure love is also, of course, God.

The road to knowing yourself as a being of love is full of trials. All of life really is a series of lessons and trials to which your soul must apply itself. You encounter jealousy, want, hurt feelings, hatred, rejection, lack of appreciation, sorrow, anger, pain, fear, grief... And each of these situations is overcome by the energy of pure, unconditional love. When you claim love as your guiding force, all troubles cease to be obstacles. They assume their proper place as lessons in love, so that your soul can journey on to higher and higher levels of consciousness. This is your life's goal.

But how can something so good hurt so bad? I hear this question in myself, and know that others ask it as well. One way to overcome hurt is to constantly be aware of how much you are judging. This is good, and this is bad. My husband should never have cheated on me. I can never trust him again. My daughter should not have fought over the family property that way. I can not find any love in her actions. I should not have allowed myself to get into this mess. These are all judgments. There is little room to be a loving being when you are judging people right and left. You box yourself into a corner from which you cannot escape. You become trapped by your own thought system, and righteously cling to notions of right/wrong that have no basis in the infinite love that is God.

Judging others leads to a rigidity that inhibits growth. You begin to expect people to behave a certain way, or else. Or else what? You won't love them any more? You'll take away love and replace it with emotional distance or hatred? You'll get even with them? You'll never forgive them?

Whoa! Slow down and think. When you do those things, you stop loving yourself. You give your power over to the darkness. Your hatred does damage toward the other person, simply by virtue of the negative energy field you create, and with a boomerang effect it does your own body harm. Hatred turns in on itself. It grows into a monster with a life of its own. Once it has found a home in your body, the monster proceeds to reproduce more monsters. Soon you have a whole pile of people and situations actively agitating within your body. Your energy centers become blocked. Love energy, healing energy, has a hard time passing through. Your light within, which exists as a result of pure love energy, starts to wane. In the case of migraineurs, spiritual energy seeking passage through your system is stopgapped at every turn. It enters through your crown, and gets turned back up into your head, causing pain, nausea, and depression. The energy is horribly, madly, painfully misdirected.

How can this be healed? How can you reestablish your internal balance? Through love. That is the only way. Putting yourself in another's shoes is one way to begin recapturing love for yourself. Let us say that a person named Jimmy has betrayed you. Imagine that you are this Jimmy who has caused you distress. Now visualize that, deep inside, Jimmy is also made by the same Creator and is possessed of the same love and light as you. Tell yourself, "I see only love in Jimmy." Feel that. Become at peace with the notion of Jimmy as a vessel containing love. Recognize that the love you feel is one and the same as the love inside all people. Know that we all are one with that love energy. We are each unique, individual expressions of the same pure, unconditional love.

Next, come back to your own energies. Forgive yourself for feeling negatively towards Jimmy. Reaffirm that, above all, your higher self is in charge. You are a being a love, underneath it all, despite all these shenanigans that take place on earth. Tell yourself, "I do not have to like Jimmy's actions, but I do have to love him." Mentally surrender the entire situation over to a higher power, and trust in an outcome based on this new affirmation of love. Let Jimmy know how you feel about his actions. And do not worry about the outcome. Inside you will know that you have done all you can do, and that you are free.

With practice, love comes more and more easily. Do not consider that the trials will end. The lessons go on and on, and you may find yourself struggling against giving your power away. It feels easy sometimes to give in to feelings of vindictiveness. Our society fosters it to a degree. Macho behavior is based on getting back, getting even, and hating back harder than the opponent. If true power were at play, however, the hero would not give his power to the lower energies (darkness) but would call up the higher energies of love and light where power is unending, infinite, and beyond human comprehension.

Best of all, once you call up your love, it works automatically through you. You do not have to work at it. Your body channels the love energy naturally, directing it where it needs to go. Saying "I of myself do nothing, but love is all that I am" is very, very powerful. If you think for an instant that you are the one who loves and others do not, you weaken the force. Look up the ego when that happens, and tell your ego to take a hike. You will use the ego for other reasons, such as getting your work out in the world, and claiming what is yours to claim. Love operates independently, holistically. It is the ultimate unifying, healing force.

Claiming oneself as a being of love leads to enlightenment, which is an interesting word to take apart. En = in. Lighten = to become light. Ment = state of being. In intensive meditation, the body feels like it is growing lighter. Light energy seems to illuminate every corner and then break out beyond the borders of the body shell. The body is filled with an awesome ecstasy.

In the healing experience, whether you achieve this through meditation or energy work done by a healer, Love and Light combine to cleanse the body of anything unlike Love and Light. I capitalize these expressions Love and Light to signify their power and also their glory and mysteriousness. We cannot know how this works. It is beyond our human understanding. But when we consider that the ancient texts in our religious traditions describe this very same healing power of Love and Light, we might also consider it our obligation to explore what this is all about both individually and collectively, not in another world, but now. That is what it was intended for. We were not supposed to be living here in darkness and ignorance. We were supposed to discover that our world begins within and radiates outward.

Along those lines, enlightenment is for everyone. And discovering your own healing gifts based on love is your spiritual birthright. You can learn to heal yourself. Contrary to common thought, learning to heal yourself is not a matter of studying, remembering, and practicing new things. It is a process of letting go of old, useless notions. Like the notion that only a doctor can heal. Most good doctors will tell you anyway that they treat symptoms, and facilitate healing, which actually comes from a God-force inside the patient. Another notion is that the intellect has any power in healing. The intellect must be relegated to the sidelines for effective treatment. It is self-limiting, and so cannot open wide enough to let the inner physician pass through. Only the heart can comprehend the physician within. It is through the heart that healing is accessed. The more your mind rests, the more effective you are in healing yourself and others.

It is never easy to explain the unexplainable. The results, however, will speak for themselves. They are real. They can be measured and recorded. So if you choose to heal yourself, get ready for full empowerment. It will change your life.

The best thing you can do for yourself is find a visualization for yourself of how love and light flow through your body in order to open you to healing. The following description may help. Read it once, then try it lying down with your eyes closed, breathing in with your nose and exhaling through the mouth, feeling the sensations as fully as you can.

The Hollow Reed, a Love & Light Meditation

Imagine your body is a light, hollow reed lying in a clear pool of water. Above you the sky is deep blue and there are birds calling to each other overhead. Feel the sun warming you. Feel a fresh current of water roll gently past both sides of your reed-body, and feel the reed-body turning slowly until it moves into a stream of warm, flowing water. The top end of the reed eventually lines up with the stream so that the stream flows directly through your head, courses through your body, and exits effortlessly out your toes in a continuous motion. You are headed downstream, carried by this warm flow, and you are aware that the water is Divine Love... Feel the water flow through you, touching every edge inside you, leaving no place unbathed, and imagine that it is smoothing you out inside so that you are perfectly clear and clean, like a straw or a tube. The water envelopes you but you stay right near the surface of this beautiful stream, watching trees and leaves and tall, green grasses along the banks.

You float along in this fashion until you become aware of the sound of a rushing waterfall. It is just ahead. You feel exhilarated by the sound of the waterfall, but before you get to the edge you rise swiftly up onto the surface of the stream, and suddenly you are being carried by a gentle wind that lifts you up, out, over the top of the waterfall. The breeze supports you as you travel through the sky, higher and higher, effortlessly. You are aware that the wind traveling through you is a wind of Divine Light. You stop to rest on a mountaintop, where Light flows through you continuously. It warms you and envelopes you. You are lighter than light. You lose any feeling of your reed-body, for now you are a beam of radiant white light expanding into the mountain below and out to the fields and trees beyond and into the sky above. You merge with the white light that is all around you. Your whole world is light and full. All is well... It is intensely quiet.

Gradually you begin to feel your form again. First you feel the outlines of the tube that is your body. Birds begin to call to each other again. A light wind caresses your body. You begin to come back to this world by wiggling your toes, then your feet, then fingers, then hands. It is nice to be lying atop this mountain, with its fresh air.

Slowly raise your hands to your heart and say to yourself, "I am grateful." Take your time getting up.

Stay in the now.

See how lovely each moment really is.

Look with your eyes and heart.

Love and light are all around you, all the time.

Chapter 14
Meditating for Real-Feel Results

There are many styles of meditation—Zazen, Vipassana, TM... No matter what the practice, though, attention to breathing—focusing on the breath as it goes in and out— is a universal aspect of meditation. Another basic in meditation is clearing the mind, letting thoughts flow freely through your head until you no longer grab onto them but simply let them pass on. By not attaching to thoughts, you grow free of the cares of daily life and the pulls of the physical world. You open naturally to the spirit within, which is one with all the universe.

Meditation is a transformative energy experience. In meditation, the lower energies are eclipsed by the higher, divine energies. White light energy can enter through the crown and circulate freely during meditation, since the energy centers within the body are becoming aligned, a process greatly facilitated by the mind's partial shutdown.

Many years ago, when I first heard that meditation could be helpful for migraine sufferers, I experimented with different forms of meditation. I remember that the experiences left me feeling very calm. However, that was not enough for me. I was in severe pain. I needed a meditative practice that would take me beyond calm, in a healing direction.

I found that meditating with focused intent opened me to infinite discoveries about self, migraine, and healing. This, finally, was effective meditation. It was meditation with a definite desired effect. It is less a method than a meditative roadmap designed to make life easier, fuller, and, ultimately, painfree. And it is incredibly simple to do.

Preparing for meditation has certain basic requirements. Choose a time for meditation when you can be all alone in a room or out of doors. There should be as few distractions as possible. (No radio, no TV blaring, nothing cooking on the stove.)

Early morning is an excellent time to meditate. So is the time just before sleep. However, there are no set rules about when to go within. The only real rules are to follow your internal direction toward establishing a good time for yourself to get centered. Many times you will face situations, those involving difficulties or confusion, that lead you to meditate at various points in the day. For ultimate effectiveness, though, it is wise to set a specific time for yourself and let your body's biocomputer become accustomed to calling up the higher energies at that set time each day. The call to meditation will become as natural as the call to eat three meals or do anything else that the body must perform in order to stay healthy and grow stronger in spirit.

Lighting incense is optional. Some migraineurs are too sensitive to scent to tolerate it. If it is not a problem for you, light a stick or cone of high quality incense and let the smoke cleanse the air of unwanted energies in the room. Sandalwood is generally good, or you may choose an incense directed toward resolving an area of personal difficulty. For example, cedar is powerful in clearing out old, unwanted energies. Hand-rolled incense from India and other countries where incense burning is a time-honored practice can be trusted for their purity.

Some people also choose to light a candle and place it on a nearby table. As you light the candle, imagine that the candle's flame represents the light of your spirit.

Sit comfortably with a pillow as good support for your back and neck. Let your hands rest gently on your thighs, preferably with palms facing upward. (If you are accustomed to sitting another way, such as in lotus position or on a meditation cushion, you may choose to do so.) Or you may lie down on a bed or mat, legs stretched out in front of you, arms lying at your sides, preferably with the palms up.

Take a deep breath in through the nose, filling the lungs and diaphragm with air; then breathe out with your mouth, flattening the diaphragm and lungs. Repeat this breathing pattern for 5 to 7 minutes. It is normal for many thoughts to flood your mind at this time. Rather than deny entrance to the thoughts, allow them to blow out your mouth as you exhale. Visualize them exiting on a stream or a gust of wind. Keep bringing your attention back to the breath.

To bring yourself quickly into the higher energies, place the right hand on top of your head, in the crown area. With practice you will begin to notice that there is one spot on your crown that radiates a heat energy, or a tingling energy. This is your highest spiritual center. Place the left hand over your heart and allow yourself to listen for a sound that comes from within. Attuning yourself to this sound takes practice. It is a sound far, far away at first, a sound created by the energy of your highest frequencies.

(It is not tinnitus, which is a ringing or jangling that some people are plagued by. Tinnitus sufferers are advised to seek out energy balancing or acupuncture to relieve the ringing, in order to become attuned to hear the true frequency beneath it all.)

In addition to the sound within the silence, look too for a light that appears in the crown area. It may be very dim at first. If you do not perceive any light at all, open your eyes and focus on the light of a candle. Then close your eyes and see that flame in your mind. This visualization process aids the eventual linkup of fire with your true inner light. As I have said many times, you must practice the art of going within. It is not usually an overnight accomplishment. For many years you have been living in the darkness of illusions brought on by the condition of the physical body. Remind yourself: "I am a spiritual being having a human experience, not a human being having a spiritual experience."

Express an invocation to meditate. The following is an invocation that may be adapted for your own use:

"Almighty Creator, maker of all things, the one wisdom, the one eternal love, the only presence and the only power, and all that is goodness, truth and the light, I am grateful for the many blessings of my path. I give thanks for divine love, protection and guidance. I know that the pure, unconditional love residing within is all that I am. I am aware that your constant and abiding love heals all pain and that your love is all that I am. I know that I of myself do nothing, that I am a perfect expression of the Creator. I know that I am being awakened to my true reality, and I am grateful."

Next, progress to the three-part affirmations that place your energies in a position of power over the lower, physical energies. The crown area represents the "I know." The forehead represents the "I am aware." The heart (biocomputer) represents "I am grateful."

Placing both hands on your crown, claim aloud, "I know I am a being of pure, divine energy."

Move both hands to cover your forehead (the third eye, or intuition and awareness center, where you "see without the eyes"), and declare, "I am aware that I am a being of pure, divine energy."

Then place your hands over your fourth chakra, the heart area, and say, "I am grateful that I am a being of pure, divine energy."

Repeat the whole sequence of hand placements with additional affirmations, such as those listed below. Depending on your needs at the time, choose to concentrate on one, two, or more of these. It depends on where you are in your own spiritual development. Choose the affirmation that speaks to your intuition at the time of meditation.

I know, I am aware, I am grateful that...

I am a being of pure, unconditional love.

I am a being of pure, divine light.

I am a unique expression of the Creator.

I am life itself.

God (the divinity) within me is all that I am.

I of myself do nothing.

All healing comes from within, from pure, divine love and light.

I am a perfect expression of the one Source, the one Truth.

All is well, all the time.

I am an open vessel for God's perfect love, and I am never alone.

I am open to hear my inner voice.

I walk by faith and not by sight.

Next, since the pain called migraine is what bothers you most, take as much time as you need to deeply feel and express the following affirmation:

This is a memory of a migraine.

"This is a memory of a migraine I once had." Proceed through the three areas to reinforce this new way of looking at migraine. Say "I know this is a memory of a migraine. It has no power anymore." Then, "I am aware that this is a memory of a migraine."

Do not analyze the statement. If you feel your logical mind straining to interrupt (and that old energy will protest, precisely because it feels like it's losing a home), affirm most strongly, "I surrender my intellect to my higher self. My higher self is in complete control at all times. I identify with the Creator, and the Creator can feel no pain. In the Spirit pain is an illusion. It is a memory of an illusion that I once had."

Relax your hands at your sides (if you are lying down) or on your thighs (if you are sitting). Breathe deeply again, in and out. Address your personal invisible helpers and guardian angels, and call upon them to work directly on your body to relieve pain and help you understand why you are facing pain at this time in your life. Always affirm that the work is already being done for you, in accordance with divine will. Divine will is healing will.

"I am grateful for the unseen energies that are now cleansing my body. I know that anything unlike perfect light and pure, unconditional love is now being removed from my body. Perfect healing has already been accomplished, and divine restoration is taking place throughout my body and in my life." Lie or sit still for several minutes after you make this affirmation, giving time for your guides to activate the healing powers within. While the unseen work is going on (usually energy balancing and clearing the aura, and can even be a type of surgery in some cases), you can aid the process by focusing on the words "divine love" and "pure light energy."

If a color comes into your head, note the color and envision which chakra it correlates to. Focus on the color, allowing it to become as vivid as possible in your mind. Visualizing purple objects or deep purple light has an especially beneficial effect. However, do not ignore another color if it comes to mind. That color will be a vital key to your own problem area, and functions as an agent of healing.

If you get caught up in thinking, you are not yet meditating. Concentrating on a color is one way to move away from the meandering mind. Another method: Allow stray thoughts to enter your mind but then send them on a voyage out your toes, mentally mailing them down through the body and out, to be received and totally absorbed by mother earth. Thoughts that keep returning, however, will eventually leave on their own accord, as your focus on breathing continues, bringing you deeper and deeper within the intuitive realms.

Finally, surrender what you can to the all-knowing, all-powerful force that is one and the same as your higher self. Say aloud or inside your head:

> "Creator of all things, the only presence, the one love, I surrender my health, my mind, my body and my earthly concerns to your loving arms. My higher self is all that I am. And I am grateful to know the truth about myself and the divine healing energy that lives within."

Feel your body fill with radiant light. Visualize light entering your head with every breath, and traveling over each and every cell of your body. Feel the warmth and tingling as light floods over all corners of yourself. Imagine this light energy extending beyond the skin, outside the borders of your physical body. Know that this energy is the force of God. Bask in the warmth and love that merge with the light. Know that this experience is your true reality. Release into the light.

Whenever you are ready, slowly begin to move your fingers and toes and let the body adjust back to physical reality. Say, "I am grateful for all the beautiful help given to me by the universe. I am aware that I of myself do nothing. The Creator expresses through me all the time in all ways. Thy will is done, and all is well."

At this point in time in spiritual awareness, many people are moving from pleas of help to affirming God's truths and love. Did you notice that the basic prayer for healing is not "Please God, let me get better?" Such a statement is an ineffectual way of using words. The words lose their power almost before they are out of the starting gate. The implication is that you are powerless in the face of a God that you have not yet internalized.

God is still regarded as Other in people who hold fast to the daily "I'm-begging-you" praying. Affirming in your heart of hearts, "I choose to believe in grace and mercy" reinforces a sense of the Higher Self within, while "Please Lord, have mercy on me"—though not ineffectual—emphasizes the separateness a human feels from the divine force driving the universe. In the most desperate of moments, when all hope seems gone, it's only natural for the latter prayer to spring forth. Over time, reexamine what words you use for prayer, and ask yourself if they truly reflect your heart.

Divinity resides within. You were made so that the God-force within could express itself through your body. Seeing yourself as separate from this God-force is the very crux of the underlying malaise in humans. It is precisely this separateness, or seeing yourself as Self and the Creator as Other, which causes imbalances, including dis-ease, in the first place. Therefore, to break through to true healing, that void must be closed firmly with the inner knowledge that you and your divine self are one and the same.

Claim your own divinity, even if you do not deeply believe it at first. As you repeat your affirmations day after day, your conviction will deepen. In time, you will come into your true reality, and old, painful ways of thinking will in and of themselves be cleared from the body.

Words are powerful. Never underestimate their power to act for you, in accordance with your personal path and ultimate purpose. In a direct way, your affirmations serve to activate the higher energies, leading to the higher self becoming more and more prevalent in your daily life. Your words guide you naturally into an unimaginably powerful process of divine intervention. Gradually, the personality and the soul move toward each other in harmony, toward perfect alignment, so that one day what you do and what you essentially are will merge completely. At that point, true healing is your blessing.

Know that healing is your spiritual birthright. Know that there is always a spiritual cause behind all suffering. Your job is merely to remember that the Creator does not have it in for you. The Creator is all-good, all-knowing, and ever-present. Your higher self cannot feel pain or suffering, just as God cannot feel pain or suffering. That is why identifying with the Creator-force is so important in healing.

Oneness, not separation, is the divine intent of the cosmos. And it is through meditation that we remember that Oneness. Because of the fact that we are in the body, living a human existence in a physical reality, it is even more important that we commit daily to going within—to remember. To feel past and future merge into now. To practice living in the now until it becomes our reality. Only then are we living fully, free of stress, whole, balanced and present.

Chapter 15
Invoking Help from Guides and Angels

One of the greatest of all illusions is that we are all alone in our struggles here on earth. No one has ever told us otherwise, in this culture, that is. Yet we are surrounded by unseen entities that exist in the form of pure energy. If we choose to become aware of the unseen entities that exist on another, higher plane, we can consciously access their help in every aspect of daily life, including healing from migraine headache. For they are here to protect, guide, and help heal us.

Of all the topics in this book, I am aware that this will seem the most like science fiction. Fortunately, there is a broadening movement toward acceptance of higher intelligences, whether they are labeled guides or angels or guardians. Gary Zukov's best-selling book *The Seat of the Soul* provides an excellent description of these unseen guides. Coming from a physicist, the information is most welcome. Psychic healers and spiritual counselors have long been aware of guides, using the information they receive from these invisible helpers to pass on to people who are seeking guidance in their lives.

In the world of unseen things, there are many levels of energy entities. The lower energies can create havoc in people's lives, if given a chance. In that realm, which literally is lower in that it is closest to the earth, earthbound spirits who departed the earth unhappy and unenlightened roam around in a kind of confusion. They are attracted to people whose inner light is strong, for they have yet to learn the lesson concerning their higher reality as beings of light. Extrasensitive people have practice in dealing with these entities, and sense their presence in various ways. We have all heard of spirits who need to make peace with relatives left behind after death. Such things do happen.

The higher entities, on the other hand, are advanced intelligences whose job it is to guide you through difficult times and, ideally, help boost you up the ladder of spiritual consciousness. Some of them are high angels, while others are lower down the rung and can be termed guides or guardians.

We all have had an experience or two (or more) at some time in life where a divine grace descended to save us from some grave harm. We cannot explain why we awoke at the steering wheel just in time to avoid hitting a truck. We cannot explain why we had a funny feeling about taking a certain airplane flight and proceeded to cancel the ticket, to discover later that the flight was doomed. We cannot produce a rational explanation about such phenomena, calling it luck or fate or chance. We joke about guardian angels, and say to each other, "Someone up there likes me," or "I was born under a lucky star."

Imagine that the self is not merely one self, but multiselves that act through us in wisdom and goodness and in accordance with God's will to take care of all the business that needs taking care of here on the earthly level. When we call upon our higher energies to work through us, to enact divine will through our presence, we give license to the legion of invisible helpers that have chosen to be with us in this lifetime. We open ourselves to a new and vast level of help.

Of course, many people are fearful of the implications of this. They like to think they are doing it all themselves. Their motto is if you can't see it, it ain't real. And if it is real, I don't want to know about it.

I know a man who is a very staunch member of the seeing-is-believing school of thought. No way could anything exist outside his realm of visual understanding. One day he found himself in the hospital after a very serious accident. By all rights, he should not have ever been able to walk again. But the perfectly freaky circumstance of his fall led him to comment, "I know I was saved by something. I don't know what or who it was, but I am thankful I have been given another chance. I know there was divine interference." He was trying to acknowledge that higher help did exist for him. While in recovery he suffered what he referred to as "visions from hell." He described people coming after him with knives, faces twisted and bodies contorted, and colors and shapes and complex plots. These were his experiences with the lower energies.

166

He concluded, "I know there is another world out there. I have seen it and felt it. It was real. It was no dream." Part of his recovery included a conscious effort to keep his own energies directed upward, so that he would not sink into the unpleasant visions. His family played a major role in lifting his energies high enough so that his angels could take over.

When I first heard about guides, I was more than skeptical. I was downright hostile toward the idea. I had been through too much pain to believe that anyone was there to help me, much less invisible entities. It was scary. But I could accept the possibility that higher intelligence existed somewhere in this galaxy or beyond.

The turning point came for me when I began to hear the names of some of my guides and angels in meditation, and I could experience their energies fluttering around my head and gently pulling at my face to let me know they were there. Furthermore, I found that calling the name of a certain guide would take me into a deep healing experience. I experienced an all-encompassing sense of love and light and well-being. Though I was in a trancelike state, I was conscious of physical work being done on me, and I emerged from the meditation knowing that the migraine was being lifted. I was aware that it had been gently but firmly dislodged from my head and was on its way out. The feeling I got was similar to the laying on of hands by my friend Martin (see Chapter One). I was tired afterward and often fell asleep. When I awoke, most if not all of the migraine pain was gone.

When you get migraines the way I did for years, and something like the above happens, you do not question whether or not it is good for you. You go back and do it again, and you trust not in how it works, but that it works.

How do guides work? Can they help you when you get a migraine? Actually, your guides are already at work if you are reading this book. They cannot tell you about themselves very well, especially if you are not skilled in the art of listening to their messages. Once you choose to find out more about invisible helpers, though, you automatically open the door to your own help. Above all, helpers are not gods and goddesses or witches or anything bizarre. They are energies created by the same Creator that made you, and they are characterized by frequencies or vibrations that are the stuff and substance of all that is good and loving. Enormous healing potential lies in accessing angels and guides.

How can you tell a guide when you feel one come forth? That is a highly individual event. More than anything else, a guide is always positive. A check against the yardstick of universal love will tell you immediately if the energy you think you feel is from a higher order, rather than a lower one. True to everything we know about angels, which mostly comes from ancient religious texts, guides operate out of cosmic truth and pure, unconditional love. They pursue no destructive course. They steer you toward everlasting wisdom and truth. They manifest energy near the crown of the head, never in the lower extremities, except when they are doing healing work on your physical body.

I often perform healing work by massaging people's feet. This is a gift I discovered very much by accident (divine accident, apparently). The first time I ever did that was many years ago, when a close friend had a severe migraine following his father's death. Painkillers did not work—at all. He was writhing in pain. Instinctively, I had him lie down and began massaging his feet. It had never occurred to me before to massage anyone's feet. Surely there was an angel on hand that worked through me that day. After about ten minutes, he fell completely asleep.

Some two hours later, he woke up, painfree.

It was to be several more years before I recalled that experience. By then I was beginning the journey of my spiritual awakening, and was learning how guides can work through light energy given off from the hands of healers. I began to share my foot massage with people who asked for help. And very often people told me that they were not conscious of when I left the room after the massage. They look at me afterwards, surprised, and say, "How long were you gone? It felt like you were still working on my feet."

Because I have become aware that not only are my guides at work, but other people's guides are being activated through this meditative massage, I tell people before I undertake the massage that they must not get up right away afterwards. Unseen work—that is, healing work performed on the body by a person's own guides—generally carries over into the ten or fifteen minutes (at least) after I have completed the foot massage. Direct energy work continues even longer if the person falls asleep. Waves of healing energy sweep over the body, targeting areas of imbalance and blockage.

It is wise to take certain protective measures before, during and after energy massage work. I generally clear the environment by burning incense or spraying a bit of ammonia in the corners of the room. I meditate first, breathing deeply, calling for my higher self to be present, and asserting that only the higher energies can work through me. I declare that there is only One Presence and One Power. I call on pure, unconditional love as the only healing force. I maintain that "I of myself do nothing; the pure love of the Creator is all that I am."

Throughout the healing session, I declare myself an open vessel for healing, and turn over the healing work to my angels, knowing they will serve to protect me from holding onto any energies that might be unleashed in the healing process. Since negative energy or blocked energy is being released during the process, it is important to claim protection, and release negative energies into the loving mother earth. I keep my feet firmly grounded, on the floor, so that unwanted energies pass right through me and become absorbed into the earth. If I feel myself tense up during the session, I consciously release that tension, imagining it to be a stream of energy that passes out my body, through the soles of my feet, into the earth. Fresh, revitalizing energy enters through the top of my head; and so the circle of energy flows down, through, out the feet—and then in again through the crown.

Afterwards, I always give thanks to the love and healing light that flowed through my body. I then wash my hands with baking soda (and sometimes my whole body depending on the nature of the healing), which serves to neutralize my energies.

One more thing. I give the person I "worked on" a big hug. For the healing experience is always a time when I too grow spiritually. Healing is not a one-way street. I see myself more as a facilitator of healing, not a healer. People often say, "I've got so much stress, you'd be drained of energy if you worked on me." Those people are operating on a misconception: they feel the stress draining their strength, and project that the same experience will happen to anyone who goes near them. In the vast majority of cases, I find myself reenergized following a massage. That's because healing work opens the self to experience the unlimited energy of the universe, which is an infinite powerful source. The battery charger is right there, if only we *choose to learn* how to plug in.

Getting back to guides. If you feel ready to call on your guides for help in healing pain, you can begin by using creative visualization. The exercise below is but one of many ways to start consciously depending on unseen guides (all-good, angelic helpers).

Allowing the Unseen to Help You

Envision your guides (or angels) as laser beams whose mission is to clear your body of anything that is unlike God-force.

While in the throes of migraine, lie back, and *allow all unseen, helping energies to work for you*, to lift the cloud of pain and push it away. Ask your guides directly if there are messages concerning the cause of your pain: Is there an unresolved conflict, or are you needing to forgive someone? Talk to your higher helpers—not exactly in traditional prayer (in most Judeo-Christian religious prayer, you end up beseeching, or pleading), but rather claiming the relief you need.

Claim that you know you have been given help for healing and you will open yourself to that help, in the name of all that is good and true and loving, and in accordance with divine will. (For a meditation to call on your guides for help, see Chapter 16, "Laying Claim to Health through Guided Meditations.")

When your guides and angels help you to heal, carrying you above the sensation of pain, you experience an invisible magic show—only there is no trick here, just your own private miracle. It's sort of like the experience the Japanese call *tenki ame*. *Tenki* means good weather; *ame* (ah' may) is rain. It is the phenomenon when, right in the middle of a rain, the sun shines through as if it did not know there was a shower going on.

Just remember, it's up to you to do the claiming. If you're having trouble getting your guides activated all by yourself, a healing facilitator can help give you a jumpstart. To learn more about guides and healing, try looking into one of my favorite books: Barbara Brennan's *Hands of Light* (see the resource list at the end of this book).

Chapter 16
Laying Claim to Health through Guided Meditations

A guided meditation is meditation that is directed in some fashion. Basically, there are two ways to enter a guided meditation: You can guide yourself, or you can have another person guide you to achieve a certain result. The basic idea is, when you speak meditational words to overcome specific difficulties such as pain and depression, over time they gain tremendous power and speed in delivering relief.

I have found, however, that it is pointless to expect a guided meditation to fully work unless I devote part of my time every day to do my homework, which consists of three primary assignments:

- daily meditation (see the previous chapter);

- inner work (such as uncovering fears, releasing anger, and learning more about deep needs— such as the need to be creative and actively nurture self-expression); and
- body work (such as exercise, massage, dance, aura scanning, and other bio-energy work).

Just as the three R's—reading, writing, 'rithmetic—long provided the foundation of education and culture, these three are the components for building an unshakable foundation of self-empowerment, healing, and liberation from physical pain. No single component may be ignored; you cannot choose one and not the others. All three must be attended to with love, care, and discipline.

Many people ask, *Why is this daily homework so necessary? They are thinking: So, are these power meditations or not? Do they work? Will they cure the pain? Why should I have to meditate every day? If these words are so powerful, why can't I just pick out a guided meditation to attack my headaches as they happen?*

The answer lies not in the fine wording of the guided meditation but in developing an ability to say those words with an ever-accelerating element of faith and trust in your inner divinity. Such daily practice in contacting your higher self, through language, and releasing to your higher self is the main highway to healing. The physician within cannot operate in the dark.

Remember, migraine seems to be preceded by unseen disease. Meditation, inner work, and body work—all of which relate to the soul's development—keep you in touch with the unseen, so that when you do turn to a guided meditation, all the angels and guides you need for help are already accessible: they are lined up and waiting, like a nursing crew in the surgical ward. The love energy that heals all wounds (the divine Love and Light within) can be called to the fore much more readily if you regularly say to yourself, "I AM a being of pure, unconditional love."

Furthermore, the messages that may be coming through to you in migraine mode can be recorded, shared, and expressed much more quickly if you are in the habit of looking to migraine as a message. Healing from the pain is swiftly facilitated once you begin to hear those messages.

Of all the meditations below, my favorite is "Memory of a Migraine." Strangely, this meditation is the one I found ludicrous at first. *What? This incredible deathlike pain is a memory? Wow.* I really resisted this concept. But over and over again it proved its worth. (Turn to Chapter 20 for more discussion on migraine as a memory reaction.)

The best way to stop a cycle of migraine is to focus on the cycle itself. Migraine cycle is a form of memory that kicks in on itself, over and over again, like a bicycle wheel going around and around. Deep-seated anger over a certain situation functions similarly, like spokes going around. And until that angry/fearful/emotional situation is faced squarely, with Love used as both weapon and shield, the memory of the discomfort persists. It kicks in. It manifests as physical pain.

Another reason I like "Memory of a Migraine" is that it tells me I can look at pain in a new way. That I am not claiming it anymore. *I am not denying that it is bringing me a message about myself, but I am no longer giving it the power it once held.* This memory is literally just that: a memory of a painful emotional time (whether it is ongoing or tied to your childhood) or a memory of a past life, and possibly a memory of a past death in an earlier incarnation. If you suspect you need help getting at an old memory, by all means seek a trustworthy counselor to help you access and cleanse that memory.

In the meantime, concentrating on this particular meditation will automatically begin to work on behalf of clearing up your energy field.

Preparing to go into Meditation

Meditation is a highly personal affair. In actuality, no special preparation is required, other than to commit oneself to quietude. There are no set rules to follow except to assert there is only One Presence, One Powerful Goodness, one moving energy-force that unites all beings.

There are, however, some aids to meditation that you may choose to incorporate into personal practice. Some people prepare the room by burning incense, such as sandalwood; some people like to play gentle music, such as music by Steven Halpern and other artists, or environmental sound recordings, like ocean waves or forest sounds.

Pre-recorded guided meditations, such as those offered by author Steven Levine, may be very useful, especially if you are in a great deal of pain and unable to read at the time. Of course, you can always make your own recordings using the affirmations here, for use at home.

Experiment to see what appeals to you and suits your needs. A person who responds to wilderness sounds, for example, may not relate well to ocean music. One woman, who was bedridden, told me that she cannot listen to water flowing because she lacked bladder control. For her, the sound of flutes playing or wind blowing through the trees was more appropriate.

Lighting a candle may help calm your mind and focus your attention. A flame always is a reminder of the flame of spiritual truth within.

Incense, music, candles—are all extras. In time, you will become accustomed to being still and deeply quiet. To enhance each meditation experience, you must get as relaxed as possible without actually sleeping. An all-around exercise for slowing down the body is the following Tense-and-Relax Treatment, often referred to as progressive relaxation technique.

STEP 1. Before Meditation: Tense-and-Relax Treatment

Lying down or sitting in a comfortable chair, mentally focus on every area of your body from the toes to the head, alternately tensing isolated muscles and then releasing them completely.

Starting with the feet, first wiggle your toes, crimp them under, and tense them up. Then relax them. Next, shake the whole foot, tense it up, hold it rigid, and then let it sink gently into the floor. Progress in this fashion to alternately tense and relax calves, thighs, buttocks, pelvis, back, chest, and so on and so forth, until you come to the face, jaw, chin, forehead, and crown. When you arrive at relaxing the crown, mentally sweep down your body to see if any part of your body has re-tensed up again. Target any body part that feels tight, and allow that area to relax. Check for places where tension hides, such as the jaw, mouth, temples, and back of the neck.

Say to yourself, "I am a being of pure, divine energy...I relax...I let go...I am safe..."

Now you are ready for a guided meditation.

STEP 2. Invoking the Higher Self

It is necessary to always call for the highest help when going into meditation, affirmations or prayers. Align yourself with pure, divine energy, by speaking aloud a statement that works for you. Do always claim that the Creator is the Only Presence and the Only

Power. At different times, I use different invocations but here is a very powerful one:

"Maker of All Things, the Only Presence and the Only Power, and all that is Truth, Goodness, and Wisdom, I am grateful for knowing my true reality. I am one with the Creator; I identify with the Creator. I know that Divine Will works through me, that I am a unique expression of an almighty Creator, and that I of myself do nothing. I surrender to my higher self, which is all Love; all Light; Pure, Divine Energy."

STEP 3: Meditations for Release from Migraine

Sit in a comfortable position and either read aloud from this book or have a friend sit with you so you can close your eyes and repeat affirmations with her/his guidance. Place your right hand on top of the crown, and hold your left hand against the middle of the chest, in the heart chakra. Affirm and repeat (out loud, if possible), whichever affirmation most closely applies to your current situation.

Keep in mind that any time you journey into the self, through silent meditation or speaking a guided meditation aloud, your entire being is involved. Mind, body and soul feel the effects of unseen energy work. It is as if you are a canvas opening to a healing artist (i.e., your own "physician within") who directs flowing lines of unseen color in waves of light, affecting every part of you from the smallest cell to the mind itself.

Therefore, after meditation do not arise quickly. Take your time. Some people use the chant "Ohm" to come back from a very relaxed state. If a friend is reading the guided meditation to you aloud, s/he can use following words to gently bring your body back into the physical realm, after allowing you to drift deeply in a quiet state for several minutes:

STEP 4. After Meditation: Re-Entry

"I am now awakening to the world around me. As I move my fingers and wiggle my toes, I feel my body tingling with energy. In my heart I feel a deep calm, steady and true, which remains with me all the time. I slowly open my eyes and look around me. I am aware. I am protected. All is well."

WORDS OF POWER: Affirmations to Use in Meditation

Letting Go

I know that I myself do nothing,

but that the Creator heals from within.

I know that the healing process has already begun,

and that every trial in my life is a lesson,

the meaning of which is made manifest to me,

through the Love and Light

that is the ultimate source, the one source, of all,

the source that is myself,

one and the same as the Creation.

I let go.

I let go, and let God.

Calling up the Healing Light

I envision the light that burns within me,

high in the crown area of my head;

even as it appears as a candle's flame

in the midst of large darkness, I know

that this light is a healing light,

a healing energy of unlimited power,

full of love and promise and truth itself.

I let the light fill me.

Pure light energy travels throughout my entire body,

healing every cell as it goes.

It is infinitely powerful.

Healing light is all that I am.

I know that anything unlike the perfect light

and perfect love of the Creator

is leaving my body now,

and has already left.

I am one with the perfect healing light.

Memory of a Migraine (Talking to the Migraine)

In this meditation, begin by breathing deeply in through the nose, then release breath out through the mouth. Breathe this way for a few minutes. Relax. Next, bring your breathing to a new pattern where you breathe in (again, through the nose), hold the breath for 7 to 10 counts, and then exhale through the mouth. After a few times of doing this, you may notice a tingling sensation in the crown area or face. Some spiritual teachers say this is a physical sign that you are connecting with your higher self, and your angels.

Place your hands on top of your head, on the crown, and affirm aloud:

> I know that I am a being of pure, divine energy.

Next, move your hands to cover your eyes and forehead:

> I am aware that I am a being of pure, divine energy.

The hands move on to the chest area:

> I am grateful that I am a being of pure, divine energy.

Repeat the whole sequence above.
Then proceed with the following affirmation:

> I know that the pain I am feeling
>
> is the memory of a pain I once had.
>
> This memory of a migraine
>
> is now being cleared from my body.
>
> Its meaning will be shown to me,

179

in accordance with God's will.

I open my self to see what this memory is,

and I know that I am purging this memory now.

I am a being of pure, divine energy,

one with God, the Creator of all the Universe.

The Creator feels no pain;

therefore, I also feel no pain.

The Creator is all-loving, all-compassionate.

The Creator does not want me to suffer,

but rather to remember that I am one with God.

Never separate, never alone.

Healing energy is all that I am.

This is a memory of a pain: It is passing.

I am a being of pure, divine, perfect energy,

and anything that is unlike the Creator

has no home in this body.

I am grateful for this clearance.

I know that I of myself do nothing, and that

Divine Restoration is now taking place.

I am grateful. I am free.

Love

I am a being of pure, divine love.

Love heals all wounds,

and love rights all wrongs.

Wherever there is fear in me,

let the all-powerful force of pure Love

reside in its place.

I know that as I am a being of Love,

everyone else I know is a being of Love,

and all I see in them is perfect Love.

I am grateful that Love is all that I am.

The healing light of Love courses through my body

and fills every cell with well-being.

Wherever I am, there is Love.

De-Stress (When There's Too Much to Do)

I surrender this day to my higher self,

and I surrender all of my concerns to the loving universe.

I walk by faith and not by sight.

I know that everything I am supposed to accomplish today

is already being accomplished,

in accordance with Divine Will.

All the help that I need is already here.

And I am grateful to the One Power,

the One Wisdom, and the One Path.

Overriding Intellect

God, I know there is but One Mind.

I am aware there is One Mind,

all-wise, all-powerful, all-encompassing.

I release any illusion of being in control.

I release my mind, my intellect, and my thoughts

to the Almighty Creator.

I am aware that the One Mind is all that I am.

I already know what I am supposed to do,

all the time.

Only God is in control.

I close down my intellect so that I may hear

the One Voice, the One Mind, which is all good,

all-loving, and all-powerful.

I open my heart to hear the words of God,

and know that God lives through me.

I of myself do nothing.

I am a unique expression of the Creator.

Facing Difficulties

I am aware that this difficulty is a trial.

I know that I am being shown the reason for this trial.

I am aware that my guides and angels protect me,

in the Light of the Creator that created all beings.

I am aware that my soul faces trials in order to grow,

183

and that true meaning is made manifest to me

in the perfect order of things,

in perfect time,

toward harmony, and toward the betterment of humankind.

I open myself as a being of Love and Light

to learn those lessons that are in my path.

Divine restoration is now taking place.

I am grateful. I embrace the lessons of life,

knowing that in the spirit, all is well, all the time.

Overcoming Depression

I am now remembering that Life lives Itself.

And I am life itself.

All that I am is life force,

life energy,

the same life energy that is the Creator;

for the Creator created me,

and lives within the Creation.

Anything that is unlike perfect love must leave this vessel.

I identify with all that is good and true.

I identify with all that is eternal,

everlasting Life and Light is all that I am.

I know that I have come here for a divine purpose,

and I open myself to walk the path of Divine Will.

I am the "I Am."

I know that mercy is on its way to me now.

I am grateful for the love that lives within.

I am a being of pure, unconditional love.

And I am never alone, for I am guided toward life

constantly, opening to live fully in each moment,

one moment at a time.

No past, no future. Only Now.

Each moment perfect, beautiful.

Only goodness can come to me.

Only the higher energies can work in me.

All is well.

Prosperity Meditation

Ask and ye shall receive.

And what is God but the Source and the Substance of all things?

God within me is all that I am, therefore

I am the Source and the Substance of all that I need.

I identify with all that is prosperous and good,

and I claim all the resources due me,

knowing that I will be provided for

as I follow my divine mission here on earth,

in accordance with God's will.

I have all that I need.

I am unlimited prosperity and unlimited love.

I am grateful, I am grateful.

Prayer for Healing

In the spirit there is no pain.

I am releasing any illusions about pain.

Anything that is unlike the perfection of the Creator

is now being removed lovingly from my body

by the healing light that lives within me.

I release my fears, my health, my mind, and all concerns now...

I send my fears back to the void from which they came,

And invite my body to fill with pure, divine love.

Bright purple light is now entering through the top of my head,

and illuminating each and every cell in my body.

This purple light is the healing light of God.

I open myself to receive any memories or information

that might help me understand the cause of my pain.

I ease into the pain.

I do not resist the pain.

I do not claim the pain, but ask instead to be shown

what lies beneath.

Is it fear?

Of who? Of what?

I remind myself that in the spirit

All is well, all the time.

The higher self is now taking over.

I do not question the vast power of God's healing,

but I allow it to lift my pain like a heavy cloud,

gently the purple light dislodges the pain.

Healing continues, unseen.

I am grateful, I am grateful, I am grateful.

Divine Restoration is taking place.

I claim my spiritual birthright to health,

the perfect, pure balance of health.

(Amen)

A Word about Using Creativity in Meditation

There is always an element of change in effective meditation. Tapping into creativity plays an important part. Eventually, the words that are best for you at a specific time will come to you as you become familiar with listening for gentle loving messages to emerge from within your heart. You will learn to take yourself to special places in meditation: a sandy beach, a grove of pine trees, or the bank of a river, where you are completely safe, all the time. This is your place, your secret space where all is well, all is safe, and you are loved all the time. This is the space you remember when you are feeling separate or lonely or frightened, for this secret place is where you and the Creator are always One.

The inner voice that is your guiding light will never tell you to destroy anything, nor will it suggest to you any messages other than perfect light, bliss, peace and harmony. Trust in your higher self. If you see a bright green color behind your eyes during the pain meditation—instead of purple—follow your instincts: green will be the best color to heal you at that time. If you find yourself crying, do not stop. Let it out. Crying is good; tears wash away pain. It is one way your body cleanses itself of old, spent, negative emotions.

After sitting in meditation, say (out loud) a simple affirmation: "I am pure, divine energy." Or: "I am a being of pure, unconditional love." Gradually, your very chemistry will change, as your faith in yourself and in your own divinity grows. People will notice the change; they will be drawn to your energy. Little by little, month by month, you will know ever more surely that, in time, you will achieve perfect wholeness and health. It's up to you to lay your claim. All the rest will follow.

Note: See www.migrainehealing.com for a meditation based on chakra energy balancing.

Chapter 17
Rx for Pain: Assists to Healing

Migraines have been around a long time, so—naturally—there are lots and lots of remedies people have tried over the centuries to prevent an onslaught and/or to treat the pain. According to some historians, migraine sufferers in ancient Egypt consumed a combination of coriander, wormwood, opium, and juniper to relieve their pain. Probably the opium did the same trick as today's narcotic painkillers (like Fiorinol, otherwise known as butalbitol) do. Anything to kill the pain, right?

Unfortunately, getting addicted to or emotionally psychologically dependent upon painkilling drugs—to the point where you take a pill to prevent even the slightest twitch from turning into a migraine—is fairly common among migraine sufferers. When, after awhile, that one pill turns into two because one isn't doing the job any more, there's a problem. When you're afraid to leave your house without a painkiller substance in your pocket, then there's a problem.

It's a troubling problem. Assuming you are caught in the world of recurrent migraines, here is a mini-guide to common aids for pain relief. Like "assists" in sports games, as in volleyball where a fellow player helps out by popping the ball up your way, these aids make it easy for you to follow through with a crushing spike for victory. They clear the pathway for the deeper, actual healing work on the cellular level, which is accomplished only by your inner physician. Assists give you a respite, a breather, from migraine symptoms. They can be very useful because, with enough rest, enough pain-free days that stretch on over a fair amount of time, you can then begin to tackle the important issues underlying migraine pain, such as where your disease is coming from in the first place.

Begin with an Affirmation Each Day

A good way to begin the healing process is to firmly declare, "I of myself do nothing. The Creator within me is all that I am." This affirmation has the power to virtually kick the healing process in motion. As various body treatments (teas, reflexology, adequate sleep, etc.) and specific affirmations are used in conjunction with meditation, the stage is set for healing to begin.

Even if you are suffering from migraines infrequently, these methods should prove helpful in staving off migraines and altering the course, duration and frequency of attacks that ensue. But, as stated in the beginning of this book, migraine is a serious ailment that should be monitored by a physician. This is not intended as a substitute for medical treatment.

Consider Prescription Drugs to Escape from Uncontrolled Migraine Cycles

I have experienced severe, recurrent migraine cycles three times in my life, where I was getting migraines at least two weeks out of every month. In a cycle, the migraine literally kicks in on itself time after time, with little relief in between. Even the slightest stress causes the migraine to crank into gear.

Depressed and living on painkillers, I was helped out of those situations twice by the drug Inderal (a beta blocker also known by its generic name, propanolol). After my doctor and I worked together to establish a dosage high enough to keep the migraines from occurring (the drug works by stabilizing the blood vessels), I was able to breathe easier, think straight, and get out of the stressful spots I had put myself in. In one case, I quit my job. While I was sick, I was simply unable to even consider that quitting was an alternative.

Anyway, the last time I was in migraine cycle, Linda worked on the spiritual causes, and I pulled through drug-free. That was two decades ago. Chances are you may not have a Linda to call on, which is why I am sharing what I have learned.

Before discussing non-drug therapies, it is important to look at some of the newer drugs for migraine treatment. In 1993, the Food and Drug Administration approved a drug that eases migraine headaches, called sumatriptan. Then-FDA Commissioner David Kessler was quoted as saying, "Sumatriptan should improve the quality of life for many of the millions of people who suffer from these debilitating headaches." He was absolutely right in his prediction. A prescription drug, sumatriptan was first available only through physicians; then it was sold in auto-injectors, a device that allows patients to self-administer the maximum recommended dose; later it came out in pill form.

Today, there are many more prescription migraine drugs that a sufferer can try, for near-immediate relief from migraine pain. These include rizatriptan (Maxalt), zolmitriptan (Zomig), eletriptan (Relpax), and others. Some of the new drugs on the market are targeted specifically for menstrual migraine pain, and government-approved trials that test drugs as treatment for hormonally-related headaches continue around the country. It would be best to talk with your physician about these options, if you haven't done so already. Depending on your personal biochemistry, these newer drugs can be literally lifesavers, especially if you are under a great deal of pressure and need that sort of immediate relief. They are the miracle drugs many of us were looking for back in the 70's and 80's. Again, when it comes to migraine pain management with drugs, this is a discussion to have with a physician. Many elements come into play: what other health conditions you have at present (or have had in the past); prescription drugs you might already be taking; possible adverse reactions; and so forth.

Aside from the -triptans, another drug that has joined the burgeoning body of pharmaceuticals against migraines is memantine hydrochloride (known also as Namenda). With more and more people becoming aware of migraine, and with research advances in brain biochemistry, it is a sure bet that still more drugs will continue to emerge from laboratories. To migraineurs and their loved ones who hate to see the suffering, this is good news.

Drawbacks to the Miracle Drugs

Drugs do have drawbacks. Take sumatriptan, for example. First of all, like most drugs, it doesn't work for everyone. Also, some people cannot take a pill when they are overwhelmingly nauseated by migraine, and they may not be capable of injecting themselves. This means they might still try to drive over to a doctor's office or hospital, which is a safety hazard in itself— then drive away with a super-strong, woozy-making substance in their system. (Like many others, this drug contains a caution against driving while you are taking it.) The alternative: They must get someone to interrupt their day and drive around in search of the necessary relief by doctor's injection. Also, surprisingly, fast-relief drugs for migraine are still not well known everywhere, so their availability is still a problem. On top of that, side effects include a "brief, mild rise in blood pressure, fatigue, and drowsiness." And people with heart disease cannot use it.

Most importantly, sumatriptan—*like all the other prescription and over-the-counter drugs available*—is not a cure. It is effective against symptoms, yes, say physicians, who have long prescribed pills to treat migraine. *But it cannot prevent migraine from happening, nor can it reduce the frequency of attacks.* In the end, treating migraine is a frustrating business for doctors, many of whom are honestly stymied by the illness and even unnerved by the extent to which their patients suffer.

Typically, in the past and even today, when their migraine patients suffered very severe or debilitating attacks, physicians asked their patients to meet them in the emergency room at the hospital where they administered shots of Demerol to quell the searing pain. If needed, they must also give out anti-nausea suppositories as well, or IV drips containing anti-nausea drugs, since uncontrollable vomiting can make it impossible for migraine sufferers to keep a painkiller working on their behalf.

Interestingly enough, I had lunch with a doctor who was engaged in one of the first trials of sumatriptan in this country— before its use was approved. He asked me to talk about the work I was doing in conjunction with migraine healing. He listened as I discussed meditation, laying on of hands, energy work, and spiritual discovery and nurturing as a way to achieve long-range, permanent healing. He seemed open to discovering new ways of treating this difficult ailment. But at that particular point in time, I could see, he was caught up with the wonders of a drug that had the power to kill pain with a simple injection. He was not ready to look at the fact that these patients had to stop their lives to come into his office, at all odd hours, take the shot, go home, feel ever so much better, and then return—again and again and again—when migraine struck. As usual, only the symptom was being addressed, not the larger question of how to live life so that pain and fear of pain were no longer primary players in the patient's life.

Back to propanolol (Inderal), briefly: there is evidence in a study in *American Family Physician* (Nov. 1992, vol. 46, #5, p. 1517) that supports the need for seriously dealing with more than just the pain (symptom) of migraine. A report from the 34th meeting of the American Association for the Study of Headache discussed a study where patients successfully defeated migraine headaches using a combination of drug treatment and relaxation/biofeedback treatments. A group of migraine patients were assigned to receive relaxation/biofeedback training alone, or in combination with propanolol (60 to 180 milligrams/day). Both groups showed significant improvement, but the dual-treatment group had significantly greater improvement as well as a quicker response to treatment.

If relaxation contributes to a quicker response to drug therapy, then, it stands to reason that developing the relaxation response—whether through biofeedback or bodywork, or meditation—could be the single most important therapy for migraineurs.

Natural, Non-Drug Assists

1. "Force" your body to relax.

The Practice of Relaxation Response

Lie down. Allow your mind to travel methodically over each body part. Starting at the feet, tense up all the toes and muscles for 5 to 10 seconds. Then tell your feet to relax, and let all the tenseness leave your toes and ankles and muscles. Keep breathing. Go slowly. Do the same activity for your calves and lower legs, tensing up for 5 to 10 seconds, to the point where you almost feel a strain in the backs of your legs; then release, relax, and let go. Keep focusing on individual body parts, one by one. Thighs, buttocks, pelvis, waist and torso, etc. (You might even ask someone to talk you through this progressive relaxation exercise.) By the time you get to your neck, face, and head, your body is already taking steps to slow down and initiate self-healing.

Additional meditations to do after the Relaxation Response: Go back to Chapter 16 for other meditations, or look to the Rainbow Meditation designed specifically to handle pain, described in Chapter 21 but also available at www.migrainehealing.com in full form. Ask someone to slowly read the meditation you have chosen, after you have gone through the basic tense-and-relax moves described above.

2. Constrict the blood vessels using physical aids.

It doesn't matter if you use a pack of frozen peas or a special migraine cooling aid such as Iceband (available in drugstores). Cold compress therapy helps your head feel better, probably by shrinking swollen blood vessels and frayed nerve endings down to size. Place the icebag either on your temples (the side of the head that's in pain) or at the back of your neck for a modicum of relief.

3. Hydrate well with drinks that aid healing.

About water... Drinking good water in the midst of migraine or during a spate of daily migraines helps rehydrate your body and flush the system of toxins. If you are the type who literally has to force yourself to keep drinking water throughout the day, then you must commit to bringing water more centrally into your life. Here are some ways:

> ➢ purchase a water cooler for home and office;
> ➢ buy a water filter for home;
> ➢ make it a practice to drink a full glass of water before ordering another drink while dining out;
> ➢ keep a filled water pitcher with a cup nearby at all times.

If you are in migraine pain and realize that you are dehydrated, bypass the water and go straight for a sports drink such as Gatorade to quickly replace any lost electrolytes (nutrients lost from not keeping your body well-hydrated). I am not exactly sure why this works, but many migraine sufferers are helped by sports drinks designed to balance electrolyte function in cells.

If your problem is the opposite—that is, frequent thirst—be sure to talk to a physician because this can be a symptom of a more serious health problem, including diabetes.

About coffee... Some migraine medications contain caffeine. Realizing that it may be helpful for them, some migraineurs believe that drinking caffeinated beverages such as coffee helps kick a migraine (presumably by the caffeine action of constricting blood vessels). Others feel it has no effect, or may even be detrimental. Coffee is an individual thing, so to discover its effect may take some charting on your part. Despite its perceived effect on your head, however, err on the side of moderation, cutting back on the amount of caffeine in your life. The reason? Caffeine stimulates excretion of urine (simply put: it makes you pee), leaving your tissues dehydrated, not well-watered.

About herbal teas... Many medicinal traditions employ herbs to treat and cure various ailments. In the book *Growing and Using Healing Herbs* (see the resource appendix), there is an interview with Ven. Chakdud Tulku Rinpoche, a Tibetan Lama (master teacher) who was trained from age five in the Buddhist monastic tradition and now teaches Tibetan medicine to Western doctors and health practitioners. The authors asked him: "Rinpoche, what is the meaning of medicine and healing in the Tibetan tradition?" His answer: "When one is learning and practicing (the medicine), this is inner medicine. When doing things on the outside, then this is outer medicine. Herbal substances temporarily cure sickness. All the causes, conditions, and results of healing ultimately lead to the Medicine Buddha [in other words, enlightenment]."

Herbal teas probably work best over time, not necessarily in response to immediate, intense pain. In other words, if you are going to experiment with herbal teas for migraine relief, consider that you should not wait until you are in pain.

The herb most often termed migraine-specific is feverfew (*Tanacetum parthenium*). If you buy the tea in a health food store or another source, follow the packet directions for best results. Feverfew is also available in tablet form. Of course, it can be grown in your garden, as well.

Another tea recommended by herbalists is white elm bark. It is quite bitter. You will want to follow package directions for a good tea infusion.

I personally have not used feverfew or white elm bark tea to the extent that I can say it contributes to preventing migraine. However, I feel obligated to list the herbs that are most frequently used for migraine sufferers.

My preference for teas that are soothing while experiencing migraine includes peppermint and chamomile. When the stomach is upset along with headache, peppermint calms and relaxes, while helping you breathe better. Chamomile tea is easy on the stomach and helps you relax and sleep.

Also, peppermint used in combination with chamomile and catnip can be good for sedation and opening clogged sinuses, plus nausea relief. If you use loose tea leaves, simply place one teaspoon each of your favorite herb into a Japanese, Chinese, or British-style teapot (the kind that has a built-in strainer) and pour in hot water; wait for a few minutes; then pour into a cup. (Flavor-wise, it's better to use less catnip than peppermint or chamomile.)

Other migraineurs find relief in drinking ginger tea and/or chewing small pieces of candied ginger, primarily to help control the nausea that often accompanies migraine.

If you are at the point in your personal program where you turn to meditation, journaling, and/or artistic expression while in the middle of migraine pain, consider making a simple sage tea. On the physical level, it helps nausea, while on the spiritual level, it helps open natural pathways to inner wisdom, and speeds oneness with the Higher Self. You can then more quickly uncover the strain on your essence that underlies the headache onslaught. You can buy sage tea or grow your own leaves to make tea. In a pinch, you can sprinkle crushed or powdered sage from your spice cabinet (about 1 teaspoon) into a slow-boiling saucepan of 2 cups water. After 3 to 5 minutes, strain the tea into a cup and sip it slowly. (You may safely add honey or another sweetener if you like. Sage tea is surprisingly sweet all on its own, though.)

Making a tea of sage plus basil leaves aims at attaining wisdom and clearance. Again, you don't need much herb to make a delicious healing tea with sage and basil. You may pour hot boiling water over a teaspoon each of these herbs in a Japanese-style teapot, or cook the tea in an open saucepan (see above description of plain sage tea).

Menstrual migraine may respond to any of the above teas. Another herb commonly associated with relieving menstrual problems is chervil.

After migraine (especially after menstrual migraine), drink Gatorade to rehydrate yourself. Later on, try some alfalfa tea to regain strength. Prepare following package directions. This nutrient-rich tea is readily available in most health food stores.

4. Check out aromatherapy options.

Aromatherapy is everywhere these days. Even Crabtree and Evelyn sell a scent you can sniff for headache relief. (Theirs contains basil and peppermint.) The chemicals of certain natural scents interact with your body to stimulate certain responses—and if you associate pain relief with these smells, aromatherapy can be a useful assist to healing.

Just beware: certain smells have an irritant effect on migraine sufferers. It is a highly individual affair. Lavender has a sleep-inducing effect on some people, for example, while others cannot stand it. Personally, I avoid eucalyptus, frangipani, gardenia, and similarly heavy scents.

5. Press the right pressure points.

There are specific pressure points on your hands and feet which correspond to the head (and head pain). These are easy to find and apply yourself, and are especially useful if you are away from home and need ways to cope with pain. Some people are greatly helped by applying pressure (pushing) on these points. Others use them for temporary relief until they can get home to bed.

For the hands, press into the soft part of the fingertips, but focus most closely on the thumb. Also, pinch-press the webbing area between the thumb and forefinger.

When applying pressure to the foot, concentrate on the large toe and generally all areas in the top portion of the foot.

You can use them yourself, or ask a friend or loved one to work on you. With the help of someone else, you can also massage the shoulder blades, the back of the neck (especially the occipital areas at the base of the neck), and certain points on the face, especially those corresponding to opening up sinuses. These are simple tools to use for healing effects. For more detailed guidance regarding pressure-point healing, see the website www.migrainehealing.com or access library books on reflexology and massage.

The very best thing to do is contact an expert in hand or foot reflexology. Reflexologists are capable of helping you completely eliminate pain or at least shorten the migraine's course. With regular treatment by a reflexologist, migraines may go away altogether.

How to apply pressure: As a general rule, using the top edge of your thumbs or digging in with the fingertips, apply pressure to headache-specific points for a count of 7 seconds, release, wait a few seconds, and then re-apply pressure. Pressure point therapy is one of the most effective hands-on treatments for headache relief, next to laying on of hands and energy-scanning (clearing the aura) which usually requires the help of a specialized, experienced healer.

6. Re-direct your body's electrical energy waves.

If you have advanced into guided meditations and have become accustomed to calling on your Higher Self to take charge, assuming an active role in directing your body's energies will help you defeat migraine pain and, in time, defeat migraine altogether.

"Migraine in motion looks like a figure eight," Linda Barnett told me. "Energy travels down through the crown, curves down into a circle around the edges of the heart, and moves back up again to the head where it circles up and around and back down again, trapped in a double circle of pain."

To break the cycle, she said, you can sit very still, place one hand on the top of your head, and the other hand on your heart or stomach. Visualize the loving, healing energy from above entering into your crown, then mentally direct this energy to pass straight on down through your heart zone, stomach, and on down, traveling the length of your body until it exits your feet and into the earth. It may help to picture this healing energy as a vibrant purple light coming from the heavens to course through your body.

Redirecting energy in this way breaks the figure eight, the trapped pain pattern, and recreates a clear, healthy energy flow from head to toe, reestablishing wholeness.

Sound therapy (e.g., using the crystal recordings made by musician Steven Halpern or Fabian Mamoun) can absolutely enhance your self-healing energy work. Thanks to many musicians who are turning their artistry into healing modalities, migraine sufferers can now buy and try out music that resonates within the heart to quicken the internal healing response. Some people find that the sound produced simply by striking a Japanese meditation bowl "calls" your natural healing energy into the heart zone, away from cycling destructively in the head region.

7. Take a hot bath in baking soda water.

When you have retired to bed with a migraine, hoping to sleep it off, but your brain—full of crazy images and words and worry and frenetic thinking—just won't let you sleep, steep your body in a hot bath that's been sprinkled with one to two cups of baking soda. You may even fall asleep, that's how comfortable a baking soda bath can be. In the time leading up to a migraine, the body's aura gets clouded with uncomfortable energies that you just can't shake (your body literally feels sticky with stress); baking soda clears that off.

8. Consider hypnosis or deep-trance work with a qualified practitioner.

There may come a time when you consider hypnosis, or spiritual trancework, as method of breaking through pain. If you think it's possible that some event or relationship from your childhood or subconscious haunts you, consider seeking out a safe guide so you can relive and purge what you need to. Why do this? One easy answer: If the procedure is done carefully and lovingly, by someone who is well qualified (you can even find professional psychotherapists who have received certification), you'll never have to do that kind of going back to the past again. An expert knows how to take you through that and put it behind you once and for all.

At the end of deep-trance work, always finish with a set of re-empowering affirmations. Example: "I am letting go of this memory. I see my body being filled with the love and light of God." Additionally, make sure to get a full-body massage from an accredited massage therapist.

Comments on Drugs and Physician-Prescribed Treatments

People have told me of many other approaches they have used on their own to battle migraine pain. Some of these treatments involve combos they invented (unbeknownst to their physicians probably). A common remedy is a decongestant/antihistamine plus painkiller (like ibuprofen); another one is stomach medicine (like cimetidine) plus painkiller. If you are trying drugs for migraine pain and not telling your doctor, you run health risks. Furthermore, you're putting yourself in a drug trap. Eventually, you're probably going to become immune to the doses. And remember: drugs do not stop migraines from happening in the first place. They are the Band-Aid on the cut, the temporary relief from a deeper, more insidious problem that still needs fixing.

The bottom line: Eventually, you are going to have to deal with the issue of stress, breathing, relaxation, self-talk, spirituality, and finding a rounded, connected, healthier lifestyle.

Author's Note: Many people ask, "Should I exercise during migraine?" I've given this question serious thought and lots of practice. I have interviewed migraineurs on the subject. I have to conclude: No, I don't think so... Exercise is not the way to go when you're in the throes of migraine. It is, however, a cornerstone in overall migraine prevention and whole-body healing—when you are not crippled with pain, that is.

A Bath to Clear Heavy, Negative, or Just Plain Difficult Energies

When you've been around people who tend to sap your energy, when you're feeling overwhelmed and stressed out, or when you find yourself walking around with an undeniably icky or bad-feeling energy, start a bath for yourself. Add 1 cup of baking soda (or more, if you like) and simply soak in it, shutting out the world for at least 20 minutes.

Baking soda has a way of cleansing and clearing the body of difficult energies, and restoring the body, mind, and soul to a more comfortable balance.

No one knows exactly why it works, but it is a valuable tool for a migraine sufferer and other very sensitive people. The more you become attuned to recognizing what feels right for you, and what does not seem right and feels out of whack, the sooner you can get into a healing bath and begin the clearing process. In many cases, a simple baking soda bath can help prevent a migraine by not allowing negative thoughts and feelings to pervade your body space or send signals that can spiral you into migraine territory.

Other times, you may discover that you are reacting on an emotional level to circumstances around you. If that's the case, after the bath, find a way to write out, talk about, or otherwise express any feelings and worries that might be bothering you.

Chapter 18
The Act of Creating

We are all artists.

This is perhaps a radical viewpoint. Consider, though, that in the broad perspective, deep inside we are all connected to creation, and the act of creating. That, I think, is enough to qualify us all as being possessed of the potential to be creative and/or make art.

People who call themselves artists are merely doing more art, actualizing themselves through more art making than others. It is a question of percentages and definitions.

One of my major life events happened at a small arts center where Linda Barnett had been invited to lead a workshop on creativity. Speaking quietly, she led a small group of eight people into a long meditation and visualization. I had meditated before, and, although it was a very calming thing to do, it had been no life-changing event. This, however, was different. This was full-scale trance activity, and it was truly fantastic. I saw alpha and omega, and wisdom of the highest order was revealed to me for the first time.

It was within my own heart all this time! Much was channeled through Linda to lead our little group into this beautiful experience, but one phrase in particular touched me so fully that I heard it, repeated it, wondered over it, and recalled it for days, weeks and months afterwards. It was: "I identify with the Creator."

I, who ran from religious dogma my whole life, hating the smugness of church and the righteous claims of those who proclaimed that their sect was the only sect that led to heaven, had found a phrase at last that resonated in my soul. It was a phrase that seemed to cross all religions, all the barriers of race and nationality. I related wholly, swiftly and directly to it: to its fairness, to its simple truth. I was and still am excited by its implications of unlimited possibilities. In one fell swoop, the sleeping artist was awakened sharply, happily from her prison bed, as if the warden had just delivered legal release papers.

"I identify with the Creator" is no light statement. It has power. In meditation, you can find out much about yourself by focusing on the phrase "I identify with the Creator." But as with all meditation, one time "ain't gonna do it." Be patient. Over time, if it is on your personal path, you will find that identifying with your creative self will play a powerful, positive role in both preventing and curing migraine.

In migraine, when the pain is intense and you are incapacitated, it is not easy to turn your thoughts toward creativity. But I have discovered that creative work that is blocked can lie at the bottom of a migraine. I think it is worth considering that in all persons, the artist within—or the creative side of each and every one of us—is crying to *express*, and magical things happen when the migraineur, even in the most desperate pain, turns to work (however briefly) with artistic materials. The magic I speak of is healing.

Art making can serve as a catalyst to connect with the physician within. In other words, the special energy required for deep healing to take place—a divine healing-energy chain of events—is set in motion sometimes by the unorthodox medicine of creative expression.

Years ago I would have completely dismissed the notion of doing drawing or writing or molding clay in the middle of migraine. I would have told whoever suggested it that he was deluded, insensitive, and unloving. Moreover, it would be evident to me that he had never experienced migraine. Today I am sure there are many people who will not ever try to express anything in any way while in migraine mode. It is all they can do to cope with the pain. But for those who are intrigued, I invite you to see what happens when you give yourself over to pen and paper, or whatever medium appeals to you—whether it is dance, singing, fingerpainting, folding paper in shapes, or cooking—during and after migraine.

Granted, this is not an easy thing to do. You will probably have to force yourself. Before you try this, though, there is one important rule to adhere to: Be as spontaneous as you possibly can. That means: Do not look back at what you do as you work. Do not judge. Embrace the concept that creative expression flows from a place over which you have no control. Allow yourself to channel the creative impulse or message that lies latent within, and allow your creative self to choose a direction for itself when you get ready to express. Above all, that means you must let go, even as you release your message.

Obviously, you should not do anything foolhardy, such as using dangerous or toxic art materials, or dancing on a cliff. Nor should you do anything that involves fine motor skills, such as wood carving. Keep it simple. Very simple. There is plenty of time later to take a sketch from a migraine episode and turn it into a real canoe, or whatever it is you decide to do. Drawing, painting, free-form writing (on paper or computer) and working with clay are four solid choices.

In the times when I do migraine-writing, I am usually not in good control of my pencil and the writing looks like scribbling. In fact, I have no recollection of what I write until I am fully recovered and review it later. But I am not out to win handwriting awards. I am out to shorten the duration of my migraine, to attend to the immediate physical need: that is, I am out to hook up with unseen healing energy, which is trying to help me pull through. Creative release ultimately serves as a tool to break through headache, pulling mind, body, and spirit into alignment.

I used to wish I had a big wall in a big loft space on the top floor of my house. I would paint, draw, and write on that wall only during migraine. It would be my Mystical Migraine Mural. If you are getting migraines on a regular basis and happen to have a spare wall, by all means help yourself if a mural appeals to you.

As of this writing, however, I get migraines so rarely I cannot justify dedicating a wall to mid-migraine expression. Partly I am sure that is because I engage in creative exercise as often as I can. I make it a daily prescription. And I am liberal in my prescription: making eggrolls from scratch counts (very meditative, very creative activity). Making up a song with the kids counts. Playing it on piano racks up more points. Writing a poem or an entry in a journal about the experience is best of all.

Consider deeply how art or a creative venture can enter your life. You do not have to do art for a living, unless your inner self demands that you take that path. Your creative activity may be writing down recipes from meals you have made spontaneously. Or it may involve interior design. Or physics. Or fixing things. If you love stories but are not a writer, perhaps you are a storyteller. Music may have been a mainstay while you were a child, but somehow you let it go, thinking it would not make a difference if you quit. Consider your alternatives, and, when you meditate next, focus on letting art come naturally to you. Trust your intuition. Go for it. Creative expression takes innumerable forms. But somewhere, identifying with the creation process can provide a way through to the other side. From illness to wellness; from feeling fragmented to feeling whole. From feeling useless, to feeling worthwhile—even if it is to discover worthiness within your own eyes.

Peter London has written a wonderful book about art and how to foster the creative self, called *No More Secondhand Art: Awakening the Artist Within* (Shambhala, 1989). About the effect art has on people, he says: "As Freud discovered, and as Jung, Rank, and later Rollo May elaborated and refined, when the conscious and the subconscious become acquainted with each other, a new persona is born. A whole, awake, compassionate person steps forward from the one who was previously fractured, incomplete, and at war within himself or herself. Those early analysts observed, as do therapists in general, a sudden burst of enthusiasm for living in such cases, a quickening of the senses, an acceptance of the self as it is and the world as it is. As an outcome of this meeting of the minds, this reconciliation, there is an inexorable blossoming of creativity" (97).

Peter London is a true champion of humanity. He recognizes that many people do not pursue art because they are caught in a mode of comparison in which they put down their own efforts even before they have begun. If you have a paintbrush in one hand, and Picasso in your head, you will not paint one stroke. The best way to free up, he says, is to give yourself permission to explore creative options. Without judgment.

London writes, "The notion that there is a right and a wrong in creative expression is inherently debilitating." Yet how many of us had bad experiences with art teachers or parents who criticized our work, judging it worthy or unworthy?! Many of us struggle with old wounds concerning art. This is Good Art. That is Bad Art.

I see only a big trap with that kind of thinking. It is a trap of the worst kind—it self-limits, putting an unnatural lid on some of the sensitive people walking this earth. Migraineurs, who are especially sensitive people, owe it to themselves and everyone around them to explore deeply the issues involving any repression of their creative/artistic side. The history of creative self is a chapter that no individual can responsibly ignore, especially if there is even a remote chance that his/her healing can be activated through this avenue.

When the urge to create is repressed—usually through a rejection experience or series of rejections by others and then the self, the ego builds a wall to avoid further violation of that sacred, spirit-filled territory that involves creative expression. To get past that wall, some readers may wish to employ the technique of re-envisioning the bad art experience. This involves calling up that experience (or those experiences, one by one) and seeing it for what it really was.

If you had an experience in which a school teacher harshly criticized your artwork in an early grade, for example, you can go into meditation to recall that time and place, very much in the way therapist/author John Bradshaw would call up an inner child experience, in order to purge it, to clear the slate. See the end of this chapter to practice a "Meditation for Re-Centering: From Repression to Expression."

Judge Not

Peter London writes, "We cannot act with integrity or be spontaneous and original when we place between ourselves and our canvas the conclusions and values of others. Right and wrong are always associated with good and bad. Good and bad are always ethical connotations; hence in judging our work (and worth) using right and wrong as our scale, we not only often come out inept, we also feel ethically deficient. Given such heavy odds that one will be judged inept and ethically unsound, is it any wonder that so few engage in creative encounters of any depth and risk?" (*No More Secondhand Art*, 57)

One thing you must do for yourself is explore. Ask why you feel the way you do about art. If you have a long list of excuses, ask yourself why you felt compelled to create that list. Throughout the day, in your regular workaday life, notice the little things that are creative. See if it makes sense to expand on them. Set no standards for your art, but just see what happens. You can always ask yourself later, "Is this true? Does it feel true?" rather than worrying about its goodness or badness.

If the great artists of the world had compared themselves endlessly to others, they would never have accomplished a thing. They all, no matter what their medium, had to operate under a self-created value system, asking, "Did I go as deep as I dared? Did I risk all? Is it my truth?" Many have written extensively about the creative process, noting that they felt a tremendous force sweep through them. The greatest of artists claim that they themselves did very little; all they did was record the art that flowed through them.

The artwork that you create, whether you are sick or well, is not the point, however. End product is rarely the point. The process is what matters. Back your personal movie up to the place where your inner child is engaging in making art. Hold onto that scene in your mind. Remember that process, remember what it feels like to live in the moment, at one with your work. Being in each moment of every day is what true freedom is all about.

And what if you instinctively know that art or creative work is what you are supposed to be doing on planet Earth?

Many of us are brought up with the refrain, "Be an artist and you will starve." Or we have come to think that artists are playing; they are not really working. At some point all the fears that come to the fore must be faced. They need to be seen in a new light of original mission and essential purpose.

Know that creating is going on all the time anyway. Work toward finding the truth about yourself and your needs. Your spiritual self always seeks an outlet for the beautiful messages it has to pass on to the world. Creative energy cannot be stopped up forever. It is too compelling. So when you explore this energy, let it satisfy you first.

What does that mean? Say, for example, that you like making pottery. This is dear to your Essence. You have some early memories of hands in dirt and mud as a child, and you sometimes tap into that sensory memory while you play with clay. To explore this natural urge, you have taken several classes in ceramics, on Saturdays. Your birthday wish list (the one you gave your husband) says you want a breadmaking machine, but in your heart of hearts, if you really gave yourself permission to dream, you would love to have a kiln at home. You could probably transform the sun porch into a studio...

For the time being, though, you keep on making pots. Your ceramics teacher puts your best stoneware plates into the Christmas show. People love them, and they sell fast. Everyone says you need to make more pottery "just like that set."

Actually, you probably would not have made plates except your teacher encouraged you to. You liked the plates, but they looked and felt like all the other stoneware plates on display at craft shows. Your ego says, "Go for it! They liked the plates! Forget those weird water vessels you've been making. No one will buy those. Get that praise! Get that money!"

But your inner self rebels. You sense it in meditation. You keep seeing yourself making water vessels. So you tell your ego: "Look, I am going to make water vessels. It may be two years before I'm ready to sell one, but when I do put a price tag on them, it will be $300.00 a pot, not $10.00 a plate. Are you with me or against me??" The ego, which is here to support you and get you out there in the world, acquiesces. It backs off to a position of support, not power. Any power the ego thought it had was illusion anyway.

Now you make your vessels. Your teacher is not thrilled, because you have announced that stoneware is not working for you. You want to do Japanese-style raku work instead. You hear of a raku teacher and make plans to start classes. When you visit your friends, they serve you hors d'oeuvres on the stoneware plates you made a year ago. They are hinting to you! Tempting the ego. You just laugh and say, "I'm glad you like these plates! Thank you for being so supportive!" They shake their heads.

The process of making the water vessels has consumed you. You draw and write in your journal about the experience. Pots emerge from your hands, are fired, and cool. You sketch and write some more. Your new teacher encourages you in this process-journey.

Strangely, you have completely forgotten all about any intention to sell the pots. When an art curator happens by your teacher's studio on a friendly visit, she takes a few minutes to watch you work. She points out three pieces, and asks if she can show them in a local gallery. You have a hard time letting them go. You have gotten used to looking at them, referring back to them as you work. Then, suddenly, you realize that you can let them go. You have mastered that shape. Your hands are holding the wet clay of a water vessel similar in "feel" to the ones that are about to make their debut in the world. You've come full circle: both the inner self and the ego self are simultaneously gratified. And all because you have been true to your higher self, first and foremost.

When I lived in North Carolina, I first became acquainted with what is called outsider art. Outsider art is made by folks who really have no plan of fame or money in mind when they make art. The artists are not living in garrets. They are people who grow tobacco or work with machinery or are housewives. Some made their giant whirligigs or wood carvings or paintings or musical compositions as the result of dream visions. Some of them are highly political in their expression, since they essentially are responding to a frustration about the way the country is run. All are testaments to the sheer will of the person, who simply could not rest until an inner message took form. When outsider art got discovered and placed in museums, no one in the world was more surprised than the artists themselves.

It is not how creative you are that counts, but the degree to which you release into your own creative expression. I believe that migraineurs are people who regularly receive messages from the higher self, and suffer when those messages cannot be decoded. Conceivably, when you find a creative outlet and retrain yourself (through practice) to channel high-frequency energy into a mode of creative expression, the energy stops turning in on itself in a mad pattern of self-destruction (migraine). It finds release. Creative expression becomes a prescription for healing.

How is that possible? Scientists have yet to document the clinical function of creative (artistic) expression. Probably one day there will be sophisticated instruments to track what happens in the body's inner and outer energies. But until that time, we can surmise that creative expression promotes wellness because it serves to clear the energies, restores Original Balance within the total energy system (body, mind and soul), and feels good afterward because a divine reconnection has been made on personal behalf.

Creativity is restorative. It is part and parcel of having been created: we are created, and we ourselves create. We create words, experiences, relationships, and art. We are constantly engaged in creative process even in spite of ourselves, as new thoughts take form within the mind. And we all have a need to feel connected with the power of creation. It used to be that Americans thought they had to retire before they nurtured the creative side of themselves. That approach works marginally at best, and only if people make it through the stress of working and living without first getting a stroke, heart attack, or cancer.

There is encouraging evidence nowadays that Americans are becoming more aware of the role of creativity and creative brainstorming, and that intuition is valuable and useful. Corporations are increasingly employing creativity specialists to help workers unleash thoughts, come up with new ideas, and play a role in co-creating future directions for the whole group. The use of imagery—creative visualization in particular—has assumed a role in healing at some of this country's most well-respected, well-established hospital settings. On the most basic-needs level, creative cooking and the culinary arts are receiving more attention than ever by men and women. All sorts of creative activities nurture, because creative expression corrals our fragmented selves back to a feeling of unity.

Beware only of attempting to control your creative activity too much; likewise if you are being controlled by someone who tries to force you to create after a certain mold. Overly controlled creativity will not feel good. And more walls can go up than come down in the process. To get the most out of your experience, meditate before creative activity to open the clearest possible pathway to your personal truth.

In summary, there are two ways to go about using artistic activity in healing migraine. One is to *do art*—engage in an art form—*during the migraine* itself. Not only is there a real chance that the pain will diminish or even disappear, but looking at the art later will give you (and your doctor, or therapist, and loved ones) important clues about the energy system that has swept through you. Art therapy for migraine sufferers has been in practice long enough for one city to hold an exhibition of paintings by migraineurs.

Another path of healing: Involve yourself daily (or regularly) in artistic or creative activity of some type. For some people, especially those who have a high need to express themselves in this fashion, following this formula may be enough to head all their migraines off at the pass, at some point in the near future. And chances are good that the world will be a richer place for their contributions, their convictions, and their example to others.

Meditation for Re-Centering: From Repression to Expression

[Author's Note: If your artistic repression stems from an intensely difficult episode, involving lots of emotional pain or abuse, please do not try this exercise alone but find a counselor to help you work it through.]

If you can think of an experience that repressed your self-expression, go back to that place and time in a state of meditation—either meditating by yourself or with someone you trust and love as your guide—and remember it as completely as you can.

Take ten minutes to become as relaxed as possible. Breathe deeply, taking air in through the nose and out through the mouth.

See yourself as a child. See the creative experience that ended in feelings of failure. If it involved a painting, see the painting in your head. If it was a musical piece, hear it. Envision the person who told

213

you that you were "no good." Remember how you felt, remember the hurt, and release any tears, anger, frustration and shame. Envision yourself walking up to the child (you) and comfort her/him. Say "I love you. You are a dear, precious person."

Next, face the teacher (or parent or other person who rejected your work) with your arms protectively around this child, your inner child, and assert confidently, aloud, "These words I speak for myself and for this child: I identify with the Creator. I am One with the Creation, and I am in harmony with all that is creative and good."

Tell the teacher, "I do not have to like your behavior. But I do have to love you, for you also are a child of the same Creator, who is all loving. I forgive you, for you acted out of your ignorance. And I forgive myself for taking on this pain. But it is not mine. I am giving back the pain and the shame, back to the nothingness from which it came."

Envision the teacher stepping back, back, back, away out of sight. Tell the child, "You are a unique, perfect expression of the Almighty Creator. That is the truth. And you are never alone. I will always protect you, and I will faithfully remind you of the truth about yourself." See your inner child turning back to resume her/his artwork. Watch the intent expression on her/his face, and bask in that glow. Imagine that you are physically transporting this child into your heart. Now the inner child is at peace. Free to explore creative expression once more.

Chapter 19
The Menstrual Migraine

Two things are certain: (1) women are more prone to migraines than men, and (2) many women get migraines or are more susceptible to getting migraines during the time of their menstrual periods. Many women have come to dread their impending periods, month after month, because of corresponding migraine attacks.

What is this all about? There are significant physiological changes that occur within the body during the menses. In fact, the nature of these changes is still unfolding. In twenty years scientists will know more about hormones, histamine, cyclical depression, and other mind-body responses associated with menstruation. Finally, at long last, women's medical interests are moving up on the medical-scientific agenda. And doubtless we'll see some fascinating facts emerge about the complex mechanisms of menstruation.

Nonetheless, menstruation and migraine will continue to occur in tandem unless we begin to look at menstruation from a higher, less tangible vantage point. To get there, it's worthwhile to examine some facts about menstruation and so-called menstrual migraines. The following information tends to be true:

- It's possible to have a period and not get a migraine.

- After a **migraine**, you generally feel much better—and view the world with fresh eyes, as if giant cobwebs obstructing your vision have cleared.

- During **menstruation**, your body clears out tissues and blood from the uterus—materials your body is not going to use at this time.

- **Before and during your period**, you may experience a number of symptoms, including (but not limited to): mood swings, depression, disorientation, clouded feeling in your head, confusion, clumsiness, diarrhea, fullness in the womanly organs, painful cramping, heightened sensitivity and reactivity to emotional stimuli (you cry "at the drop of a hat," or feel overwhelmed at the beauty of a certain painting or song), touchiness when interacting with other people, feeling like you want to retreat or become a hermit, feeling somewhat limited or "tied down" in the sense that you're consciously or subliminally aware of the need to know where the nearest bathroom is, and generally feeling more vulnerable than at other times of the month.

- **Before and during migraine**, you may experience a number of symptoms, including (but not limited to): mood swings, depression, disorientation, clouded feeling in your head, confusion, clumsiness, fullness in the temples and sinuses, flashing lights and colors, heightened sensitivity to physical stimuli such as noise and light, hyper-reactivity to emotional stimuli (you cry "at the drop of a hat," or feel overwhelmed at the beauty of a certain painting or song), touchiness when interacting with other people, feeling like you must retreat, and feeling limited, disabled or "tied down" in the sense that you must head for a dark, quiet room away from the sounds and sights and stresses of the world. And generally you feel much more vulnerable compared to when you don't have migraine.

- Some artists report that **menstruation** brings on creativity, that some of their most vital work occurs during menses.

- Some artists report that **migraine** events bring on spurts of creativity, that some of their most vital work occurs during or as a result of migraine.

- **When *menstruation* hits**, once a month, women are reminded of the difference between themselves and men by the physical reality of menstruation (blood, the need for pads, and, possibly, need for medication), and they mentally mark this in some way. (Examples of mental marking: you wonder about the whole phenomenon; you wish your mate could just once go through it, too, so he could know how it feels; you think about other women and how they deal with it, especially your mother; you may question your ability to meet crises with children or work or spouses, since your focus is on getting through the period with as few accidents and as painlessly as possible; you're in awe of the forces of nature; and so forth.)

- **When a *migraine* strikes,** typically, many women are reminded of the difference between themselves and their men simply by the physical gender-reality of migraine (since it's long been termed a woman's disease) and they mentally mark this in some way. (Examples of mental marking: you wonder about the whole phenomenon; you wish your mate could just once go through it, too, so he could know how it feels; you think about your mother if she also suffered migraines; you question your ability to meet crises with children or work or spouses, since your focus is on getting through the migraine event intact; you're in awe of the forces of nature; and so forth.)

Migraine and Menses as Spiritual Events

The similarities between menses and migraine are striking. But instead of concluding that the two M&M's must inevitably be tied together, what if we were to look at both events as spiritual events?

What if we were to consider them both as times of clearance, when the body and mind work together in a sweeping fashion to cleanse, rebalance, and reaffirm connection with forces larger than the self?

We know that menstruation is a time of heightened sensitivity and awareness, and that migraine as an event is similarly characterized by super-sensitivity. By definition, in my book, that makes them both events of the spirit—or, more clearly, events that have the potential to carry you deeply inward, back to the point of remembering a higher power, and allowing that higher power to reign over the daily forces of ego, self, personality and role definition.

In recent years, women have begun to discover new dimensions of menses: There are now menstruation-related seminars celebrating goddess and fertility and rites of passage. There are books now on how to embrace menstruation, and enjoy it rather than vilify or hide it. The discussions between men and women grow franker and more honest when it comes to this formerly taboo topic. And there are lots of books exploring historical and cultural aspects of menstruation. For example, many of us have heard about women in certain societies (other than our own) who live in separate lodgings during the duration of their periods; or we learn about menstruating women who weren't (and aren't in some cultures) sanctioned to cut meat or prepare other foodstuffs; and other cultural dos and don'ts concerning women and their bodies.

All of this exploration is positive, I feel. I think it opens the road toward women being able to claim their own truths, needs, feelings and experiences about menstruation. And because I cannot truly speak for anyone other than myself, I will say here what has worked for me.

Menstruation signals a time of heightened sensitivity. It signals a time of becoming ripe to hearing essential truths from within. It signals a time to pull back, to whatever degree I feel necessary, from the world.

I cocoon and nest when my period comes. I plan ahead so that the most demanding elements of my life are handled at other times of the month. I reserve the right to go into deeper meditations during the menses, and put aside secular work to delve into mysticism, messages from my angels, and creativity in all forms: music, literature, art, freeform writing, dressing up, inventing artful and delicious cuisine.

As with migraine, I view menses as a time of clearance: a time when all the cares of the world are swept away, an entering into a newer, higher plane of being.

A strange and wonderful thing happened when I began to see the onset of my period as a spiritual time. Migraines lessened in severity. They occurred less and less frequently. One day I realized that the two events—the M&M's as I used to call them— did not have to happen together. *Migraine is not an inevitability during menstruation.*

The bottom line is, that menstruation for many women remains a time of vulnerability, emotional fragility, and hypersensitivity. Denying this reality is to invite migraines, for as mentioned earlier, migraine is spiritual energy mis-directed. When menstruation is at hand, and the head and heart and entire body system open ever wider into a realm of spiritual connectedness, the woman who keeps right on trucking, pushing past deadlines, stuck in mind-logic mode, never slowing down, never stopping to acknowledge the sacred space she's entering is the same woman whose messages of the spirit get jammed. She is susceptible to migraine.

By contrast, the woman who accepts heavenly direction with grace and receptivity—an attitude and a way of be-ing that is cultivated through meditation and stillness—will have a far better chance of averting migraine. She knows she's dealing with a physical event of spiritual magnitude, and pampers her body accordingly.

Thinking about it won't get you there. You can't think yourself into spiritual receptivity. But here are some concrete things you can do to break the monthly cycle of M&M's:

➢ Meditate daily.
  Take classes in meditation, if you aren't able to accomplish it at home on your own. There are many wonderful teachers out there. Have faith in the Chinese proverb: "When the student is ready, the teacher will come."

➢ Practice deep, rhythmic breathing daily.

➢ Explore and release your anger daily, as well as any feelings that are complex and difficult, frustrated, or simply sore. You can do this by talking to a trusted friend, writing in a journal, simply listing troubles on a piece of paper, seeing a counselor regularly, and working to get rid of the Control Freak within. (You don't really want to control everything anyway: it's much too much work.)

➤ Nourish your social life, and hug your friends and loved ones frequently.

➤ Nourish your spirit...
...whether it's through a weekly commitment to the local Food Bank, taking a course on watercolors, reading inspirational books, or playing the piano. (Beware the common phrase "I don't have time for it." Whenever you say that, follow it with this cynical question, "Do I have time to suffer a migraine?" Argue with yourself.)

➤ Develop a plan for being nicer to yourself when your period comes.
This should not be a cop-out plan that you can pass on to others (examples: "Hey, I really suffer from my periods. So, everyone, look out, and leave me alone.") What you're striving for, instead, is the opposite of a pity party. You can cut back on commitments during the week that your period is due (e.g., don't pick that week for carpooling), schedule a massage, take a hot bath every night, read a good book, and journal or draw in solitude. Be creative. But schedule at least a full hour daily just for yourself.

Separating the M&M Memory

One of the most important tasks you'll pursue in un-doing menstrual migraine is training the mind to regard menstrual migraine as a memory of something that used to happen.

This powerful re-training technique is explored in Chapter 20. It involves telling the heart, your biocomputer, that you wish to change your electrical circuitry. Over a period of time, simply repeating the words "This is a memory of a migraine I once had" will be sufficient to stop the nagging headache pain and release it out into the universe as just old energy, old thought. But this new software is not installed in one day. It takes time, much repetition, patience, and faith.

10 Actions to Alter the Menstrual Experience

Ultimately, you alone are the only one who can create a new, enriching experience during your menses. Suggestions:

1. Privately regard your period as high holy days.

2. Claim to be SuperGoddess, not SuperWoman. If you have been experiencing menstrual migraines, look at that fact squarely and face up to the possibility that certain tasks, events, demands, people—whatever—do not fit well into your period. Let part of the housework go, or turn it over to someone else in the family or hire a professional, or do what you have to do in order to keep stressors at a comfortable low. (Remember: Stressors are not inherently bad: they're just those things that happen at you. It's how you deal with them that counts.)

3. Postpone, postpone, postpone (if possible). Deal with the most demanding elements of your work before and after your period, whenever feasible.

4. Retreat when necessary.

5. Love your body. Take long baths. Get massaged. Rest. Breathe deeply. Let your eyes take long looks out over expanses to relax from the up-close perspective of dishes, computer screens, TV, and "close" work. Go to bed earlier.

6. Go within—meditate—more than once a day.

7. Investigate your self. Write down your thoughts, insights, ideas that come about through meditating. Special task: Review how you first learned about menstruation. Explore the full range of emotions and memories you've attached to having your period. See if there's a pattern that doesn't feel right. Find ways to honor the womanly depths and aspects of your soul. Do a self-portrait: Paint or photograph or write about yourself now.

8. Drink teas (especially raspberry, alfalfa, and peppermint) for menses, and eat smaller, more frequent meals that are low in fat and high in complex carbohydrates, instead of huge sit-down meals. (Many women report feeling better by grazing in this fashion: it provides their system with a steadier flow of nutrients, yielding more energy and a more even temper.)

9. Identify, and then honor, what works for you. If, for example, you suddenly dive into an emotional tailspin, look at the events *preceding* the event so you can avoid a recurrence. Perhaps you'll notice something important: for example, maybe a tailspin happens every time a particular friend calls to gossip for an hour. Give yourself permission to say, "Look I can't talk right now. Let's talk next week." Chances are, either the information will be irrelevant by then, or you'll be better equipped to listen to it.

10. Do freeform singing, talking, drumming, and anything else that involves releasing you from your usual routines, usual songs, and overly controlled rituals. Plan a trip to a museum or a beautiful cathedral, just so you can stare at paintings of cherubs and angels. Be creative.

PART FOUR

LIBERATION
Living Your Truth

The surrender process that is an integral part of deep-state meditation yields a powerful, paradoxical consequence that can only be achieved through direct, personal experience: While meditating, you die into each day, and you are reborn into a truer self—a self beyond self.

"How can I stop having migraines?" is a question I am often asked. "Is there a formula—a list of things I can do—to keep migraines from happening?" By the time you reach the last page, you will have all the tools you need to get started with exactly that: a list of things you can personally commit to doing which will help prevent migraines. But skipping ahead will not do much good. The chapters that conclude this book are geared toward actively helping you move completely past the old state of affairs in your life, so that a new, joyful present can take over—in mind, soul, and body.

When headaches are not caused by tumors weighing on the brain or by a separate, outside, mechanically induced condition, there is a strong chance that they are much more responsive to a committed centering process. At the very beginning of the book is a Chinese proverb, which goes: "When you have a disease, do not try to cure. Find your center, and you will be healed."

Centering suggests many things to many people. It conjures up images of deep breathing; knees folded in meditation; hands folded in prayer-mode in front of the heart; or feeling loved and connected and well. Some of those images are evidence of centering methods and expressions of feeling centered. But what many people don't know is that finding one's center is not the equivalent of feeling deep peace or finally discovering who you are. It's not a said-and-done experience. Finding one's center is a daily event that defines what your truth is to be, as fully and completely as it possibly can be, at every point in your life experience. Finding center is an experience that is continually full of surprises. It is the single most delightful way to live life, once you embrace it. And not coincidentally, it is the one way to experience liberation.

How can you find your center? How can you become free to be the self beyond what you think your self is?

Finding your center invariably requires *dropping your notions, illusions, and delusions of self* and entering a meditative state to become ever more honest with yourself in a deeply satisfying way. Finding center is the result of literally abandoning your life and turning it all over to God on a daily basis. It does not mean abdicating responsibility. To claim you are leaving it all in the hands of God and lying back to eat bon-bons is cop-out, not liberation.

What does it mean, exactly, to be honest? Why do you still get migraines if you—and others—think of yourself as an honest person?

People often talk about honesty; it has long been a highly valued character trait. One of Shakespeare's most-quoted lines (from Hamlet) is "This above all: To thine own self be true." Going back a few more centuries, Socrates advised: "Know thyself."

What is involved in honesty? What is true? How can anyone be sure of what true means—when so many people seem to have differing versions of the truth? How is it possible for someone to swear that he or she is telling the truth?

Have you noticed that more questions than answers keep coming up?

There is a reason for that. Imagine that, for one day, you could see much more than just your side of the story. You could see through the eyes of each person you come in contact with. You could experience events from behind the veil of each person's collective set of experiences. You could feel each emotional response around you. You could view and experience every encounter, every twig and leaf and air blown piece of dust with a multitude of combined impressions that would fill in every single blank, create a whole jigsaw puzzle image with every piece intact—and multidimensional at that. You would be...omniscient.

Then, you would know what truth really is.

Being Honest

Deciding to become more centered is Step One to living a genuinely truthful life, which subsequently leads to feeling genuinely whole (healthy). Because what I am describing is such a personal experience, one that consists of learning about your true self—primarily through meditation, there is not much for me or anyone to say about your truth except that it surely exists. Only you can further uncover what you can truly become and know as truth. The smart place to begin is with setting aside quiet time for yourself, and then choosing to have a one-on-One relationship with that which knows the whole truth about everything, a.k.a. an omniscient Creator.

But there is a small obstacle. Here it is: We humans fool ourselves every day. (Some of us are better at it than others.) That's why some folks do a quickie prayer as they drive through a changing red light. Or why some athletes eat a lucky Arby's meal or wear a certain color or item of clothing when they are about to compete. Their belief system gets bound together with material manifestations that suggest a belief in fate, in the Big Unknown outside self. And yes, even when confirmed seekers of the spiritual life go into meditation, they/we often fool themselves/ourselves. Our thoughts might be: "If I say my mantra (secret, high-energy chanting word) enough times…[I will have a good day/Things will go well for me, etc.]." Or, "If I zone out by saying a hundred Hail Marys…[I will then have a good day/Things will go well for me/My friend will get better, etc.]."

In a nutshell, these thinking patterns are nothing more than attempts at control—not letting go. They are deceptive ways to assume control over how the day will go, or worse—to dictate the course of events, as if we ourselves were the Highest Power.

At the core of centering is turning everything—including self—over, and recognizing that "Hey, I really don't have the power to experience the world through the eyes and lives of other people around me." What you have is you. You and the big unknowns of life. No more fooling, no more little lies. Once this concept takes root, you can open to the path that is laid out *for you*.

And this brings the discussion to a tricky word that is impossible to define but crucial for centering: Faith.

Anxiety as Crisis of Faith

The best way to measure your faith factor is to look for anxiety. Got anxiety? If you suffer anxiety, examine your tendency to want to control things, events, or people. Faith is knowing that you don't have to control; you can simply respond with an inner sense that mystery can be a very good thing. A baby's sigh is mysteriously unpredictable—and it is a sweet thing to hear. Writing the words to a song as they enter your head—that's a mysterious process generally thought of as a good (even miraculous) thing. Having a revelation experience is a mysterious event that changes your life forever—again, a very good thing.

If I said that all of the universe and all God-force supports the intrinsic value of each and every higher self on earth, would you believe me? Or would you still deliver an excuse as to why things are not going well with your health:

My son has arthritis, so I can't relax.

There's no money in painting portraits, so I can't do it even though I love   it.

My family wouldn't understand if I meditated.

I have to get to my job at 6 a.m., so I can't take care of my health.

(Etc.)

Life will go on; you will encounter more and more trials, some manifested in debilitating migraines; and "the world is a rough place" will be your motto.

Alternatively, you can give faith a chance. Faith is knowing (without directly seeing) that there is always a larger force at work. You can fight it, but it does not disappear simply because you are bull-headed about it. You will come back and back and back to this point, until you learn the lesson you came here to learn: find your center. Faith will follow. And the truth of that is what will, eventually, set you free.

I can't prove it, though. That's up to you.

Building Faith: A Hands-On Activity

Begin keeping a separate record of events—a Faith Book—that help you remember that in the spirit, all is well, all the time. This may take any form that is most useful to you: a journal, computer document or folder, or even an audio tape or home movie that you can keep adding to whenever you realize that your prayers are being answered. Anecdotes—the stories you tell to others, and the stories you hear or read about that constitute daily miracles—are true faith-builders. Do not hesitate to include memorable dreams or especially deep, bliss-filled meditations and inner journeys that awakened you to spiritual wonders.

Helpful Ideas: To begin this progressive actualization of your personal faith foundation, you can go back in time. Start your sentence with "I remember when…." Recount the most amazing things that happened when you were at low points of your life. Write down the names of people who called you just when you needed to hear their voices. Recall the good that goes on all around you. Think back to an event which seemed truly unfair to you at the time—but which turned out to be a blessing that, in retrospect, had a better ending than you could have dreamed up yourself. Consider how you met the most important people in your life, and how you happened to meet. All of these ideas qualify as entries in this special Book Of Faith that you can keep close to you and re-read whenever your faith gets shaky.

Chapter 20
Memory of a Pain

Can migraine be a memory—manifested as pain? Could it be that, like a rat that's found an efficient course through a maze, once a migraine is triggered, the headache "tracks" itself along the same familiar, well-traveled pathway of debilitating pain, nausea and general "shut-down"—even to the point where it sticks to a predictable time schedule? (If you are like many migraine sufferers, you probably have a pretty good sense of how long a typical migraine experience lasts for you.)

In coaching me with affirmations to manage an oncoming migraine, Linda Barnett predicted that my most powerful tool would be to simply say, over and over to myself, "This is a memory of a pain I once had. It no longer has any power over me. This is a memory of a pain." Then, she encouraged me to examine events of the preceding day to see where I might have stirred up some old, lingering, emotional pain.

At first, I really thought she was crazy. But I chose to suspend my disbelief since she did, after all, have this magical ability to heal my head while saying a phrase that made no logical sense: "This is a memory of a pain."

I knew I was feeling pain. That was tangible. *But my teacher was asking me to consider what was going on in my life—conscious or unconscious—that may have caused an old, unresolved emotional hurt to resurface.* In every case, if I dug deeply enough, I could wind my way back to the very beginning of the pain event—the maze's starting point. Perhaps it was an old feeling of not measuring up to my father's hopes for me, and feeling angry that he wanted me to be a lawyer instead of a writer. Perhaps it was nothing that happened at work or at home, but, rather, an anniversary trauma. A look at the calendar revealed some date that I had forgotten about: April, the month my divorce was finalized. Or, perhaps, three years earlier, someone in my family had a terrible fall and I felt guilty because I wasn't there to prevent it from happening. Whatever the cause and progression of the old hurts we hold, the next step to take—in order to clear those old triggers once and for all—is to forgive. Once we go the distance, and forgive those people who hurt us, then forgive ourselves for being crippled by that hurt for so long, then and only then does the affirmation "This is a memory of a pain" start to "work" very fully, and miraculously, on our behalf.

Interestingly, research published in the mid-90s showed that brain scans of migraine patients studied within six hours of the start of migraine attacks revealed overactivity in the brain stem at the base of the brain. The scans also showed a possible migraine "generator" at the point where the brainstem joins the midbrain. The attacks, surmised German researchers at the University of Essen, might occur when this generator lost normal control over brainstem centers that regulate how we perceive pain as well as the expanding and contracting of blood vessels. The generator "continues firing even when the headache is gone," said the lead neurologist.

To see the full power of the memory response, let's look at it another way:

We've all had experiences where we meet someone who looks or acts like someone else we know. "He looks so much like my best friend from high school!" you may be saying to yourself. And despite the fact that you've just been introduced to this person, you feel close to him, and feel like he may instantly understand you better than the other strangers you've just met. There's no foundation to these thoughts—except for the memory response.

Conversely, you may meet someone who triggers an instant dislike from you—and it's linked to an association with someone who led you to a strong distrust and disdain. It could be anything from her posture to her tone of voice. If it's her perfume, though you may not be consciously aware of it, that scent is going up your nose's nerve pathways and "talking" to your brain, which is working hard to process all this information. Later, much later, you're trying to figure out why you reacted so negatively to this person whom you've just met, and you say, "Aha! I've got it. She somehow reminds me of Great-Aunt Sue, who used to force me to eat liver and onions even though it always made me throw up." Now the association is complete, the incident remembered—and, finally, once you've called up a big dose of unconditional love for Great-Aunt Sue, and then forgiven yourself for not being able to stand up for yourself (after all, you were a child then), the whole matter clears.

Your next step is to thank the stranger who brought up those lingering, unforgiven moments still churning in your solar plexus. And you thank The Great Forces That Be for bringing the experience to your doorstep.

End result? You're freer than you were when you woke up this morning.

In declaring the migraine to be nothing more than a memory, you accomplish two main goals:

1. You disarm the headache itself, through neurolinguistic (nerves-and-language) programming. The brainstem overactivity becomes disrupted when you actively declare that you do not perceive pain in the same way you did in the past.

2. You open yourself to discovering all the wounded, saddened places in your memory banks—as if you were opening damaged files in a computer—which gives you an automatic opportunity to "fix" those places through the healing power of love, should you so choose.

Remember—it's always a choice. It is choosing to heal that makes all the difference. Each time you choose to view a migraine headache as a memory of a pain, and then ask for guidance in locating the source, and subsequently love yourself and others through all that went before, you actively shorten the life of the migraine itself. It loses power, for you are creating new "reaction software," so to speak. Instead of immediately zapping onto the old migraine path, which only triggers more of the same pain, you're now creating a new *reaction pathway*—one which bypasses the brain and drops directly to the heart zone for spiritual healing, the only true, lasting healing there is.

To find the faith it takes to believe in "memory of a pain" self-programming, it helps very much to record your migraine experiences as you go. I found that, at first, the migraines lasted as long as they always had—48 hours. Naturally, I questioned the method. But something in me persisted in trying. Gradually, months later, I could look over my journals and see that the headaches were ending earlier—first 30 hours, then 24 hours, then 20, then 8 and so on. These discoveries yielded that elusive force field called faith. I could see for myself the real change.

As faith strengthened, healing stuck. The new truth replaced the old pain memory, opening up a shortcut to pain relief that bypassed the long, pain-ridden hours of the past—like a high-tech Bullet train speeding the body back to balance, past rusting, long-forgotten railroad tracks that no longer had any use.

Through the pain response, my body had been signaling me all along. Now that I finally paid attention to it, everything shifted gears—toward health.

Re-programming Memory Lane

Ever catch yourself traveling the same route to work? Or insist on taking the same highways and byways when you visit a certain friend? And do you ever get upset when you find yourself forced into taking a detour—only to discover it's a better route than the roads you've been following by force of habit?

The following passage is a powerful affirmation which, repeated faithfully every day, can effectively re-program the pain pathways that your memories get stuck on when they start traveling around your body system. It's not that your memories need to travel the same well-grooved nerve paths they've been shooting down; it's that you allowed them to get stuck there and now they can start carving new, painfree paths to travel on. The more you unravel the bound-up sadnesses and hurts of your past, doing the hard work of embracing them and crying and letting them go, the more you need to allow the heart to etch out new, healthier nerve pathways for your memories to travel safely on. That way, in the future, when difficult

231

memories are evoked, they do not automatically head down the Migraine Highway, but instead get routed toward the heart, where the unconditional love of God heals them before they ever have a chance to cause pain.

Memory Affirmation

Place your hands on top of your head, on the crown, and affirm aloud: I know that I am a being of pure, divine energy.

Next, cover your eyes and forehead with your palms, and say:
I am aware that I am a being of pure, divine energy.

Placing your hands over your heart, say:
I am grateful that I am a being of pure, divine energy. I open my heart to receive all of my memories, all of my migraine thoughts. I claim new pathways for my emotions to travel. I let go of all of my memories and all of my pain, and relax here—safe—in my heart.

> Divine Restoration is now taking place.
> I am grateful.
> I am free.

Chapter 21
Helping the Migraine-Prone Child

It's one of your worst nightmares—that your child might follow in your footsteps and be afflicted with migraines. Because migraines tend to "run in the family," mothers with migraine are always on the lookout for migraines in their children. It is important to recognize the possibility, but equally important to not obsess over it.

There is one good thing that comes of this knowledge: At least you know what to look for. Imagine being a parent who does *not* have any direct experience with migraine... What would you—as an inexperienced parent—think if your daughter's teacher called to say, "Your child says she has a terrible headache, she feels like vomiting, and the headache is getting worse and worse"?

Hundreds of children suffer migraine headaches without having a clue as to what they are experiencing, much less how to relieve the pain. It can be very frightening. In some cases, it takes years until the parents and child learn what's really going on. By then there can be a lot of damage done, by siblings, friends, and, unfortunately, even parents who accuse the migraine-prone child of "faking it to get attention" or "taking to bed early to avoid doing homework" (or housework).

As a child, I suffered from headaches more than my brothers or sister. Nausea came easy to me: I was the one who got carsick, not my siblings. In my early teens, when I got my period, it often began with a run to the bathroom—to throw up. In college, overwhelmed by PMS, I'd find myself walking into walls or furniture. Thinking back, I am quite certain that these symptoms were all precursors to migraine.

First Migraine

I remember my first true migraine headache. I was 17 years old, about to finish a year of school in a small Japanese city, as a high school exchange student. I was not only far from home, I was 7,000 miles away from home. It was a hot day—high noon—and the sun seemed to blast down on me as I walked home from school toward my host parents' house. It was a Saturday (Japanese kids attend school full days during the week, and from 8 to 12 on Saturdays).

To get a sense of how scary the first headache can be, I include here an excerpt from my diary:

> "I shall never forget Sat. the 17th—I had planned to go on a picnic and hike with Motoko [my best friend] along the quaint road leading to the sea behind the Uchiyama's house. We had planned to take pictures and relax on this day—from way back when...
>
> In the first period [at school] I developed a headache that continued and steadily grew worse during the hot day. By 12:30 I could barely face Motoko to tell her of my plight—but I had to break the news that it would be impossible for me to go...Naturally, she was disappointed and so was I ... but the pain, the throbbing (concentrated on the left side) was something I have never experienced before in my life. I washed my eyes, reddened from crying, in the lav, and took the first bus home. My whole body felt weak and my mental system went haywire with exhaustion. I didn't know why I was so torn up—perhaps a combination of the conflicting emotions I have regarding my return home—I want to go—and I want to stay—I fear going home, yet I want to so very badly (insecurity?)—but I really scared Okaa-san [my host mother] and Otoo-san ["Father"—who was, fortunately, a physician by profession] with my incessant and unexplainable tears and the pain of my head. Okaa-san laughed—the typical Japanese cover-up—because, as she said afterwards, she was very worried. Otoo-san was obviously upset and sent me to bed having swallowed

2 green pills and a headache pill. [I discovered later he treated me for anemia as well as migraine.]

Lying in bed up there [in my room], my lungs and whole body felt tight—constricted and very strange—almost as if I were in a coma, and my headache was raging inside the left half of my head. I honestly and truly thought I was going to die.

I drifted off into a restless sleep and awoke about 3 hours later with Okaa-san standing over me: my body was *beta-beta* (clammy) with sweat and I sat up to find that the pain had diminished to that of a regular headache and with relief we went downstairs..."

My host father, Dr. Nishida of Imari City, diagnosed the episode as "hen-zutsu." I hurried to look up the new word in my Japanese-English dictionary. Migraine! Oh, no. Immediately I flashed back into scenes that occurred throughout my childhood: my mother suddenly and inexplicably incapacitated, everyone tiptoeing anxiously between the rooms of the house, fierce anger from my father if we dared disturb my mother, who was lying in a completely darkened room, shades drawn, with ice cubes wrapped in a washcloth that never moved from her forehead, except to change refresh the cubes.

I knew now how my mother felt. And I hated it. I now understood her better. But aside from drugs and rest, I had no tools to handle the pain. She passed on what she knew about the flashing lights and the pain, and later, after her hysterectomy, she told me that the migraines had all but ceased. Occasionally they recurred. The miracle I had to wait for, I thought, was menopause.

Could I endure the thirty years or so of torture? Some part of me said, "No." I vowed to learn a way through. It took twenty years in all, but what I have learned I am passing on to one of my daughters, who manifested migraines early on.

The beauty of teaching children spiritual centering for treating their own headache symptoms is that they are so open to imagery and positive visualization. Also, as a parent, you are in a unique position of being able to spot trouble in your child before it manifests as migraine. The most important thing to remember is that the migraine-prone child tends to be highly spiritual. She or he is an open vessel, so to speak, through which spiritual energy passes through and gets expressed in some form or another. This child is highly sensitive, therefore, not only to criticism and harsh words, but to all sorts of energy influences. Being around people with negative or destructive energy on a constant basis is not healthy for this child, because she easily takes on that energy, especially if that person is close to her or if she has stresses in her life—a cold or flu, difficulty adjusting to school, or changes.

Prevention Tactics

The migraine-prone child can and should be encouraged to develop healthy lifestyle routines, and stick to those routines that work best for her. Lifetime habits are learned early on; best to get it right in the formative years. The following are some of the most valuable migraine preventatives I have learned from experience:

1. Honor the **Sleep** Schedule

Place the child on a rigid schedule of regular, full sleep. Both parent and child pay for it later if there is leniency here. The occasional sleepover with friends is fun and good for her socially, but be prepared to spend the following day at home, so that your child can catch up on her rest. Scheduling too much activity back to back does not allow the sensitive child to process what she's been experiencing, take the time to express it verbally or artistically, and get back to center.

2. Set a daily **Quiet Hour**

Whenever you sense the need, encourage naps. During the days when there is no school, always maintain a daily Quiet Hour (usually at the same time, like right after lunch). Depending on the child's age, he or she may wish to read, or draw quietly, or listen to you read.

3. Find an **Indoor-Outdoor Balance**

Playing out of doors is important for children's mental and physical health. However, do limit exposure to direct sunlight (two to three hours) if the child is engaging in strenuous activities, such as summer camp. Find out from the counselors if the children have shady areas to play in, and how much time they spend in the blazing sun compared to an air-conditioned room or cool space.

Don't let yourself get paranoid about oversunning—just watch it, that's all. Keeping a child indoors too much is no good either—the balance is what you're striving for.

4. Encourage **Water**

Provide plenty of fluids, especially water, and encourage the child to get in the habit of taking in fluids. Sometimes children forget about such things—they're having too much fun. Before you know it, they are dehydrated, and the body becomes stressed.

In some schools children are only allowed to drink water from the fountain at specific times of the day. The teachers claim it is a disciplinary issue; I claim it is a health issue, and would appeal to the principal if necessary to ensure my child's ready access to drinking water.

5. Foster **Creative Expression** daily.

Encourage your child to express herself daily. Self-expression takes many forms, and it should be easy to see which format your child is most drawn to. Encourage artistic and creative expression, whether it is building things, inventing things, drawing, painting, dancing, claywork, writing, and so forth.

6. Promote the joys of **Physical Activity**

Make regular physical activity a part of daily life, but take care not to push a non-competitive child into stressful competitive situations. In other words, swim team is fine so long as it remains fun, and the child does not complain chronically afterwards of headache or stomachache. Remember, though, when a child is down with a headache, physical activity is not (to my knowledge or experience) curative.

7. Honor **Feelings**

Ask your child how she feels about her day, and make time to become familiar discussing feelings rather than events.

8. Consider **Small Groups**

If possible, place your migraine-prone child in a smaller class situation. Being around 30 to 50 other children can make it hard for the sensitive child to concentrate—too much wild energy flying around! Her grades will suffer, as will her behavior reports. Ideally, a class with no more than 20 is good; unfortunately, in public schools these days, that's practically unheard of. Scheduling one-on-one situations can help balance that situation: for example, the music lesson after school should be one-on-one or take place in an extremely small group, and so forth.

9. Embrace natural **Spirituality**

Foster visionary expression and a rich spiritual life in your child. When your child seems naturally drawn to images of angels, it is because of a natural understanding that angels and guides are with her constantly, working to keep her anchored in the light. If your child has a dream to share, listen closely to her. Instead of doing dream interpretation for her, allow her to find some meaning in the dream herself.

10. Become **LOVE**

In your own meditations, and at any time during the day, mentally draw the child into your heart area and surround her with pure, unconditional love. This is one way for your higher self to connect deeply and directly with the child's higher self, promoting the balance you both need to maintain.

11. Be a role model for **Meditation and Strong Foundations of Self-Help**

Invite your child to meditate with you, and practice guided meditations with him/her. That way, the practice of centering through becoming still and opening the heart and crown will become second nature, a definite boon to self-healing. Many children respond positively to environmental tapes, musicians (including Enya), and meditating outside in nature.

Techniques for Treating Pain

"It hurts, Mommy." Sometimes a child does fall off center, or an important message of spiritual nature is being blocked from entering—and migraine strikes. When that happens, the very first thing you should do is sit still for a few minutes. Expel any fear within yourself. With the right hand on your crown, and left hand over your stomach, let your feelings come forth. If you are anxious, panicky, fearful for the child, or in any way lacking faith in the self-healing process (and hence, in a higher power), give yourself a large dose of forgiveness for feeling this way. Say to yourself, "This is a memory of a fear I once had. This is a memory which has no power whatsoever."

Now move the left hand up to your heart area, keeping the right hand firmly atop the hot energy spot on your head (the crown chakra). Say aloud, "I know that I am a being of pure, unconditional love. I identify with all that is loving, and healing, and good."

Meditate on the color green or rosy pink to pull out love energy. Feel yourself engulfed by colored light.

Now, remember deeply that the body is equipped with natural painkillers that are far stronger than any substance created in a lab. Remember that both you and your child are completely capable of opening up channels to let those painkillers activate naturally and purely, with the help of your angels and guides. Know that healing energy flows by itself, after you have released control, after you have surrendered to a higher power. Let the knowledge of true healing, the ancient and true memory of the body's power to heal itself, resonate within your heart.

Love clears anything unlike itself from the body. Therefore, if you take five or ten minutes to clear fear from your energy field, you will find yourself calm and ready to assist the child in healing.

In some areas of the country, researchers are finding that children with migraines respond beautifully to biofeedback and visualization techniques. Rather than training the children into taking drugs, they are teaching them ways to center themselves and access natural healing. They are teaching them self-empowerment, the way to true and lasting health.

Every child has a memory image to focus on for healing: a beautiful place, a good time, a happy self in a happy, loving situation. You can help out by having your child lie down, and concentrate on a good memory image. "Tell me what you see...Tell me about a beautiful place you know..." is one opener to get your child talking.

If the child cannot talk her way into that image, it's up to you to gently guide her way into a beautiful space. Use your intuition, describing in great detail a warm beach, a sunny meadow, a mountaintop... Because the migraine sufferers hands and feet tend to be cold, you might guiding the meditation in this direction: "Imagine that you're lying in a warm, sunny spot. There's a light breeze blowing gently over you, but the sun is warming every part of your body. It feels like the sun is aiming warm rays of sunshine right on you, on every part of you, touching your chest, and legs, and arms, and melting into your skin, making your toes and feet warm, and your hands warm and your fingers warm..."

Advanced Healing

It is not unusual for a child to fall asleep simply by being talked into calmness. But a migraine in its advanced stages may require more. Some parents may wish to use aspirin and acetaminophen (Tylenol) as an aid, which is fine so long as the drug is not portrayed as a cure-all but merely as an occasional aid to healing. (In truth, I think it works only by helping the child fall asleep more quickly.) Whatever you do, don't give your child a pill and then walk away assuming all is well. Your participation in the healing process is crucial, not only as healer but as a teacher of how to heal.

In my own experience with my migraine-prone daughter, a combination of the following two therapies is a quick route to healing even the most horrendous migraine.

Foot Massage: Position yourself at the foot of the child's bed, on a chair or stool. Starting with the left foot, begin massaging the child's feet, using both hands, taking care to push gently but firmly, mostly using thumbs. Pay special attention to the big toe, especially the side edge of the toe and the base, as well as the pads of the other toes, and the heel. There are important pressure points all over the feet, which correspond to all the organs and sites within the body; touching them serves to open up the meridians (channels) for healing. Messages travel from site to site, brain releases sufficient chemicals to numb pain, and the body relaxes enough to allow a major re-balancing.

Rainbow Meditation: While working on her (or his) feet, go through an entire rainbow meditation. Talk your way up, slowly, through the seven colors of the rainbow—in order:

red
orange
yellow
green
blue
indigo

241

violet

Do this in the fashion that suits the situation:

1. If she is in mild pain and can talk aloud, have her describe each color, taking two to four minutes describing all the things she sees in her mind's eye that are red, then orange, then yellow, green, blue, indigo, and purple.

2. If it seems better to keep her quiet, go through the colors aloud, taking lots of time for each color image to take root, enabling waves of colored light to flow through both healer and child. For example, you might start out, "I see a deep, dark red...a rose, a beautiful red rose with soft red petals...and an apple, bright red, sitting in a bowl with lots of other pretty red apples..."

Then comes orange, then yellow, and green: "I see a big green can of paint, and I dip my paintbrush into the paint, and it's a magic paintbrush, which can color every cell inside my body, from my head down to my toes..." And so on. Be creative, talk softly, and really concentrate on each color. It helps, I find, to close your eyes when doing a rainbow meditation.

And even if the child is quiet throughout most of the talk-through, he or she might join in from time to time, with inner observations such as, "I see a blue, blue boat on the blue ocean..." You can say back, "I see it, too...It's beautiful, isn't it?" Or, "I see my yellow dress..." and you reply, "I see that dress on you. It's such a beautiful yellow, isn't it?" Enjoy minutes of total quiet between you, just allowing the color to wash over you and into you and out beyond the borders of your body.

3. If the child is in so much pain she cannot bear to hear your talking, go through the rainbow colors in your mind. Infuse them into the energy of the foot massage. Imagine the colors flowing one by one through your palms and into the foot.

Rainbows are truly one of the greatest gifts we are given here on earth. We can physically see rainbows with our eyes, and yet we can walk right through them. The memory of any rainbow has the power to bring us into the light of healing. Therefore, *stop when you do see a rainbow*. Pull the car off to the side of the road, and soak it in. You may be drawing on that image in time to come.

Become Sensitive to Your Child's Surroundings

It goes without saying that a child's room can be decorated in such a way as to promote active, fulltime balancing. Go for ivory or peach-colored walls with as little clutter as possible, and put up a photo of a rainbow, a painting or two by your child (and chosen for framing by your child, not you), a poster of a favorite animal, a soft sculpture or image of a cherub or angel, a picture of the family at a happy time, a wilderness calendar with pictures of trees and natural wonders, and so on. You get the idea. A child's space needs to be a haven, prepared and maintained so that it is as close to the inner image of "safe space" as possible.

Think twice before buying commercialized toys and posters and coloring books. Children are attracted to them, but they have a way of squelching a child's natural need to create from scratch. Stock the child's art corner with blank paper and sharpened pencils, regular and colored. Keep a box of jumbo colored chalks by the back door, ready for sidewalk drawings and outdoor games. Buy a small, durable, school-quality blackboard that is portable, and can be used anywhere.

Whatever you do, allow your child's natural talents to unfold. If you want him to draw, and he or she would rather build, you must respect that urge, and respond accordingly by providing an environment where the activity of building can flourish. Ask a child what she/he needs to create—to make a list (parents: resist the urge to prompt!)— and you will be amazed at how specific the child can be: "I'd like my own table, some wood, some sand, ..."

My parents were university teachers, and, having lived through the Depression, they were fairly frugal. They would save the unused portions of small blue college examination booklets and give them to us kids to play with. At age six, I wrote my first "collection" of short stories in one of those booklets. I've been writing ever since. My brother would draw in his; he still draws. The point is, you cannot know what lies in store for your children. But you can be sure that their mission will manifest in some form, at some time, fairly early on.

Wise and loving is the parent who not only encourages creative expression in children, but helps the child achieve discipline (not constraint—discipline) to become more fluid with every aspect of the chosen creative medium, for that expression will serve an individual throughout a lifetime as a direct link to the Creator-force within. This binding, loving connection, this wholeness, nurtures a self that feels well and healthy and good. Like the rainbow, expression heals.

We can chart all the changes I've talked about with machines, showing how brain waves move from beta waves to alpha and theta and so on. One day in the future the school nurse will be able to hook up a child with migraine to a physical device that will instantly induce a trance state, inducing healing waves to clear out the headache. Medical (allopathic) intervention to speed healing takes all forms, and I am not going to disparage any device or treatment that diminishes pain. But it seems to me that equipping the child to access the physician within, while she is still at an age where that is relatively easy to do (i.e., before the self-healing ability has been socialized or ridiculed out of her) is preferable for two basic reasons.

One, from a practical standpoint, it makes sense because the child is not dependent upon an Other—someone else, a machine or a drug—for help. Two, from the standpoint of personal mission, there is a compelling need to do all we can to encourage the teachers among us to express themselves. And migraine-prone children definitely come here on a mission of spirit. Their sensitivity pains them since society is generally not receptive to the message they carry.

Hope for the migraine-prone child lies in improving the tolerance and understanding of everyone; and in embracing the interlocking S's—Sensitivity and Spirituality—recognizing their blessed merits in the physical and metaphysical realms.

Chapter 22
Migraine as Metaphor

A long, long time ago, as Japanese legend says, the Sun Goddess had a quarrel with her brother. So angry was she that she entered a cave and refused to come out. The world was plunged into darkness... No amount of coaxing could lure her out, and a terrible cold threatened to kill every living thing. Finally, in desperation, a plan was hatched: A great mirror was brought to the cave entrance and the Sun Goddess was tricked into peering outside her self-imposed prison. Blinded by her own light, the Sun Goddess reentered the world, accepted the apologies of her brother, and proceeded to warm the world once more. Everyone rejoiced...

This tale of the mighty *Amaterasu Omikami*, Sun Goddess, is much like migraine. It is a direct metaphor, in fact, for migraine. In migraine, we seek a darkened, closed-off environment (cave), unable to bear the hyper-bright light, the hyper-loud sounds of the world, the bombardment of all sensory experiences upon our highly sensitive selves (hurt from quarreling). The legend is our own tale of cocooning, going within, and then getting back, overcoming disappointments, and finally emerging from the cave to perform the work of a powerful light being. The goddess (god) within us can sometimes be thrown off course, into darkness, by a crisis of imbalance; then, after the crisis passes through her, she is warmed by her own vast sunniness. She remembers her true worth, and true nature—the sun being the ultimate metaphor for the great creator spirit with which we are one, which is the source and substance of our being.

But the Sun Goddess is more than a myth and a metaphor. Each conversation we hear on a day-to-day basis, each person who connects with us, each nuance of weather and each occurrence big or small plays a role in our personal metaphor, which we can consciously choose to see, experience, be receptive to, and learn from.

Migraine sufferers have a tendency to want to control events around them. But that controlling, manipulating tendency is gratifying only when we perceive that things are going "our way." We have trouble seeing that trials come to us because it is the only way we can grow—a way to learn to release the illusion that we are solely in control.

Instead of being trapped in the controller pattern, we truly become empowered by viewing ourselves as co-Creators of our own lives. If we accept the premise that soul, mind and body are integrally interconnected, it stands to reason that when the body feels good, the soul and mind are also at ease. We spend a lot of time and effort and money trying to make our bodies feel better. We go to doctors at the drop of a hat, buy new clothes when we don't need them, and work on the physical attributes that make us attractive to others—hair, nails, and so on. *And after all that, we still get migraines.*

What is wrong? Very simple, really. We have got it backwards. The world does not get created from the outside in; it is created from the inside out. If we expended even a fraction of that same time, effort and money on nurturing the spiritual, intuitive side of ourselves, all the rest would fall in line. But these are just words. Only by reversing the direction of energy, that is, turning to the inside and watching how it manifests in the outer world, can we free ourselves from pain.

Nearly everyone has experienced the ability to look at The Big Picture. Somehow, at some time, you were able to see what was going on in your life as if you were watching a film of your life. Maybe you connected with this feeling in a dream, or when you had someone read your tarot cards, or you simply saw things more clearly than usual. "Oh," you said to yourself, "so that's what's going on!"

Imagine, though, being able to view the world with this video awareness every day of your life. Imagine that you are able to view the entire scope of events, including the migraine you got last night, the odd behavior of a co-worker, the rain that woke you up at 3 a.m., the interaction with your children, etc., etc. Even if you are able to accomplish this for five minutes in your day, you gain a unique sense of being a co-Creator of your world simply by being able to see through godly eyes. The sense of control that you deeply desired before would now be fulfilled in a far more balanced fashion, for you are recognizing two things simultaneously:

1. There is no need to control, or connive, and you can finally relax about that point. Universal law is in place, and the best you can do is align with that flow.

2. Rather than focusing on controlling, which is a restrictive force by definition, you focus now on creating the kind of inner and outer life that you feel most comfortable with. As you focus on creating goodness through releasing into goodness, you automatically "walk the walk, and talk the talk" as they say.

The area of the body that corresponds with "I walk by faith and not by sight"—the awareness chakra—is located in the forehead. To improve your third eye vision, there are many helpful exercises you can do, and many helpful books. Perhaps the easiest way to begin is to focus on the color indigo, either in meditation or by wearing the color or putting a large painting of indigo in front of you. The best indigo painting I know of is the night sky. The deep blue-purple that envelopes the world about midnight is healing in itself, and just standing under the stars is an exercise in appreciating The Big Picture.

Pursuing active avenues such as the martial arts also promotes this awareness, this knowing without seeing. An advanced practitioner of the Japanese self-defense art called aikido, for example, has developed an intuitive sense regarding other people's energies that can save his own life, as well as the lives of others. He or she knows through long-nurtured intuition when someone with negative energy is approaching, long before there is any evidence, and reacts instinctively, calmly, protectively—readying against an attack without thinking twice about it.

Another way to promote third eye awareness is by writing or talking about yourself, as if the story was fiction or a fairy tale or a play. If writing is not something you enjoy, you can paint a picture of yourself on a daily or weekly basis, showing all the elements that are going on around you. There is a rhyme and a reason to all of the events going on around you. A synchronicity exists. You will, with practice, begin to recognize important patterns through this self-analysis process, which can be infinitely useful to you in breaking free from pain, old patterns, old and self-destructive compulsions, obsessions, and manipulative methods, including trying to control others around you.

If you are ready to see the Really Big Picture, imagine a picture of the soul (your soul) choosing to come to earth, arriving at the parents and location it chose, and seeking to break old karma—those situations you seem to get yourself into over and over again, taxing and perplexing you greatly. Your whole life may look like fiction, after you've finished examining your own timeline. And indeed, not only is fact stranger than fiction, if it feels like you're living in fiction that is only because you are living a metaphor of your own making. Change happens for you only when you work through old situations with love and keen awareness, putting passion aside, and choosing to learn about the big picture.

In one of the Star Trek series, there is an episode where one of the heroic characters, Captain Picard, ends up on a planet he has no intention of visiting. After fighting the reality of being there, he eventually finds himself sitting down, in the unlikely position of having to tell a story to a dying man: The man knows his life is at an end, and he begs of Picard, "Tell me a story!"—in order to ease his pain and smooth his passage into the life beyond. The story Picard chooses to tell, unwittingly (or so it seems) parallels his own situation. He is dealing with his own personal metaphor, and this shocks him deeply and fills him with an awakening. In this case, compassion was the key that served to bring out inner meaning.

In compassion we put ourselves aside; without even trying, there comes a beautiful death of the ego, something essential to this process of developing third eye awareness. Coming into spiritual awareness necessarily demands a death of the old. When it's happening, it feels like sickness or death, but is actually—in The Big Picture—a cleansing process, a divine clearing the way for the new self, the aware self, to emerge.

To give another example of metaphor as part of the stuff and substance of daily reality, there is the real-life story of a woman I once knew. It took Emma* (not the actual name) years to get up the courage to leave her husband, a man called Albert. He had abused her throughout the marriage, and now that she had small children—two little girls—she became afraid and aware that she did not want to have them grow up with an abusive father. She left the state, and started life anew.

Although she reestablished herself, within two years she began to falter -- money troubles, relationship problems, lack of solid direction. One year later, she announced to me she was getting remarried. After a beautiful wedding on top of a mountain ridge, with hawks and eagles soaring overhead, Emma was completely ecstatic and positive about the future. Interestingly enough, her new husband's name was Albert. She laughed about it with friends. Eleven months later, she fell apart. Her life was a mess. She admitted to being once again in an abusive, unfulfilling relationship. She came apart at the seams. "It wasn't a joke," she said after entering a women's shelter. "I even married someone by the same name. I knew deep inside that he was the same kind of man. I looked for it, and I got it. But I am not going to get myself in this mess again. I'm going to look at the clues I'm given—all the clues."

The point is not that every Albert is abusive, but rather that we keep on walking into the same karmic situations that have caused us trouble because until we learn what it is we need to learn from that situation, it will keep on coming back. Only by developing an awareness, by being able to step outside of ourselves, can we break old, destructive patterns in our behavior.

A very similar situation existed with Allie. She was deeply dissatisfied with a publishing job she'd held three years. Allie was a creative person, involved in puppeteering and writing dramatic plays outside her job. She eventually became so stressed out over her work, though, that her health began to suffer. She put out applications for a new job, but nothing opened up for her. She grew more and more frustrated.

A meditator and former teacher of TM (transcendental meditation) for many years, Allie tried to work things out by putting the situation in the framework of her inner life. Still, no movement. No escape from the job. No answers from within. But one day, in the middle of a one-week vacation where she spent her days working on a play, the whole scene of her life was revealed to her. The key? Talking it out with a sympathetic ear. The relationship with her boss proved to be the seat of all her pain and frustration. It was not so much what he did, but that he reminded her of most of the other employers she had previously worked for. There was an aspect of authority that continually presented itself in her life—in fact, as she realized, she was more or less following it around and it continued to cause her grief.

Her solution: to deal with the cause of that grief, which originated with another relationship (an early relationship) in her past. She then turned her focus toward becoming fully aware of the dynamics of that relationship and working through the difficulties: re-feeling the old pain and rejection, and, finally, finding love within her heart to dispense toward herself and the man involved. Allie had discovered that if she walked away from the problem one more time, she would only end up in the same boat again. It was a classical karmic situation, and only by going back to the beginning, in a sense, could she crack the karma and open up to a better, brighter path.

Once upon a time, much like the time of her mother and her mother before her, a girl child was born. She was a sensitive child, as all children are, but even more so than others: She befriended those who had no friends, defended mice and other small creatures from the torment of cats, and hid from her brothers who wanted to play war in the fields behind the barn. She preferred to get up long before the others in the family, to crouch in the middle of a meadow to examine the smallest buttercups, and pick the ripest wild strawberries for the breakfast table. Cereal tasted so much better with sweet berries...

In fact, the above story is mine. The meadow exists in my mind, as well as in the tangible town of Temple, New Hampshire. I still am sensitive. I still get up earlier than everybody. I still find everything I need in the meadow above my grandmother's house: earth, fruit, flowers, sky.

See the Themes in Your Life

It's time to begin a fresh autobiography now. As you turn to your BEING Journal, begin to see your own story in metaphors, as told by yourself, as honestly and completely as you can.

The metaphors within your life will unfold all by themselves. Make two lists. On one list, talk about those times of your life when you did not have migraines. (If you have been doing all the exercises listed in each chapter, look back over the lists you made earlier to see if certain themes exist.)

Was there a time when you did not feel pain?

What were the circumstances?

What were the salient elements of those time periods? Pretend you are a fiction writer, or a storyteller, and you're looking over these lists for recurring circumstances, or themes, to give you a sense of what makes you happy, stress-less.

On another list, discuss the times when migraines were (are) occurring regularly. How do those elements compare with the times when migraine was (is) a daily or weekly affair?

There are clues in both lists. It is up to you to recreate and claim those circumstances associated with wellness.

Everything you need to know about yourself, and how you can live most comfortably, is right there within your own wisdom.

Chapter 23
Master Plan for a Pain-Free Life

To build the strongest, most stable structure—one that keeps you warm and safe and dry, and lets in lots of light—an architect must first create a master plan. Then, those who erect the building must follow that master plan. Using a master plan insures that the building will succeed, not fail; will please, not disappoint; will house its inhabitants for generations to come, not fall apart in the first windstorm.

To live in a body that is in charge over migraine pain, a body that is *as migraine-free as possible*, you must create a Personal Master Plan (PMP) for yourself. Then you must follow it—diligently. Diligence is the price you pay if you want the headache battle to be over, once and for all. But diligence is not an unhappy thing. The steps you outline in your master plan are much like the steps you already take to keep your mind and body healthy. For example, you brush your teeth to preserve your mouth and dental health; you bathe or shower to keep bacteria from settling on your skin and causing infection; you call your mom or dad to keep in touch and to relieve your anxiety about their well-being; and so forth.

Likewise, you must create a plan, a routine, for yourself that serves to prevent migraines from happening. Obviously, your plan should fit you. If you tend to get migraines during menstruation, one of the first things you must incorporate into your PMP is to mark your menstrual periods on your personal calendar and make it a rule to not overtax yourself during that week, but to nurture yourself instead (e.g., schedule a foot massage with a reflexologist, get to bed early, do something artistic like molding clay or writing poetry). Generally, during ovulation and menstruation, give yourself permission to SLOW DOWN. Go within, and maintain contact with your higher self.

If it's allergies that kick off your migraine reaction, be sure to follow some "allergy rules" before allergy season starts (e.g., see your doctor for an allergy prescription that won't depress you or cause you to feel sleepy during the day; vacuum the house regularly; and stay indoors on high-pollen days, etc.).

In other words, for situations that you've discovered are linked to recurring migraine in your life, add those helpful rules into your PMP. Here are several fundamental tips that will serve you well as you lay the foundation of a migraine-free life plan:

1. Meditate every morning. That way, you'll start every day off right. If you simply can't make time one morning, do it later on that same day. The sooner you meditate and/or pray for 20 to 30 minutes without fail every day, the sooner you will heal.

Meditation is the single most important practice a migraine sufferer must employ to overcome suffering. It is the only way to remember, daily, that *the world works from the inside out; not the other way around.* Meditation and prayer allows you to come to center, which gives you the strength you'll need to cope with the hundreds of daily challenges that come your way. Like a buoy on the ocean, you'll always be able to bob up from all the waves that—at first appearance—threaten to buffet and drown.

I am a big fan of morning meditation. Here's why: When you meditate in the morning, all the experiences that come your way during the following hours of the day take on new meaning. Problems become lessons that your soul needs to learn and overcome with compassionate response; the smallest, sweetest things that happen feel like mini-miracles, and fill you with natural joy.

2. Get regular exercise. Your body needs to move and be pushed to perform *every single day* in order to be whole. Organs, tissues, and cells all depend on you to exercise regularly in order to improve blood flow and clear the body of toxins.

Get the big "E" for Exercise onto your calendar now. Literally. Pick up a pen and write "E" on each day of your personal calendar. Then, fill in the details daily. For example, a first week of "E" notations might look like this:

Monday	E: walked dog 15 minutes
Tuesday	E: swimming—6 laps
Wednesday	E: walked dog 12 minutes; 1/2 hr Pilates tape
Thursday	E: shot hoops on basketball court w Jamie, 20 minutes *(fun! haven't done that in years)*
Friday	E: went to my first contra dance (scared at first but had a great time)
Saturday	E: walked the dog 10 minutes; went to mall and walked it end to end
Sunday	E: 40-minute hike/walk in the park w Jamie; Pilates tape 1/2 hr.

Lift weights, walk, swim, play tennis, run, do yoga, learn the hula—just do anything that moves you out of a sedentary position. Explore what feels like the right activity for you. Engage in T'ai chi, aikido, golf, or any activity that feels like it's opening you up.

3. Get massaged (or receive some form of body work) on a regular basis. Massage therapy (whether it's Swedish-style, foot massage, cranial-sacral, or acupressure) assists your body as it gets rid of waste products (lactic acid buildup in muscles, for example) and it both clears and re-stimulates the lines of energy (meridians) that allow the body to heal itself. Perhaps one of the most important benefits of massage, though, is its effect on your lymphatic system. Your lymph nodes, while not touted too much in everyday conversation, are an absolutely critical component of total health. They need touch, though, in order to stay well—and neither meditation nor exercise works directly on lymph health the way massage therapy does.

4. Purge anger and conflicted feelings. Find someone you can talk to about anger and unsettling emotions. (And yes, we all have them. Don't skip this one.) This person may be a counselor, sister, priest, or trusted friend. Perhaps you will form a support group of migraine sufferers, or a support group of four or five friends, to talk out your disappointments and uncover hidden angry thoughts together. Perhaps writing in a journal can serve as a confidante, but if you're still getting migraines, consider finding a counselor as well. (See the Appendix for help in finding a counselor.)

5. Remind yourself of the power of Light and Life-force. Remind yourself of what you have learned, and what you must do to keep on track. You can post little (or large) signs in strategic places (the car, bathroom mirror, kitchen wall, etc.). For example:

> **"BREATHE"** is a good word to post. This is especially useful for migraine sufferers, who often get their brains going so hard and intensely, that if they stop to ask, "Am I breathing?" the answer is commonly "No, not really."

> **"CLAIM IT."** This means, simply, claim what you want, what you need for personal growth and harmony. Many people, especially people who have had pain as their constant companion for a long period, have grown disheartened: they quit claiming for themselves long ago, without really knowing it. At different stages in this process called living, you may alter the sign to specifically claim something elusive. For example, change it to say **"CLAIM WELLNESS"** or simply, "I am claiming all that I need in order to Be Me."

> Another useful sign: **"I have all that I need."**

> And in the kitchen or bathroom where you tend to spend time first thing in the morning: **"I qualify this day with absolute perfection."**

Sometimes, reminding yourself of Holy Spirit is as simple as hanging a crystal in your front window, or placing a beautiful, polished stone in your pocket along with your coins. For others, wearing a crucifix serves the purpose.

6. Do something creative. It doesn't matter what it is—from watercolor painting to cooking—just do it. We get so caught up in exercising the left side of the brain (the side that handles practical, logical, linear tasks) that our right brain—the creative, artistically motivated side—hungers to get busy, so it can offer fresh solutions to old problems. Creative activity acts as a release valve to prevent our becoming too wound up.

7. Get your zzzzs. Honor your body; go to bed on time. No excuses!

8. Focus on your heart to beat anxiety and overcome the need to control others. Whenever you start to feel frantic, or you're thinking too hard about anything, or people aren't acting the way you want them to behave, command yourself: "Drop your brains into your heart." How? Just focus your mind on your chest area; imagine you are thinking through your heart. When you do this, you naturally slow down and remember the ultimate truth—that you can't control anyone or anything around you. You can, however, turn over your life to a higher goodness and trust that "In the Spirit, all is well, all the time." So, you can, after all, *relax* as you walk through life.

9. Share. People who are isolated or feel isolated and lonely tend to get sick. (They also die sooner, according to health statistics.) Share your time with others—and make sure there's a fair portion of scheduled sharing time. For example, you might set Sunday nights aside as Family Night—a time when everyone eats dinner together, talks together, shares what's coming up in the following week, whatever. Also, volunteer somewhere, whether it's at church, an after-school tutoring program, hospice center, Boys and Girls Club, homeless shelter—anywhere other than home. (Just be sure to volunteer at one place only—migraine people are notorious for overloading themselves with extra responsibilities—and then they end up having to quit everything because they get overloaded.) The point is to maintain good social contact.

Another option for regular social interaction may be to join some form of formal group that offers therapeutic value for your soul's growth, such as Alcoholics Anonymous, Overeaters Anonymous, Workaholics Anonymous or any of the other "Anon" groups; a parenting/parent support group; or a quilting circle, Rotary Club, arts alliance, and so forth.

Sharing how you feel is in itself a healing activity.

10. Become a healing facilitator for others. If you find yourself drawn to the healing arts—massage therapy, reflexology, yoga, breathwork, reiki—go for it! Take classes if you want training, and read everything you can about the healing art that appeals most to you. And don't discount martial arts when making a decision—aikido, for example, is a martial art form that requires you to practice forgoing physical strength and supplanting it with spiritually charged life-energy strength, or ki (in Japanese it's "ki"; in Chinese it's "chi"— same thing).

There's a saying among people who do healing work. It's "Heal and be healed." That's because when you become more familiar with ki and energy flow in yourself and others, you naturally receive a healing effect. It's never a one-way process. (P.S. If your alternative healing practitioner takes all the credit for making you feel better, get yourself a new healer. The healer doesn't heal—she or her acts as a channel to facilitate healing.) The specific feel-better chemicals released in energy-healing work are only now being charted by Western scientists.

But why wait until the chemistry is charted? Get started— now.

11. Learn to love the quiet. Every day, set aside time for solitude.

12. Limit TV. Some people say that TV relaxes them. But does it really? Ever take your blood pressure readings throughout a night of TV viewing?

Relying on TV as a de-stressor backfires for most people, given the current levels of violence, the focus on harsh news and traumatic happenings, and commercial push. Soundtracks themselves in shows and advertisements alike are designed to jolt the human system and get the adrenalin flowing—at predictable, frequent intervals.

(If you restrict your viewing to Sesame Street, tame animal documentaries, and comedy, then maybe you can skip this suggestion.)

At any rate, cut back. Way back. Or keep it off all together if you like, especially if you sense this will help you heal from a long stretch of migraine attacks.

13. Eat fresh foods. When you spend more time in the produce section and less time in the canned, frozen, and dough-y (bread, pies, pastries) aisles in the grocery store, you can literally eat your way back to health. Fruits and vegetables provide a large variety of nutrients to nourish your body and help ward off stress. There are the calming B vitamins and the blood-friendly antioxidants (betacarotene, and vitamins A, E, and C, for instance) for a healthy heart, lungs, and immune system. Zinc, calcium, potassium, and other minerals promote healthy blood vessel tone, bone health, and a strong immune system. Fiber promotes bowel health. Putting produce first is a first step toward a healthier, leaner body system. In a "luxury society" such as ours (one characterized by having more food and money available—compared to third-world countries), it tends to be true that weighty foods like meat, sugar, doughy foods, and fats become "primary on the plate"—with veggies and fruits relegated to the role of "side dishes." The result: imbalance and heaviness (both mental and physical). An easy way to reverse the heavy "luxury-lifestyle" eating habit is to *make produce primary on the plate*. That way, everything else (fats, meats, etc.) becomes a side dish, served in scaled-down quantities that are much closer to what nutritionists call a single portion size.

14. Stop Smoking. No whys or wherefores. You know why. Just do it.

15. Develop a new set of triggers—health triggers. Instead of wasting your time trying to pinpoint and avoid foods and other physical "things" that trigger pain, find triggers that induce well-being—and use them to the hilt.

Visualizations, meditations, writing, swimming, calligraphy—all influence the immune system. They are those "things" that, for you, make your system well and keep it well. When you actively pursue your health triggers, you condition your body to wellness and quick healing. Keep a list of health triggers handy. Use it as a checklist, especially if you start feeling headachy. Instead of asking yourself, "Did that chocolate milk bring on this headache?" ask yourself, "What health triggers can I use today?"

(Exception: MSG in food is something migraine sufferers should always steer clear of. It attacks the brain stem. If a Chinese restaurant can't make you an MSG-free meal, don't patronize the place. A good chef can always make a good meal without depending on monosodium glutamate.)

16. Get lots of natural light every day, and enjoy the healing effects of being in nature. Get outside as much as you can. In winter, if you are house-bound and aren't getting enough light indoors, consider buying all-spectrum indoor lamps. A pretend sun is better than no sun. Just be careful not to stay in direct sun for extended periods of time.

17. Laugh.

18. Express joy—often.

19. Follow the 7-Day Mental Diet. (See Chapter **7.**) Watch your thoughts, observe your thinking patterns, and—basically—strive to replace the woe-is-me, Eeyore approach to life with the ever-optimistic Pooh bear approach. (Recommended reading: *Winnie-the-Pooh*. Read these stories to yourself, read them to your kids, have your kids read them to you. Or, if you don't have children, read them to your spouse or partner.)

20. Create your own Master Plan. This is the final, ultimate key to mastering migraine.

Exercise: Design Your Own Master Plan

The copy-able list below contains eight baseline tactics for preventing migraine, but leaves space for you to describe the specific times, methods, or schedules you will follow daily.

1. Meditate.

2. Move (exercise).

3. Get a massage. *(Recommended: every other week or at least once a month.)*

4. Purge anger. (Discuss how you will regularly discuss or dig into unsettling emotions.)

5. Use reminders of Spirit.

6. Do art (do something creative).

7. Get enough sleep.

8. Focus on your heart to beat anxiety and stop controlling others. List those people whom you try to control the most, and those situations that are most anxiety-producing. This helps you become aware of the need to drop your focus from the head zone to the heart zone.

Fill in the blanks below with your own reminders of finding your center and staying centered.

9.

10.

11.

12.

Finished Making Your Personal Master Plan?

Upon completion, post this list in a place where you are going to see it daily. If a To Do list approach works better for you, copy it, and make it a checklist that you date and check off daily.

When your migraines have receded, and your life has begun to turn itself around, be sure to give thanks to yourself—every day.

Thank yourself for loving yourself enough to embrace your spirit and engage in the largest, greatest task we all face during our tenure on earth: enabling the soul to transcend the stuck place it got into, and move onto the next set of challenges.

Lastly, give thanks to the unseen goodness—the all-loving life-force—that brought you in touch with your own true, lasting healing power.

Shalom

APPENDIX

The Migraineur's Guide to Helpful Resources

See the author's site at *www.migrainehealing.com* for updates on migraine healing aids, workshops, news, retreats, and links to other sites.

Physical Therapy: Ready-to-use Cold Compresses for Head and Neck
Cheapest: Keep a bag of frozen peas in your freezer. (Mothers of small children know this is the fastest therapy for a bruised body, since it quickly conforms to the body's shape.) The only problem is that the peas get soggy pretty quickly, so this is best used for temporary relief, while you prepare a washcloth with ice cubes.

Next cheapest and available through the local pharmacy: Cooling headbands and neck wraps, usually with a gel component that cools easily in the freezer.

Audio and DVD Aids to Spiritual Development
Sounds True is a company that features audio recordings and DVDs "helping you explore: myth, psychology, healing, the spiritual life, creativity." Go to the website: shop.soundstrue.com or call 1-800-333-9185 to get the catalog.

Recommended Reading
Bradshaw On: The Family, and *Healing the Shame That Binds You*, by John Bradshaw (Health Communications, Deerfield Beach, FL, 1988).

Chakra Therapy, by Keith Sherwood (Llewellyn, St. Paul, MN, 2002).

The Confident Woman, by Marjorie Hansen Shaevitz (Three Rivers, New York, 1999).

The Dance of Anger: A Woman's Guide to Changing the Patterns of Intimate Relationships, by Harriet Lerner (Harper, New York, 1997)

Going Within: A Guide for Inner Transformation, by Shirley MacLaine (Bantam, New York, 1990).

Hands of Light: A Guide to Healing through the Human Energy Field, by Barbara Ann Brennan (Bantam, New York, 1987).

Healing Into Life and Death, by Stephen Levine (Doubleday, New York, 1987).

Health and Healing, by Andrew Weil (Houghton Mifflin, Boston, 1988).

How to Use the Science of Mind, by Ernest Holmes (Dodd, Mead, New York, 1950).

No More Secondhand Art: Awakening the Artist Within, by Peter London (Shambhala, 1989).

Ordinary People as Monks and Mystics, by Marsha Sinetar (Paulist, Mahwah, NJ, 1986).

Present Moment, Wonderful Moment: Mindfulness Verses for Daily Living, by Thich Nhat Hanh (Parallax, Berkeley, CA, 1990).

The Seat of the Soul, by Gary Zukov (Simon & Schuster, New York, 1989).

The Superwoman Syndrome and *Superwoman Doesn't Live Here Any More*, by Marjorie Shaevitz (Warner, 1984).

Transformers, The Therapists of the Future— Personal Transformation: The Way Through, by Jacquelyn Small (DeVorss, Marina del Rey, CA, 1982).

Unfinished Business: Pressure Points in the Lives of Women, by Maggie Scarf (Ballentine, New York, 1980). A national bestseller on women and depression.

CPSIA information can be obtained at www.ICGtesting.com
Printed in the USA
BVOW08s0417051215

429410BV00001B/4/P